Writing the Black Decade

After the Empire: The Francophone World and Postcolonial France

Series Editor: Valérie K. Orlando, University of Maryland

Advisory Board

Robert Bernasconi, Memphis University; Claire H. Griffiths, University of Chester; Alec Hargreaves, Florida State University; Chima Korieh, Rowan University; Mildred Mortimer, University of Colorado, Boulder; Obioma Nnaemeka, Indiana University; Alison Rice, University of Notre Dame; Kamal Salhi, University of Leeds; Tracy D. Sharpley-Whiting, Vanderbilt University; Nwachukwu Frank Ukadike, Tulane University

Recent Titles

Writing the Black Decade: Conflict and Criticism in Francophone Algerian Literature, by Joseph Ford

Performing the Pied-Noir Family: Constructing Narratives of Settler Memory and Identity in Literature and On-Screen, by Aoife Connolly

The Algerian War in Film Fifty Years Later, 2004–2012, by Anne Donadey

Remnants of the Franco-Algerian Rupture: Archiving Postcolonial Minorities, by Mona El Khoury

Theory, Aesthetics, and Politics in the Francophone World: Filiations Past and Future, edited by Rajeshwari S. Vallury

Paris and the Marginalized Author: Treachery, Alienation, Queerness and Exile, edited by Valérie K. Orlando and Pamela A. Pears

French Orientalist Literature in Algeria, 1845–1884: Colonial Hauntings, by Sage Goellner

Corporeal Archipelagos: Writing the Body in Francophone Oceanian Women's Literature, by Julia L. Frengs

Spaces of Creation: Transculturality and Feminine Expression in Francophone Literature, by Allison Connolly

Women Writers of Gabon: Literature and Herstory, by Cheryl Toman

Backwoodsmen as Ecocritical Motif in French Canadian Literature: Connecting Worlds in the Wilds, by Anne Rehill

Writing the Black Decade

Conflict and Criticism in Francophone Algerian Literature

Joseph Ford

LEXINGTON BOOKS
Lanham • Boulder • New York • London

Published by Lexington Books
An imprint of The Rowman & Littlefield Publishing Group, Inc.
4501 Forbes Boulevard, Suite 200, Lanham, Maryland 20706
www.rowman.com

6 Tinworth Street, London SE11 5AL, United Kingdom

Copyright © 2021 by The Rowman & Littlefield Publishing Group, Inc.

All rights reserved. No part of this book may be reproduced in any form or by any electronic or mechanical means, including information storage and retrieval systems, without written permission from the publisher, except by a reviewer who may quote passages in a review.

British Library Cataloguing in Publication Information Available

Library of Congress Control Number: 2020948469

ISBN 978-1-4985-8186-8 (cloth)
ISBN 978-1-4985-8188-2 (pbk)
ISBN 978-1-4985-8187-5 (electronic)

Contents

Acknowledgments	vii
Introduction: *Writing the Black Decade*	1
1 Rethinking Testimonial Literature in Rachid Mimouni, Assia Djebar, and Maïssa Bey	33
2 Exploring Complicity in Salim Bachi	61
3 Beyond a Grotesque Aesthetics of the Black Decade in Habib Ayyoub	85
4 Specters of the Black Decade in Kamel Daoud's *Meursault, contre-enquête*	99
5 Deconstructing Oppositional Criticism in Mustapha Benfodil's *Archéologie du chaos* (*amoureux*)	121
Conclusion: Beyond the Language of Crisis and Conflict	139
Bibliography	145
Index	161
About the Author	169

Acknowledgments

Conflict is so often a force that divides, throws people into the unknown, and strips us of common and familiar points of reference. But, conflict can also unite people in social and political solidarities that extend far beyond our immediate communities. This solidarity has been my overriding experience of working with the many writers and scholars included in this book. I must, first of all, thank the Algerian writers, scholars, and friends who generously gave time to work with me on my project during multiple visits to Algeria and Paris between 2014 and 2017. If this book is any good, then it is probably largely down to those who have helped and supported me along the way. In Algiers, Habib Ayyoub, Mustapha Benfodil, Muriam Haleh Davis, Belaïd Djefel, Rachid Guesmia, Hamid Grine, Selma Hellal, Attika-Yasmine Kara-Abbes, Khedidja Khelladi, Amara Lakhous (in person and subsequently via Skype), Djamel Mati, Guillaume Michel and others at the Centre d'études diocésain, Les Glycines, and Youcef Saïah each in different ways gave me an indispensable sense of the localized dynamics of writing and publishing in Algeria. In Paris, Zineb Ali-Benali gave her time generously, kindly providing feedback on my plans for the initial project as well as procuring a hot-off-the-press copy of Kamel Daoud's *Meursault, contre-enquête*.

I am grateful to colleagues at the University of Leeds where I completed the PhD thesis upon which this book is based and to more recent acquaintances at Durham University and the Institute of Modern Languages Research, who have supported me in writing this book. I was privileged to be supervised by Jim House and Andy Stafford who supported and continue to support my research in ways that go beyond the call of duty. The feedback received from my examiners Jane Hiddleston and Max Silverman was central to helping me reshape the thesis into this book. I have also been lucky to have critical friends who read earlier versions of various chapters, including Sarah Arens, Pat Crowley, and Andy Stafford. They, along with Lexington Books' anonymous reviewer, provided much constructive advice for rethinking some of the material here. I would like to thank my very patient editors, Holly Buchanan, Nicolette Amstutz and Megan Conley, at Lexington Books, and the series editor Valérie Orlando.

Some of the material published in this book appears in "Deconstructing the Grotesque in Contemporary Francophone Algerian Literature, or: How to move beyond the 'zombified' State?," *Irish Journal of French Studies* no. 20 (2020), "Rethinking Urgence: Algerian Francophone Literature after the 'décennie noire'," *Francosphères* 5, no. 1 (2016), and "Algiers, Paris, New York: Migrating Terror," *Bulletin of Francophone Postcolonial Studies* 5, no. 2 (2014). I would like to record my thanks to the editors of those journals for allowing me to reprint that material here. I must also thank Editions Barzakh for giving permission to reprint parts of Yassin Temlali's *Algérie: Chroniques Ciné-Littéraires de Deux Guerres* (2011), Marie Virolle at Marsa Publications for allowing me to reprint parts of Amina Bekkat's interview with Habib Ayyoub that originally appeared in *Algérie Littérature/Action* no. 57–58 (2002), and again, Mustapha Benfodil whose image of his 2012 installation in the library of the University of Aix-Marseille adorns the cover of this book.

Finally, my deepest thanks go to my family and friends (too many to name individually—and too risky that I miss someone out!) who have been present throughout this project and helped in different, but equally important ways.

Introduction
Writing the Black Decade

This is a book about how literature—and the way we read, classify, and critique literature—impacts our understanding of the world at a time of conflict. My specific focus is Algeria and the conflict that engulfed the country in the final decade of the twentieth century. Known outside Algeria as the Algerian Civil War of the 1990s, Algerians themselves adopted the euphemism "décennie noire"—the "Black Decade"—to describe a period of violence that is widely considered to have begun with the cancellation of the first democratic elections in Algeria's history in 1992 and ended with the rise to power of Abdelaziz Bouteflika in 1999, president until he was ousted amid mass peaceful protests in April 2019.[1] In the pages that follow, I trace how Francophone Algerian literature, and the literary, cultural, and academic criticism that surrounds it, has mobilized visions of Algeria over the past thirty or so years that often belie the complex and multilayered realities of power, resistance, and conflict in the country. I argue that, while it is frequently understood as an illuminating and emancipatory mode, literature—and the ideas we have about it—can, in fact, restrain our understanding of the world at a time of crisis and further entrench the kinds of polarized discourses that lead to conflict in the first place.

Because of its interest in both literary and critical accounts of the period, *Writing the Black Decade* draws on the main corpus of seven Francophone Algerian writers and, as such, offers a partial view of the numerous literary works produced across French, Arabic, and Tamazight in the years during and since the end of the 1990s conflict. It is important to note here that, throughout the 1990s and since, French-language writing has by far received most media attention in France and internationally.[2] Francophone Algerian writing, unlike its Arabic and Amazigh-language counterparts, has also featured prominently in historical and academic accounts of the 1990s conflict and features on various university curricula in French- and English-speaking contexts.

In his book, *The World, the Text, and the Critic*, Edward Said stresses how "texts have ways of existing that even in their most rarefied form are always enmeshed in circumstance, time, place, and society."[3] He continues:

> Whether a text is preserved or put aside for a period, whether it is on a library shelf or not, whether it is considered dangerous or not: these matters have to do with a text's being in the world, which is a more complicated matter than the private process of reading. The same implications are undoubtedly true of critics in their capacities as readers and writers in the world.[4]

Said's point here is that reading and writing is not something cut off from society or politics, and the conflicts that occur within or between societies and opposed political factions; rather, literature—and importantly reading and criticism—are "worldly" because they *constitute* the world in which we live. For our purposes, then, literature both "uncovers" the world at a time of conflict and "opens up other possible worlds."[5] While many will understand the notion of "opening up" as form of positive illumination, I argue that we must also address the instances when literature, and the ideas we have about it, negatively impact our world.

Coming at the question of literature's "worldliness" from the perspective of politics, French philosopher Jacques Rancière argues that "aesthetics" is at the center of any practice of politics.[6] Challenging Plato's foundational division between "the sensuous" and "the intelligible," Rancière shows how citizens gain access to the political realm via an "aesthetic regime" that has the capacity to reconfigure preexisting relations of power between State and citizen.[7] This is important for our study of literature and criticism because it allows us to see more clearly how writing, and the aesthetic more generally, might feed into the everyday practice of a "democratic politics" of contemporary experience.[8] I am not so much focused on defining literature in the book but on how representational practices and mobilizations of the literary interact with the aesthetic realm of politics. My argument here is that conflict inevitably produces writing that is deeply interested in the aesthetics of politics (more than, say, the politics of aesthetics). Hence, "writing" includes not just what we might ordinarily understand as "literature" produced by *literary* authors but journalism, historiography, and academic literary criticism.

As the reader will glean from the discussion that follows, it is difficult to offer a narrative of the 1990s conflict without being seen to take a "side" or articulate a bias in focus or approach. Those viewing the crisis through the lens of art and literature have been accused of oversimplifying a complex period in Algeria's history, as well as creating overly generalizing visions of Algerian society and culture.⁹ Literature is undoubtedly the object of my study, but I do not use it as a lens through which to apprehend social or historical facts about Algeria or its citizens; on the contrary, I take literature as my focus in order precisely to scrutinize the tendency of some journalists, historians, academic literary critics, writers, and publishers to perpetuate myths about Algerian society, history, or culture. I also look at the preexisting mechanisms that allow for this scrutiny to take place.

Given this book seeks to unearth and critique various other commentators' ideas about literature, it will be important for me to briefly articulate my own perspective.¹⁰ My "idea of the literary" is taken from postcolonial criticism, which has, in turn, acquired its *ideas* from French thinkers such as Jacques Derrida, who stress literature's "*suspended* relation to meaning and reference"—that is, its mutual "dependence" on and "distance" from society, politics, or history.¹¹ Literature's "suspense" means it is not reducible to any normative political or ideological discourse, but it is able, as Nicholas Harrison suggests, to give "room" to readers to think in creative and critical ways about making and remaking the world.¹² Thus, while I remain skeptical of claims that literature plays an emancipatory role during times of conflict such as the Black Decade, I gesture toward the notion of a critical space where the literary and the political might intersect.

AN OUTLINE OF EVENTS

Any summary of the period that became known as the Black Decade risks failing to capture the myriad elements of the crisis or the complex historical context in which it occurred. As the historian James McDougall writes, the crisis became almost impossible to analyze, given that any account was likely to also express one of the many "competing narratives."¹³ This book is explicitly not a history of the Black Decade, but for the sake of clarity, I give a brief outline of the events in question here, before exploring the importance of the interaction between narratives of the conflict and literature in more detail later in the introduction.

On October 5, 1988, young, mainly male, disenfranchised Algerians took to the streets in demonstrations during which the armed forces rounded up protesters, killed up to 500 and tortured many more.¹⁴ Accused of propagating a system of corruption within the government, the Algerian president, Chadli Bendjedid, responded by introducing wide-ranging constitutional reforms which would end the one-party rule of the Front de libération nationale [National Liberation Front] (FLN)—in power since independence from France in 1962—and pave the way for Algeria's first free multiparty elections.¹⁵ In the first round of the elections, which took place on December 26,

1991, the Front islamique du salut [the Islamic Salvation Front] (FIS)—one of the many parties legalized by Chadli—won 188 of the 232 seats contested, with a further 198 to be balloted in the second round, a majority of which the FIS was predicted to win.[16] On January 11, 1992, Chadli was forced to resign and a transitional body established by senior generals of the Algerian military, the Haut Comité d'Etat [High State Committee] (HCE), took control. On January 12, the second round of the election was canceled; a state of emergency was declared on February 9.[17] Mohamed Boudiaf, one of the founders of the FLN, was chosen to lead the transitional government but was assassinated by one of his bodyguards in June 1992. With the sudden extinction of this moment of hope, the crisis deepened and violence increased, with anything from 100,000 to 200,000 killed. As Jacob Mundy has stressed, "Whatever political character the violence had in relation to questions of democratic governance and party participation in early 1992, this character seemed to bear no relation to the killing that escalated from 1993 onward."[18]

In the years that followed, Algerian academics, writers, and journalists were targeted in a series of attacks, thought to have been orchestrated by disenfranchised former members of the FIS, who had joined its armed faction, the Armée islamique du salut [Islamic Salvation Army] (AIS) or one of the elements of the Groupe islamique armée [Armed Islamic Group] (GIA).[19] On May 26, 1993, the novelist Tahar Djaout was shot as he left his home in a suburb of Algiers; he died in hospital a week later. One of the first writers to be killed, Djaout was also the cofounder of the radical independent newspaper *Ruptures*, which had launched in 1993. For many a staunch defender of freedom of expression in Algeria, Djaout's death led to his writing becoming a symbol of the war and cornerstone of anti-Islamist discourse.[20]

Some of the most shocking violence to be documented would take the form of massacres perpetrated between 1994 and 1998.[21] Those receiving most international attention were the massacres that took place between August and September 1997 at Raïs and Bentalha, where more than 700 people are reported to have been brutally murdered.[22] What was different about these massacres was that in the numerous accounts emerging from survivors, the army was accused of not intervening, despite being stationed nearby and, in the case of Bentalha, apparently standing guard at the edge of the town.[23] As with the (brief) international attention they brought to the Algerian crisis, these massacres would give rise to the famous and still unresolved 'Qui tue qui?' [who's killing who?] question. Accounts of the massacres were published in France; Nesroulah Yous's *Qui a tué à Bentalha? [Who killed at Bentalha?]* (2000) was one of the several texts that accused the Algerian army of staging the violence of the 1990s through widespread infiltration of the GIA made by special forces officers.[24] Information, albeit limited and likely biased, was creeping out of the crisis to, as Martin Evans and John

Phillips put it, challenge "the official script of the 'good army' versus the 'evil terrorists.'"[25]

Situating the roots of the 1990s crisis in an identity-based struggle that had long been playing out within the upper echelons of the one-party FLN State, Hugh Roberts underlines the importance of understanding the FIS as an offshoot of the Islamist elements of the FLN that had fashioned itself as a State with an Arabic, Islamic, and socialist identity.[26] Indeed, the FIS actively appropriated the language of revolutionary legitimacy, painting the FLN as a group of "corrupt apostates" who had stolen the revolution from its people, undoubtedly helping its success in the first round of the elections.[27] Although often presented as an emerging "civil war," where the legitimate government faced an illegitimate "challenge" from an Islamist opposition, and despite the extreme violence, the conflict became notable for its invisibility on the international stage as well as for its lack of a clear sense of who was responsible for the violence.[28]

One consequence of the historical vacuum facing scholars and critics throughout the years of the Black Decade—coupled with the inaccessibility of Algeria to foreign journalists and scholars—was that the violence of the 1990s was never clearly situated in historical conditions, but rather filled with a series of competing narratives within and outside Algeria. Written, on the one hand, by Algerian writers who had largely fled the country and taken refuge in France, testimonial accounts (packaged as literary texts) began to enter the Parisian publishing market. Meanwhile, on the other hand, political scientists began to fill the historiographical void with studies that attempted to understand the dynamics of violence without clear access to empirical realities on the ground. In both cases, writers and critics relied on preexisting narrative tropes about Algerian violence—inherited largely from the War of Independence of 1954–1962—that succeeded, at best, in perpetuating obscure or ambiguous accounts and, at worst, reproduced a set of reductive stereotypes that pitted supposed factions against one another in a battle of identities and cultures. As Walid Benkhaled and Natalya Vince highlight, these "mutually exclusive" divisions were drawn along binary lines and took the form of a despotic "system" set against a "downtrodden" population, a backward-facing "tradition" versus a forward-looking "modernity" and a supposedly violent political Islam set against a purportedly "progressive" secularism.[29] Linked to this, cultural and linguistic identities were also weaponized with supposedly "progressive" Francophones pitted against more "regressive" Arabic-speaking intellectuals.[30]

As it pertains to Algeria during the 1990s, literature and its designation as a predominantly emancipatory mode is tied up with important questions of the mediation of literary narratives about conflict via the news media, literary journals, and academic criticism, as well as the normative status of "testimonial literature" and its supposed ability to communicate "facts" about what had become a largely invisible conflict to the outside world. These mediating spaces of literature can be divided, broadly speaking, into four main categories: news, journalism and literary criticism published in journalistic outlets; history and political science; academic literary criticism; writers and publishers themselves. In the discussion that follows, I focus on these four mediating spaces of literature with the intention of explaining how they relate in specific ways to the 1990s conflict. Readers who wish to skip ahead to the main content of the book can go directly to the chapter overviews (20–23) and main chapters, which serve as self-contained studies of the writers and works examined.

NEWS, JOURNALISM, AND LITERARY CRITICISM

If the vacuum in news from Algeria led to the propagation of a series of narratives and stereotypes about the violence occurring throughout the 1990s, these reductive images have long outlasted the conflict itself. For Natalya Vince, this is exemplified in the reporting of an incident that took place some thirteen years after the end of the Black Decade, when a gas facility, located in the east of the Algerian Sahara, was seized by Islamist militants in January 2013. The presence of foreign workers at the installation meant the hostage situation made international headlines. As Vince explains, while clearly lacking expertise on Algeria, the media narrative quickly related the hostage-taking, and the subsequent intervention by the Algerian army, to Algeria's "savage" and "bloody" past in the War of Independence and violent "civil war" of the 1990s. Accounts of the incident reproduced the "Orientalist stereotype of Algerians" as, bluntly put, "a bunch of crazy hothead machos, for whom human life means little and pride everything."[31] If this example does not contain explicit references to writers or literature, the stereotypes are part of a story crafted in the news media that takes inspiration from Orientalist conceptions of "the East" propagated in European art and literature.[32]

Other examples of this kind of reporting can be found across French newspapers throughout the 1990s and since the end of the Black Decade. In the French daily *Le Monde*, Catherine Simon captures the general tone of many journalists when she describes the conflict as a "guerre fratricide qui déchire l'Algérie" [fratricidal war tearing Algeria apart], while Jean Roy in *L'Humanité* recounts the 1990s in terms of a "barbarie qui sévit en Algérie" [barbarism prevailing in Algeria].[33] Even since the end of the conflict, French newspapers have aligned their coverage of Algerian writers with often reductive accounts of the period of upheaval. As I show in chapter 4, accounts of the French release of Kamel Daoud's novel, *Meursault, contre-enquête* (2013) [*The Meursault Investigation* (2015)], resort to the same violent imagery employed in the French press throughout the 1990s.[34] For instance, the French weekly news magazine, *Le Nouveau Marianne*, recounts the story of the Black Decade as a time when "les djihadistes des GIA, les groupes islamiques armés, égorgeaient l'espérance" [the jihadists of the GIA, the armed Islamic groups, slaughtered/cut the throats of hope].[35]

In his recent history of news in colonial Algeria, Arthur Asseraf writes how news is a "story" that is "understood to be factual by its audience [. . .] *distinct* from fiction, regardless of whether it is accurate or not."[36] And yet, as we can see in the abovementioned examples, the "story" that fills the information vacuum is based largely on *imagined* tropes about Algerian history and culture that are based in Orientalist *fictions*, not fact. Of course, what is important here is how "stories" and "facts" are received by readers of newspapers and testimonial narratives coming out of Algeria during the 1990s.[37] By packaging testimonial accounts as literary texts, and literary texts as testimonial accounts, literary critics working for French newspapers effectively became reporters of "news" from Algeria, while more mainstream news journalists became increasingly acquainted with a form of literary criticism.

At the same time, Algerian writers often work as journalists. Of the writers I consider in this book, three have worked or continue to work as journalists. Most notable are Kamel Daoud, who, as I examine in chapter 4, worked as a prominent and controversial columnist throughout the Black Decade, and Mustapha Benfodil, whose work I explore in chapter 5. Though Benfodil has recently become notable for his involvement in Algerian protest movements, his status as a journalist has no doubt made his literary work more visible. Contrastingly, Daoud's literary success has led to his resurgence as a journalist writing in French and international outlets in the wake of the Black Decade.

The Algerian writer Maïssa Bey, whose work I explore in chapter 1, picks up on this interweaving of journalism and literature in the title and preface to her 1998 collection of short stories, *Nouvelles d'Algérie*. The text, which begins "[v]oici des nouvelles d'Algérie" [here are/is some short stories/news from Algeria], plays immediately with the ambiguity of the French term "nouvelle," which means both "short story" and "news," and thus draws the reader's attention to the appropriation of literature for the purposes of communicating "news" as well as the infiltration of the "news" media by testimonial literature. Bey's subtle play on words helps us to see how news from Algeria during the 1990s had increasingly become separated from fact and more aligned with rumor and fiction, while literature had become increasingly more proximate to news. As Paul Silverstein demonstrates, rumor and conspiracy theorizing became a strategy for Algerians in France to feel part of a "transnational imagined community" engaged in the politics of the conflict.[38] And news of the publication of the latest testimonial text from Algeria often became the occasion upon which this community would be informed by French reporters about new information emerging out of the country.

While journalists and literary critics working for French newspapers during this time were probably unaware of it, the work they did in framing literary testimony as news is likely to have contributed to a "culture of conspiracy" that reinforced "an alternative truth regime" among Algerian exiles in France.[39] According to Silverstein, what was presented as "moral critique" took on "the ironic guise of hyper-nationalist rhetoric," because "a critique that questions [. . .] paradoxically legitimates State power at the precise moment of its greatest challenge."[40] Indeed, as Charles Bonn wrote in the late 1980s, ideological discourse only worked to symbolically reinforce the nation-State if the people were permitted to continually question State power.[41] And, as I address in the discussion of academic literary criticism later, there is an important link between the ethical claims made about literature in times of conflict and how literary texts are understood to play an oppositional or contestatory role in relation to political power.

HISTORY AND POLITICAL SCIENCE

With reliable information limited, many historians and political scientists who sought to make sense of the initial history of the 1990s were entering into the battlefield of "competing narratives" as stressed by McDougall.[42] Some fell back on oppositional tropes and recidivist narratives abounded both outside Algeria, where historians had little access to information on the ground, and inside Algeria, where citizens were faced with obfuscatory and conflicting narratives offered by the authorities.[43]

One of the most prolific historians of Algeria publishing work during the Black Decade was Benjamin Stora. Famous for his historical work on the War of Independence and his biography of the dissident Algerian nationalist Messali Hadj, Stora is widely acknowledged to be the most influential French-language historian of Algeria and, according to Benkhaled and Vince, has been one of the most influential figures for scholars across the disciplines seeking to interpret the Black Decade.[44] While, within Algeria, images of the repetition of the War of Independence in the period of the Black Decade appeared very real, these images were also being used in an essentialist and reductive manner outside the country.[45] An image repeatedly evoked was that of the "once oppressed" Algerian slipping into the position of the "oppressor."[46] In a 1995 article in *Les Temps Modernes*, Stora draws attention to this narrative of repetition—what he explicitly names the "récidive."[47] Citing Albert Camus's "Discours pour une trêve civile en Algérie" from January 1956 in an epigraph to his article, Stora aligns the two periods of war. The epigraph, which reads "L'histoire se répète comme une bouche sanglante qui ne vomit qu'un bégaiement furieux" [the story repeats itself like a bloody mouth vomiting in a furious stutter], finds its way into Stora's text which asks of the possibility of naming the 1990s a "deuxième guerre algérienne" [Second Algerian War].[48] While offering a critical reflection of the instances of repetition, Stora nevertheless adopts the language of "first" and "second" wars that reduces Algerian history to a story about violence. And though he ultimately rejects the idea of the "second" war, he does view the crisis years of the 1990s as "a consequence of failing to work through the trauma of the war of independence."[49]

Throughout and since the end of the Black Decade, the dominant languages of conflict and power have also actively drawn upon narrative tropes inherited from the War of Independence. While McDougall underlines how the multiparty experiment of the early 1990s constituted a "shop window"—a mirage of democracy that was in effect about splitting the opposition and forging new "networks for clientism and patronage"—increasingly entrenched narratives of opposition would come to have a material effect on the performance of violence during the height of the massacres in 1997.[50] Here, "ritualistic violence," where corpses and severed heads were exhibited in public or left on people's doorsteps, deployed "well-known scripts" drawn from the War of Independence where the bodies of Algerian soldiers were left in public spaces. For McDougall, the reality was not so much that of a recidivist "return of the repressed," but rather part of "calculated *mises en scène*" that sacralize violence and ruthlessly divide the population pitting a glorified armed insurrection against groups of dehumanized victims.[51]

Another influential commentator criticized for his use of recidivist tropes is the political scientist Luis Martinez and his book, *La guerre civile en Algérie* (1999), which was published in an English translation just one year later in 2000.[52] In his review of the text, Roberts questions the way Martinez uses symbols of past conflict to frame and explain the Black Decade. Adopting an "imaginaire de la guerre" [imaginary of war] and advancing the pathologizing trope of "war in general" to explain how Algerians traditionally use violence to attain power, Martinez reads the actors of the conflict in overly symbolic terms.[53] As Roberts comments, in Martinez's vision,

> The emirs of the GIA are to be understood as the latest in a series of emblematic figures dominating Algerian history, all of whom exemplify in different guises, the idea of "the political bandit," a series which begins with the Barbary corsairs of the pre-colonial era, followed by the caïds [. . .] and the colonels who commanded the guerrilla units of the *Armée de Libération Nationale* (ALN) during the war of independence.[54]

As Roberts concludes, "the Martinez thesis boils down to a reformulation, within the trappings of academic sophistication, of that very old, and unmistakably cultural-essentialist, idea, to which the *pieds noirs* were so viscerally attached, that *les Arabes* are cut-throats."⁵⁵

It will have been difficult, near-impossible perhaps, for historians like Stora or political scientists like Martinez to see the theatrical maneuvers by the State, without gaining some distance from the conflict. As I discuss later, more explicit uses of theatrical language and aesthetics by the Algerian State came several years after the end of the conflict in 2005. Nevertheless, the imaginary and symbolic lenses that some historians and political scientists came to rely upon further consecrated the reductive international media narrative that the Black Decade was a conflict rooted in cultures of "Arab" violence.

After coming to power on the promise of legislating the end of the conflict, Bouteflika's government called precisely on the theatrical and aesthetic languages that had dominated throughout the 1990s to bring about a renewed sense of national unity. A continuation of earlier policies drafted by Liamine Zéroual (president of Algeria between the disbanding of the HCE in 1994 and the election of Bouteflika in 1999), the new president's flagship policy was the "Concorde civile" [Civil Concorde], which promised amnesty to members of armed groups. On paper, the amnesty did not excuse the more serious crimes of rape, murder, or torture, but the reality was that the new laws meant a broad amnesty and constituted an attempt to impose an "official silence" on the violence of the 1990s, including on crimes that were sanctioned by the armed forces or security services.⁵⁶ The law was voted in by referendum, with 98.6 percent in favor (based on an apparent turnout of 85 percent) and was, in 2005, further consecrated in the "Charte pour la paix et la réconciliation nationale" [Charter for Peace and National Reconciliation].⁵⁷ Deploying an explicitly theatrical language, the 2005 charter labeled the Black Decade Algeria's "tragédie nationale" [national tragedy] and outlawed any appropriation of its "blessures" [wounds] for destabilizing the nation-State, security forces, or damaging Algeria's image on the international stage.⁵⁸ As Laurie Brand writes, the charter implicitly recalled the anti-colonial war, as the security forces were placed alongside "the people," who had *together* "struggled nobly against a vicious enemy."⁵⁹ The fact that Bouteflika, and the authors of the charter, chose to use an aesthetic frame was not just an acknowledgment that what had been lost during the height of the violence of the 1990s was a narrative order, but that regaining control of the discourse required reestablishing a "shared language of power" in which citizens could also have a stake in the narrative that would, in turn, allow them to access social and political capital.⁶⁰

Historical and political science literature published in recent years moves toward a critical appraisal of the centrality of symbolic narrative to the way the Black Decade has been narrated inside and outside Algeria.[61] Indeed, many writers publishing inside Algeria from 2000 onwards experimented with literature and the capacity of the literary form to stage the kind of critical distance required to gain a fuller understanding of the political manipulation of history, symbol, and the aesthetic during and after the 1990s. As such, writers have increasingly been able to unveil the way contestatory narratives of conflict had been central to making the political present in Algeria, based as it was on an intensely polarized opposition between State and Islam.

Of course, while binary and recidivist narratives were played out during the 1990s conflict in Algeria, they were set within more widespread trends in political and conflict science that turned toward notions of culture, identity, and "civilization" as a means of mapping out a parallel void in the great unknowns of the new post–Cold War era. After the fall of the Berlin Wall in 1989, political theorists plotted new narratives in what they claimed was an attempt to predict what might happen in a future that would no longer be defined by ideology, but by identity. One of the most (in)famous of these hypotheses was advanced by the political scientist, Samuel P. Huntington, whose 1993 essay, "The Clash of Civilizations?," strikingly captured the shift in conflict science from studying political, economic, and ideological power to privileging notions of culture.[62] Alongside Bernard Lewis's earlier essay from 1990, "The Roots of Muslim Rage," Huntington posited that conflicts between Islam and the West would be at the center of a new global politics.[63] Drawn along "cultural fault lines," a series of "basic" differences between civilizations—and principally religions—would come to dominate future conflicts.[64] In an article that is itself replete with Orientalist stereotypes and culturalist and identitarian language, Huntington fails (or has little desire) to recognize how the "fault lines" of religious identity were in fact being weaponized by those in power for *ideological* ends. Taking the incendiary speech of figures such as Saddam Hussein and Ayotallah Ali Khomeni as evidence of a clash of civilizations, Huntington mistakes *political appropriations* of the language of clashing cultures for an *empirical* reality.[65] As Mundy writes, what was not considered by Huntington and Lewis—and those conflict scientists who willingly took up their simplistic language—was the idea "that 'civilization' and 'identity' were part of the 'cultural logic' of a nascent geopolitics that no one could explain without reproducing this logic's self-image."[66] In other words, the "clash of civilizations" was a self-fulfilling prophecy whose polarizing narrative served to further perpetuate conflict.[67]

Huntington and Lewis's narratives gained traction because of the simplicity of the binary narratives they employed. In the context of the Black Decade, observers willingly co-opted their language of culturalist opposition to "Islamize" the violence, especially when reporting on the massacres of 1997–1998.⁶⁸ While initially a product of the void of history after the end of the Cold War, and of the political fallout of the early 1990s in Algeria, binary conflict narratives such as those adopted by Huntington and Lewis have a troubling legacy, especially in the significant, and yet most likely factitious, links between violence and identity that have been repeatedly drawn since September 11, 2001.⁶⁹

To return to Mundy's observation that the character of the violence after 1993 had little relation to debates over democratic governance in 1992, it is nevertheless the case that political parties, such as the Parti de l'avant-garde socialiste [Party of the Socialist Avant-Garde] (PAGS)—former Parti communiste algérien [Algerian Communist Party] (PCA)—and to a lesser extent the Rassemblement pour la culture et la démocratie [Rally for Culture and Democracy] (RCD), created their own self-fulfilling narrative in their extreme opposition to political Islam.⁷⁰ As Malika Rahal shows in her investigation of the PAGS archives, continual references to the need for "radical suppression" of Islamists foreshadowed the polarized conflict of the Black Decade.⁷¹ As Rahal writes,

> Constant references to a threat to come, the apocalyptical anguish expressed and created by such discourse, emphasized by the frequent reference to the Iranian revolution of 1979 and the threat of the Islamic Republic that followed, acted as a means to construct the enemy and accelerate the descent into civil war.⁷²

As self-fulfilling prophecies, these oppositional narratives offer political (the case of the PAGS) and scholarly (in the case of Huntington and Lewis) cover for violence. Far from learning lessons from the mistakes of the past, many commentators have continued to rely on these self-perpetuating narratives of cultural conflict, often implicitly advancing their own reductive narratives of the post–Cold War order.

ACADEMIC LITERARY CRITICISM

Much existing academic criticism produced about literature in times of conflict focuses on the notion of "post-conflict." This is because literature is very rarely produced in the immediate moment of conflict, but part of a process of reflection that occurs after the putative end of conflicts. In their edited volume, *Post-Conflict Literature: Human Rights, Peace, Justice* (2016), Chris Andrews and Matt McGuire argue that in the age of the spectacular, literature can offer an "alternative discourse" to work through the "invisible injuries" of the past.⁷³ However, while we must clearly recognize that the practices of reading and writing can be forms of what Mireille Rosello has called the "reparative in narrative," it is also vital to acknowledge how the literary as an idea has been appropriated and weaponized during and after times of conflict.[74]

While often more circumspect than journalists and literary critics writing in newspapers, academic literary critics, like historians and political scientists, are not immune to the dangers of reductionism. Indeed, Andrews and McGuire go on to define literature as a form of "counter-history"; here, the literary text is a privileged site for capturing "experiences of vulnerability and loss" as well as for addressing the "political and ethical responsibilities that emerge as a result."[75] The problem with this definition is that, in their attempt to understand "post-conflict literature," Andrews and McGuire attribute an antagonistic, or conflictual, "retrospective ethos" to literature.[76]

In attributing retroactive ethics to literature, moreover, Andrews and McGuire's approach aligns with those scholars of literary and memory studies whose work draws directly on certain kinds of "testimonial literature" produced at times of conflict. In her 2012 study, Névine El Nossery asks how the ethical could be seen to coexist with the aesthetic during the Algerian conflict of the 1990s. Yet, the critic's characterization of literature as a "weapon" against the rise of Islamic fundamentalism and State violence constructs a "mutually exclusive" vision of Algeria that reductively pits a "downtrodden" population against the backward-facing violence of Islam and the State.[77] El Nossery is not alone here. In the introduction to their 2010 special issue, "Ecrire en temps de détresse" [Writing in Times of Distress], which is partially focused on the Black Decade, Belaïd Djefel and Boussad Saïm underline how the writer leads in a "bataille du sens" [battle of meaning] fought to "apprivoiser le mal" [to win over evil].[78] Other academic literary critics, such as Patricia Geesey and Mildred Mortimer, have tended to focus on the singular status of "dissident" women writers during the Black Decade.[79]

Rather than attempting to understand the complexities of the roots of the Black Decade, some academic literary critics have repeated simplistic stereotypes about Algerians when referring to the violence. In a chapter on the representation of women in Albert Camus, published in the prestigious Cambridge Companion series, Danielle Marx-Scouras deploys a grotesque imagery of attacks on women in Algeria to advance a reductive idea of the country as "giv[ing] birth to fundamentalist terrorists who thought nothing of raping their sisters and slitting the throats of their mothers, of bashing the heads of babies in the name of 'justice.'"[80] By invoking the image of the nation "giving birth" to terrorism, and further defining the conflict as a "'second' Algerian War," Marx-Scouras reinforces the idea that the conflict was rooted in a culture instinctively prone to recidivist violence. This is despite

Marx-Scouras's own critique of a "cultural radicalism" in France that, she says, "cannot accommodate the Other."[81]

Indeed, a posthumous Camus, whose name and work enjoyed a resurgence among journalists, historians, academic literary critics, and writers during the Black Decade, was at the core of what became an "ethical" response to the crisis years of the 1990s. Stora's mention of the Algerian-born writer's 1956 "Discours pour une 'trêve civile en Algérie'" to contextualize the 1990s conflict was symptomatic of a more general tendency to view the 1990s through the lens of Camus's "ethical" position on the War of Independence.[82] Here, Camus's apparently nonviolent stance came to offer a kind of "third way" for writers and critics who understood the 1990s conflict to be the result of an increasingly polarized discourse of State versus Islam. Academic literary critics such as Christiane Chaulet-Achour have extensively documented the reappearance of Camus's name and work during the 1990s, but some critics have gone further and moved into the realm of literature, as they themselves reimagine Camus's response to the contemporary crisis.[83]

In the 2004 proceedings to a conference held on Camus and Algeria, Alek Baylee Toumi—an Algerian academic living in the United States and the brother of then Algerian minister of culture, Khalida Toumi—published a curious play entitled *Albert Camus: entre la mère et l'injustice* [Albert Camus: Between the mother and injustice].[84] The play, which was subtitled "plaidoyer pour la réhabilitation d'Albert Camus en Algérie" [plea for the rehabilitation of Albert Camus in Algeria], continued Camus's 1957 cliffhanger short story "l'Hôte" [The Guest].[85] While Toumi adds a more finite ending to Camus's ambivalent short story, the "genèse" [genesis] to the play, published in the same proceedings, fuses Camus's ethical pronouncements with Toumi's own biography in the conflict of the Black Decade:

La passion du théâtre, Américain d'origine kabyle, ni complètement Algérien, ni Français, en exil aux Etats-Unis, dans un entre-deux devenu un entre-trois, la peste galonnée, la barbarie des GIA, nouvelles "misères de la Kabylie" en 2001, ma famille menacée, une sœur condamnée à mort, des islamistes qui sont allés pour égorger ma propre mère à Alger, une seconde guerre d'Algérie qui a déjà fait plus de cent cinquante mille victimes civiles. Si ces morts pouvaient renaître, ne diraient-ils pas tous, à l'unisson, qu'entre ma mère républicaine et la justice intégriste, "je choisirai ma mère avant la justice."[86]

[The passion of the theatre, an American of Kabylian origin, not completely Algerian, nor French, in exile in the United States, in a space "between two" which has become a space "between three," the tasselled plague, the barbarianism of the GIA, new "miseries of Kabylia" in 2001, my family threatened, a sister condemned to death, Islamists who went to slit the throat of my own mother in Algiers, a second Algerian war that has already led to more than 150,000 innocent deaths. If the dead could be reborn, would they not all declare, in unison, that between my republican mother and a fundamentalist justice, "I would choose my mother before justice."]

We can see here how what is initially broached as a reparative retrospective ethics becomes part of a personal and political pursuit, as Camus's infamous statement about choosing his mother over justice is refigured in the contemporary context of the 1990s conflict as a choice between a "republican" mother and "fundamentalist" justice.[87] Here, ethics is marshaled to produce yet another "mutually exclusive" vision of contemporary Algeria that pits progressive secular republicanism against political Islam.[88]

This return to a Camusian "ethics" is also present in Aziz Chouaki's 1997 play, *Les Oranges* [Oranges].[89] In the play, Chouaki imagines Camus dividing a symbolic Algerian watermelon into wide round slices so that everyone can have "un peu de cœur" [a bit of its heart].[90] For the narrator, the question is no longer about the controversial reception of Camus's *L'Etranger* [*The Outsider*] (1942), or doubts over pronouncements that he preferred his mother to justice, but a down-to-earth humanist ethics that recognizes the plurality of what he calls "la grande famille des oranges" [the big family of oranges]—a symbol for a pluralistic and inclusive Algerian identity.[91] Just as Toumi turned playwright, Chouaki turned critic when he published a short piece, "Le Tag et le Royaume" [The Tag and the Kingdom], in the same conference proceedings.[92] Chouaki describes his, and his fellow writers', exile from Algeria in terms of a repetition of the departing French settlers after independence in 1962: "Pour nous, écrivains algériens d'exil, version années 90, on a vécu le remake pied noir de 62. La valise ou le cercueil exactement. Au point où il n'est pas faux de dire qu'on est des pied noirs [*sic*] de deuxième génération, comme un deuxième ressac de l'histoire." [For us, exiled Algerian writers of the 1990s, we experienced the pied-noir remake of 1962. The suitcase or the coffin indeed. To the point where it is not untrue to say that we are second generation pied-noirs, the backwash of history.][93] If such rehabilitations of Camus might for some spark a reconciliatory note, they also confuse politics with ethics and advance recidivist narratives of recent Algerian history in the process.[94]

While, of course, ethics is a foundational part of readers' relationship to literature—and the ideas we have about literature—scholarship focused on the ethical capacity of literature to "tell" conflict has tended to eschew political considerations, particularly the way in which literature has been received and understood in different ways by different critics. One reason for this is that these critics appraise literary texts in the present moment and thereby are more likely to fall victim to a dominant language that prevails at that moment.

But this process is a mutually constitutive one because critics are central to producing the dominant frames through which readers apprehend literature and attribute to it an ability to recount a history of conflict.

Hafid Gafaïti is one of the very few to admit complicity in perpetuating polarizing ideas about the 1990s conflict. Revisiting the work he published at the height of the violence in 1997, Gafaïti explains how commentators understood the Black Decade as a "war of languages" that opposed supposedly "progressive" Francophones and "regressive" Arabophones.[95] Describing how he himself had fallen into this "simplistic perspective," the critic demonstrates the need not just for further analytical nuance but for a more self-reflexive scholarship among academic literary critics.[96]

In the introduction to their book, Andrews and McGuire embrace T. S. Eliot's understanding that literature "give[s] shape and significance to the immense panorama of futility and anarchy which is contemporary history."[97] However, by adopting Eliot's idea of literature, the editors appear to reduce history to the event itself, without noting the work of history as an academic discipline in unpacking and scrutinizing the narrative of events that Eliot uses to frame his presentation of "contemporary history" as "futile" and "anarchic." The problem here is twofold: first, history—and the work of historians—risks being obscured; and second, literature is privileged as a singular site or lens through which violent events acquire meaning. Throughout this book, I show how literature is never alone in the process of illuminating violence, encountering history, or mapping out new political futures. Rather, literature is part of a complex web of discourses that make the world.

WRITERS AND PUBLISHERS

The 1990s were, as Stora has argued, a time when Algeria became increasingly "invisible" to the outside world.[98] However, this was also a moment when Algerian literary testimonies, as well as other nonfictional testimonies, experienced an upsurge in publications, notably within publishing houses in France.[99] Prized for its graphic, shock realist, representations of the violence in Algeria, this body of writing became known as "écriture de l'urgence" [emergency writing] and has variously been described on a scale ranging from a necessary work of testimony, or of anamnesis regarding the silences of the period, to a problematic body of writing which plays to a thematic demand in order to appeal to a mostly French readership.[100] The problem was that it was far from clear which works could be placed within "écriture de l'urgence" and what were the formal or generic markers of this designation. Applied by journalists and academic literary critics to a host of writers producing work during the 1990s, the term came in some ways to characterize a heterogeneous body of literature in overly homogenous terms. The headline-grabbing terminology also led some writers to ultimately denounce what they saw as an overly realist or referential genre developing within French publishing houses.[101]

Throughout the period of the Black Decade, publishers offered confused and confusing narratives of their own texts. The case of Fériel Assima's *Une Femme à Alger* is instructive.[102] The publisher's blurb on the back cover describes the work as both "témoignage sans complaisance" [uncompromising testimony] and "littérature" [literature]; and, while the book is described as apolitical, it nevertheless carries the subtitle "*chronique* du désastre" [chronicle of the disaster].[103] As Pamela Pears argues, front and back cover iconography, as well as the accompanying paratext, are part of both selling Algerian literature—in particular women's writing—and exerting "control over [its] critical reception."[104] The confusion about the role of testimonial literature in communicating "news" from Algeria reveals how publishers and journalists alike had little interest in promoting or assessing the literary qualities of texts, seeking instead to privilege their capacity to tell and sell.

Whereas writers might have intended to offer a more ethically sensitive response to the violence they had witnessed during the years of the conflict, they initially neglected to see that their literary texts were part of a growing market for testimonial literature in France. As Tristan Leperlier and others have noted, the focus on women writers emerged in an increasingly conservative and neoliberal Parisian publishing market that, in its drive for profits, developed an Orientalizing impulse, falling back on gendered and ethnocentric colonial stereotypes.[105] In his study, Leperlier details how women writers were put under pressure to change the focus or style of their literary works in order that they conform to a certain expectation among French publishers.[106] In her account of leaving the French publisher Editions Julliard for Editions du Seuil, Leïla Marouane stresses how the former had wanted to impose "une certaine image de l'Algérie et les espaces thématiques à traiter" [a certain image of Algeria and the thematic areas to be addressed].[107] Marouane describes how her editors at Julliard encouraged her to write "dans un registre précis, défini par lui, c'est-à-dire une écriture féminine, avec en sus Shéhérazade des Mille et Une Nuits et la danse du ventre" [in a precise register, defined by them, that's to say a feminine writing, akin to Shéhérazade from the Thousand and One Nights and belly dancing].[108] In addition to these Orientalizing narratives was a referential aesthetics—where, for instance, place names had to clearly resemble contemporary Algeria—and an expectation that women writers would "speak for" a broad community of women conceived to be under attack in their country. In this way, publishers and critics called upon the tropes of a "culture war" or "clash of civilizations" discussed earlier—only this time, women writers were co-opted into the polarizing conflict narrative.

As I show in chapter 1, the role of the Algerian writer as "spokesperson" was put under the spotlight by Assia Djebar some ten years prior to the outbreak of the conflict of the 1990s.[109] Critics such as Deepika Bahri develop the notion of "native intelligence" as central to market, pedagogical, and cultural spaces defined as postcolonial literature, where the minority view is privileged as "authentic" and where the "native informant" fulfills the demands of a "needy metropolitan audience."[110] Relatedly, Ato Quayson has stressed the risks of "misapprehending postcolonial literature as being a simple reflection of conditions in postcolonial societies"—as "a form of testimonial."[111] Meanwhile, Harrison points toward Gayatri Spivak's signaling of the German distinction between *vertreten* and *darstellen*; both can be translated as "representation" but the first refers to political and the latter to artistic representation.[112] For Gillian Beer, women writers are at particular risk of being adopted as "tokens" of a broader constituency of women. As she writes in 1989,

> *I* am not a representative woman representing all women: I am not speaking on behalf of all of us, or occupying the space of those who differ from me. The demand that as women we claim women as our constituency may rapidly move from desirable solidarity to tokenism. So the woman finds herself there *in place of* a wide range of other women, uttering wise saws on their behalf, creating the uniformity of universals all over again.[113]

Here, Beer unpacks how women writers in particular are co-opted into a "uniformity of universals" defined along patriarchal norms. It is interesting, and perhaps not a coincidence, that this gendered collapsing of the political into the artistic occurs at the same time as the emergence of postcolonial studies as a recognized discipline in the West.

The tendency to understand the postcolonial writer as "spokesperson" is further complicated by the ways in which a previous generation of Algerian writers, publishing before and immediately after the War of Independence, related their literature and poetry to an "engaged" or "revolutionary" mode of expression. As Jane Hiddleston has demonstrated, writers such as Kateb Yacine, as well as non-Algerian theorists Frantz Fanon and Jean-Paul Sartre, drew an explicit connection between poetry and revolution.[114] As I show in chapters 3 and 4, Kateb, Fanon, and Sartre are certainly visible in the literary expression of contemporary Algerian writers. However, the legacy of these "engaged" figures also poses problems for writers who must contend with a very different, often obscured or conflicting, set of historical and political circumstances.

Another legacy of the generation of writers that lived through the War of 1954–1962 is that their defense of writing in the colonial language of French meant that the "progressive ideals" associated with fighting for Algeria's independence came later to be linked with Francophone writers who, in turn, were understood as fighting a rising religious fundamentalism or oppressive Arabophone one-party State.[115] Yet, as we have seen, the idea that the Black Decade was a "war of languages" that opposed Francophones and Arabophones has not only been found to be overly simplistic but can be seen to contribute to a self-fulfilling Manichean discourse that relied on false notions of a culture war or clash of civilizations.[116] Many of the writers I study here attenuate that more simplistic narrative of opposition, deploying literature in different ways to complicate existing conceptions of the Algerian writer and to throw into doubt the contestatory status of their own art.[117] Indeed, writers themselves become conscious of a need to understand their politicized status, or the ways in which journalists, historians, and academic literary critics understand and use literature (consciously or unconsciously) for political or ideological ends.

Toward the end of the 1990s, we see an increasing heterogeneity of the literary field in Algeria. Facilitated by the emergence of new publishers based in Algeria, and not confined by the demands of the French market, Algerian writers who had not published works during the years of the Black Decade found a new home for their literary works.[118] Emerging in 2000 as one of the most dynamic independent publishers in Algeria, Editions Barzakh published what its cofounder and director Selma Hellal referred to as "manuscrits dans [les] tiroirs" [manuscripts in drawers]—texts that Algerian writers had written throughout the 1990s but were unable to publish.[119] Contrary to the thematic demand of the French publishing market, publishers in Algeria were open to experimental texts that revisited the events of the 1990s in more oblique ways.

Named by some academic literary critics as the "1988 generation," writers such as Salim Bachi, Habib Ayyoub, Kamel Daoud, and Mustapha Benfodil have been celebrated for their opposition to State discourse.[120] However, the reality is more complex. While writers might initially appear to pursue a form of opposition similar to that adopted by the revolutionary generation who fought against the French colonizer, they can also be seen to become increasingly aware of the ways in which these expected forms of opposition are, in the wake of the 1990s, co-opted into an overarching spectacle of power. As I discuss in chapter 3 with reference to Achille Mbembe, the danger here is that writers end up "ratifying" a hegemonic narrative the "regime" seeks to advance of itself.[121] Such encounters with opposition, and the building up of greater knowledge about the workings of oppositional discourse in Algeria, are vital in assessing literary texts written in the aftermath of the Black

Decade, as well as the ongoing revolutionary activity of the "Hirak," which began in February 2019.[122]

Having changed the constitution to allow him to stand for a fourth presidential term in 2014, Bouteflika and his supporters proposed his candidacy for a fifth term in early 2019. This was despite the president having suffered several severe strokes and being unable to govern for many years. Credited for bringing an end to the violence in the years immediately after the Black Decade, Bouteflika—and the obscure figures around him known by Algerians as *les décideurs* [the decision makers]—became increasingly unpopular. After he submitted his candidacy in February 2019, citizens took to the streets across Algeria in peaceful mass demonstrations. While protests countering his reelection to a fourth term in 2014 had failed, the demonstrations of 2019 forced Bouteflika to resign on April 3 and led to the arrest of key figures around him.

The president's resignation indicated a shift in power dynamics at the core of the Algerian State, but the protests of the Hirak were rooted in a longer history of political and cultural critique in Algeria that has used aesthetics to break free of what had become a "zombified" state of political discourse.[123] The work of the journalist, political activist, and writer, Mustapha Benfodil, is indicative of the way literature can be used to deconstruct dominant understandings of power and opposition. As I show in chapter 5, the experimental form of the novel moves readers beyond a polarized conflict narrative of the Black Decade at the same time as offering new and inventive ways of understanding power and resistance through the medium of art and literature.

CHAPTER OVERVIEW

Chapter 1 is unique in that it draws on several writers producing testimonial literature during the Black Decade. Meanwhile, chapters 2–5 each take a single author as their focus. By looking at a sample of works produced during the Black Decade itself, I hope to give readers an initial sense of how different forms of testimony framed distinct narratives of the unfolding conflict.

In its first part, chapter 1 examines how the Algerian writer Rachid Mimouni uses testimonial literature to reduce the Algerian crisis in its early years to the narrative of "clash of cultures" and "civilizations" advanced by political scientists such as Huntington and Lewis. Focusing on Mimouni's political and literary texts, I show how the writer plays on general and specific anxieties about Islamism and the role of Islam in 1990s Algeria and France.[124] At stake here is the question about the degree to which writers publishing work between the political unrest of 1988 to 1992, and prior to the intensification of the violence after 1993, are wittingly or unwittingly complicit in entrenching polarizing narratives that come, as Rahal writes, to "construct the enemy" and thereby "accelerate the descent into civil war."[125] In a second part, I shift my focus to two Algerian women writers, Assia Djebar and Maïssa Bey, who simultaneously produced and scrutinized the possibility of testimonial literature during the 1990s. By examining the interrogative forms they adopt, I critically assess how, while predominantly male writers fused fiction, autobiography, and history to "express the experiences of many," these women writers acknowledged the unreliability of the "truth" testimony purports to tell.[126]

Chapter 2 explores how Salim Bachi picks up the pieces of the self-fulfilling political myth of the "clash of civilizations" that writers such as Mimouni incorporated into their testimonial literature. Reacting by moving away from a referential mode and delving deep into myth, Bachi initially rejects testimonial literature, noting his own preference for the more reflective form of the novel. However, in the final parts of the chapter, I show how Bachi paradoxically returns to a form of referential writing in order to scrutinize the return, after September 11, 2001, of the harmful myths of the "clash of cultures" and "civilizations" in the media and dominant political narratives. As with other writers, Bachi can be seen to fall into the trap of repeating recidivist tropes, but his works reveal the changing ideas he has about literature. The shuttling between different narrative forms is a movement intimately linked with the author's concern for the ways myth and the mythologizing process are embedded in the writing of Algeria's history by journalists, historians, academic literary critics, and writers themselves.

In chapter 3, I examine how Habib Ayyoub uses literature to interrogate narratives of opposition during and since the end of the Black Decade. While initially deploying grotesque images of leaders to undermine and "combat" the dominance of the Algerian State apparatus, I show how Ayyoub's literary texts end up developing a more complicated understanding of how citizens and commentators are complicit in the ratification of a dominant spectacle of power that relies upon a "shared language" of resistance established during the War of Independence.[127] Less successful in the global literary marketplace, Ayyoub has struggled to gain recognition outside Algeria, but his works are interesting precisely because they are more directly aimed at an Algerian audience and thereby "give voice" to experiences and perspectives that might otherwise be dismissed.[128] For instance, where Ayyoub's early texts, produced in the immediate aftermath of the Black Decade, capture more explicit satires of grotesque leaders, his recent writing offers a more comprehensive and self-reflexive examination of the historical narrative offered by the State. By staging the play of collaboration and resistance between "ruler" and "ruled," Ayyoub's texts begin to map out the possibility of escape from a fixed discursive structure of power that traps citizens and commentators alike.

Chapter 4 continues to interrogate the thematic of opposition, examining how Kamel Daoud fashions himself as the embattled public intellectual par excellence. In a return to Albert Camus's political and literary legacy, Daoud's *Meursault, contre-enquête* offers both a celebration of Camus's writing and a self-conscious reflection on the place of literature and reading practices in contemporary Algeria. Throughout this chapter, I show how journalists, academic literary critics, and publishers have been complicit in reproducing orthodoxies of opposition, as well as appropriating the period of the Black Decade to further consecrate Daoud as a legitimate "spokesperson" for his Algerian compatriots. Despite Daoud's seeming ability to engage in forms of self-reflexive literary writing, his rise to prominence as a journalist leads him back to some of the more reductive stereotypes prominent among writers such as Mimouni. Ultimately, I argue that Daoud and his supporters actively fashion the writer as an oppositional "spokesperson" for Algeria, using Camus's contested relationship with Algeria as a model, and the Black Decade as a contextual backdrop.

In chapter 5, I turn to the work of the Algerian journalist, political activist, and writer Mustapha Benfodil and his avant-garde novel, *Archéologie du chaos (amoureux)* [*Archelogy of Chaos (lovers)*] (2007). In a first part, I show how Benfodil uses literature to deconstruct the language of oppositional discourse that prevailed during and after the Black Decade. I argue that, by drawing attention to the failure of artists, writers, and protest groups to meaningfully contest a dominant spectacle of power in Algeria, Benfodil's text is (similar to Ayyoub's) able to deconstruct narratives and tropes of opposition that have co-opted citizens into the State's own "shared language" of resistance.[129] However, while Ayyoub offers a text-based deconstruction of the spectacle of power in Algeria, Benfodil goes a step further by taking his text to the streets and reading it aloud in public displays of dissent. In a series of what the author named "Lectures Sauvages" [Wild readings], Benfodil and his supporters read passages from his own work and that of other Algerian writers whose work had been banned in Algeria. While the publication of Ayyoub and Benfodil's texts were not subject to any challenge by the State apparatus, the "Wild Readings" led to Benfodil's arrest and detention. In a final part of the chapter, I show how Benfodil's literary and linguistic experimentation anticipates the public performance of his works, as he attempts to uproot and transfigure the various forms of binary thinking that have configured a stagnant Algerian politics and society throughout and since the end of the Black Decade.

While I resist the temptation to frame literature as a "counter-history," each chapter seeks to reveal the unique capacity of literature to deconstruct dominant frameworks of reception that perpetuate reductive accounts of Algerian society written by some journalists, historians, and academic literary critics, as well as the way in which dominant ideas of power, resistance, and conflict come to shape our understanding of literature. This reciprocal vision of literature in its productive and consumptive spaces (in the shared realm of the writer and the reader or critic) is captured by Said when he underlines how texts and critics alike are "always enmeshed in circumstance, time, place, and society."[130] Taking Said's insight as my starting point, this book attends both to literary texts and the way narratives of time, place, culture, and society determine their reception in the world. Far from simply being forms of contestatory or emancipatory discourse, I show how literature, and those narratives that it either forges or is forged by, can entrench polarized discourse, engender new conflicts of their own making, and ultimately create a map for peace.

NOTES

1. As James McDougall notes, the term "décennie noire" was used from around 2002 onwards to name the violence of the 1990s in Algeria, even if it had initially been used by some to describe the economic crisis and corruption of the 1980s. See James McDougall, *A History of Algeria* (Cambridge: Cambridge University Press, 2017), 385, n. 10. I use the English term "Black Decade" without quotation marks from now on.

2. For a list of books published during the period, see Hadj Miliani, *Une littérature en sursis? Le champ littéraire de langue française en Algérie* (Paris: l'Harmattan, 2002), 237–41. The same is true of films produced about the Black Decade, which have generally been funded from France and are produced in French. See Walid Benkhaled, "Algerian Cinema between Commercial and Political Pressures: The Double Distortion," *Journal of African Cinemas* 8, no. 1 (2016), 87–101.

3. Edward W. Said, *The World, the Text, and the Critic* (Cambridge: Harvard University Press, 1983), 35.

4. Said, *The World*, 35.

5. Pheng Cheah, *What Is a World? On Postcolonial Literature as World Literature* (Durham: Duke University Press, 2016), 129. While I am sympathetic to Cheah's understanding of literature as world-making, I remain cautious about attributing a normative function to literature, as he does in his book.

6. Jacques Rancière, *The Politics of Aesthetics: The Distribution of the Sensible*, trans. Gabriel Rockhill (London: Continuum, 2004), 13.

7. Rancière, *The Politics of Aesthetics*, 14. See also, Margus Vihalem, "Everyday Aesthetics and Jacques Rancière: Reconfiguring the Common Field of Aesthetics and Politics," *Journal of Aesthetics & Culture* 10, no. 1 (2018), 1506209. doi: 10.1080/20004214.2018.1506209

8. Davide Panagia, "'*Partage du sensible*': The Distribution of the Sensible," in *Jacques Rancière: Key Concepts*, ed. Jean-Philippe Deranty (New York: Routledge, 2014), 96.

9. Walid Benkhaled and Natalya Vince, "Performing Algerianness: The National and Transnational Construction of Algeria's 'Culture Wars,'" in *Algeria: Nation, Culture and Transnationalism 1988–2015* ed. Patrick Crowley (Liverpool: Liverpool University Press), 243.

10. As Nicholas Harrison argues, "Any critic dealing with literary texts *needs* an 'idea of the literary.'" See "Preface," *Paragraph* 28, no. 2 (2005), iv.

11. Nicholas Harrison, "Who Needs an Idea of the Literary?," *Paragraph* 28, no. 2 (2005), 12.

12. Nicholas Harrison, *Postcolonial Criticism: History, Theory and the Work of Fiction* (Cambridge: Polity Press, 2003), 137.

13. McDougall, *A History of Algeria*, 292.

14. Martin Evans and John Phillips, *Algeria: Anger of the Dispossessed* (New Haven: Yale University Press, 2007), 105.

15. Hugh Roberts, *The Battlefield Algeria 1988-2002: Studies in a Broken Polity* (London: Verso, 2003), 107–08; see also Evans and Phillips, *Algeria*, 103–04.

16. McDougall, *A History of Algeria*, 289.

17. McDougall, *A History of Algeria*, 289.

18. Jacob Mundy, *Imaginative Geographies of Algerian Violence: Conflict Science, Conflict Management, Antipolitics* (Stanford: Stanford University Press, 2015), 61.

19. The AIS was the successor, in 1994, of the Mouvement islamique algérien [Algerian Islamic Movement] (MIA), both of which sought to force the Algerian State into legalizing the FIS. The various groups making up the GIA, on the other hand, sought to overthrow the State. See Roberts, *The Battlefield Algeria*, 269.

20. Dominique Fisher, *Écrire l'urgence: Assia Djebar et Tahar Djaout* (Paris: L'Harmattan, 2007), 21.

21. These massacres, with approximate numbers killed, are documented in Youcef Bedjaoui et al., *An Inquiry into the Algerian Massacres* (Geneva: Hoggar, 1999).

22. Evans and Phillips, *Algeria*, 237–39.

23. See Roberts, *The Battlefield Algeria*, 309.

24. Nesroulah Yous, *Qui a tué à Bentalha?* (Paris: La Découverte, 2000). Also notable was the testimony of former special forces soldier, Habib Souaïdia, in *La sale guerre: le témoignage d'un ancien officier des forces spéciales de l'armée algérienne* (Paris: La Découverte, 2001) which was released, as with Yous's book, by the left-wing publisher La Découverte, previously Les Editions de Minuit.

25. Evans and Phillips, *Algeria*, 240.

26. Roberts, *The Battlefield Algeria*, 110; 259. I capitalize the word State when referring to the political category, so as not to confuse it with other uses of state (as in "state of discourse," for instance).

27. McDougall, *A History of Algeria*, 296.

28. For discussion over the naming of the conflict, see Luis Martinez, *La Guerre civile en Algérie, 1990–1998* (Paris: Karthala, 1998).

29. Benkhaled and Vince, "Performing Algerianness," 252.

30. See Tristan Leperlier, *Algérie: les écrivains dans la décennie noire* (Paris: CNRS, 2018), 105–62. The split between languages has been consistently instrumentalized by those in positions of power to bring about a simplistic binary division between Algerians using the French language, the so-called *hizb fransa* [the party of France], and those using the official language of Modern Standard Arabic. Hafid Gafaïti has noted how the simplistic Manichean opposition between Francophones and Arabophones denies the complexity of the realities of the violence of the 1990s, while Rahal has shown how these conflicts and instrumentalizations of language can be traced back to factional struggles between the various congresses and associations organizing at the beginning of the Algerian independence movement. See Hafid Gafaïti, "The Monotheism of the Other: Language and De/Construction of National Identity in Postcolonial Algeria," in *Algeria in Others' Languages*, ed. Anne-Emmanuelle Berger (Ithaca: Cornell University Press, 2002), 20–21; see also Malika Rahal, "Fused Together and Torn Apart: Stories and Violence in Contemporary Algeria," *History & Memory* 24, no. 1 (2012), 133–34.

31. Natalya Vince, "In Amenas—A History of Silence, not a History of Violence," *Textures du temps*. http://texturesdutemps.hypotheses.org/576.

32. Edward W. Said, *Orientalism* (New York: Vintage, 1978).

33. Catherine Simon, "L'écrit-survie de Maissa Bey," *Le Monde*, October 17, 1997. https://www.lemonde.fr/archives/article/1997/10/17/l-ecrit-survie-de-maissa-bey_3775463_1819218.html; Jean Roy, "Boudjedra se dresse contre la barbarie," *L'Humanité*, January 7, 1994, Centre cultural algérien, Paris.

34. Kamel Daoud, *Meursault, contre-enquête* (Algiers: Barzakh, 2013/Arles: Acted Sud, 2014). I refer throughout to the original Algerian edition of the novel.

35. Martine Gozlan, "Kamel Daoud contre l'idéologiquement correct," *Le Nouveau Marianne*, November 7, 2014, 64.

36. Arthur Asseraf, *Electric News in Colonial Algeria* (Oxford: Oxford University Press, 2019), 3, my emphasis.

37. It is worth noting that a lack of widespread internet access during the 1990s meant that printed newspapers and testimonial texts carried significant weight for French readers and those Algerians living in France.

38. Paul Silverstein, "An Excess of Truth: Violence, Conspiracy Theorizing and the Algerian Civil War," *Anthropological Quarterly* 75, no. 4 (2002), 644.

39. Silverstein, "An Excess of Truth," 646.

40. Silverstein, "An Excess of Truth," 646.

41. Charles Bonn, "Littérature algérienne et conscience nationale: après l'indépendance," *Notre librairie*, no. 85 (1986), 37.

42. McDougall, *A History of Algeria*, 292.

43. The historian Benjamin Stora notes how the reporting of terrorist attacks in Algeria was banned in 1994. See Benjamin Stora, *La guerre invisible: Algérie des années 90* (Paris: Presses Sciences Po, 2001), 25.

44. Benkhaled and Vince, "Performing Algerianness," 255.

45. As Rahal underlines, when formulating approaches to writing history, scholars of Algerian history and culture must take into consideration the fact that Algerians

have suffered a great deal of exposure to violence. See Rahal, "Fused Together and Torn Apart."

46. Benjamin Stora, "Deuxième guerre algérienne? Les habits anciens des combattants," *Les Temps Modernes*, no. 580 (1995), 242–61.

47. Stora, *La guerre invisible*, 56. On the idea of "codes of violence" during this period, see also James McDougall, "Savage Wars? Codes of violence in Algeria, 1830s–1990s," *Third World Quarterly* 26, no. 1 (2005), 117–31.

48. Stora, "Deuxième guerre algérienne?"; see also, Albert Camus, "Pour une trêve civile en Algérie," in *Essais* (Paris: Gallimard, 1965 [1956]), 991–99. For more extensive discussion of Camus and Algeria, see David Carroll, *Albert Camus the Algerian: Colonialism, Terrorism, Justice* (New York: Columbia University Press, 2007).

49. Benkhaled and Vince, "Performing Algerianness," 255. See also Leperlier, *Algérie*, 178.

50. McDougall, *A History of Algeria*, 298.

51. McDougall, *A History of Algeria*, 132–33.

52. Martinez, *La Guerre civile en Algérie*; Luis Martinez, *The Algerian Civil War, 1990–1998*, trans. Jonathan Derrick (New York: Columbia University Press, 2000).

53. Roberts, *The Battlefield Algeria*, 256.

54. Roberts, *The Battlefield Algeria*, 255.

55. Roberts, *The Battlefield Algeria*, 256. See also David Macey, "The Algerian with the knife," *Parallax* 4, no. 2 (1998), 159–67.

56. See George Joffé, "National Reconciliation and General Amnesty in Algeria," *Mediterranean Politics* 13, no. 2 (2008), 213–28.

57. Evans and Phillips, *Algeria*, 263.

58. Ministère de l'Intérieur et des Collectivités Locales, *Charte pour la Paix et la Réconciliation Nationale* (Algiers: MICL, 2006).

59. Laurie Brand, *Official Stories: Politics and National Narratives in Egypt and Algeria* (Stanford: Stanford University Press, 2014), 180.

60. Muriam Haleh Davis and Thomas Serres, "Political Contestation in Algeria: Between Postcolonial Legacies and the Arab Spring," *Middle East Critique* 22, no. 2 (2013), 105; Benkhaled and Vince, "Performing Algerianness," 265. As Homi K. Bhabha observes, the nation is characterised by an "impossible unity," comprising "myriad actors and forces" that are "continually changing." See Brand, *Official Stories*, 13.

61. See, for instance, Mundy, *Imaginative Geographies*; Brand, *Official Stories*; McDougall, *A History of Algeria*; Rahal, "Fused Together and Torn Apart."

62. Samuel K. Huntington, "The Clash of Civilizations?," *Foreign Affairs* 72, no. 3 (1993), 22–49.

63. Bernard Lewis, "The Roots of Muslim Rage," *Atlantic Monthly* 266, no 3. (1990), 47–60.

64. Huntington, "The Clash of Civilizations?," 25.

65. Huntington, "The Clash of Civilizations?," 35–36.

66. Mundy, *Imaginative Geographies*, 66.

67. See Chiara Bottici and Benoît Challand, "Rethinking Political Myth: The Clash of Civilizations as a Self-Fulfilling Prophecy," *European Journal of Social Theory* 9, no. 3 (2006), 315–36.

68. Mundy, *Imaginative Geographies*, 68.

69. See Mundy, *Imaginative Geographies*, 66.

70. Mundy, *Imaginative Geographies*, 61.

71. Malika Rahal, "1988–1992: Multipartism, Islamism and the Descent into Civil War," in *Algeria: Nation, Culture and Transnationalism 1988–2015*, ed. Patrick Crowley (Liverpool: Liverpool University Press), 95. See also McDougall, *A History of Algeria*, 297.

72. Rahal, "1988–1992," 95.

73. Chris Andrews and Matt McGuire, "Introduction: Post-Conflict Literature?" in *Post-Conflict Literature: Human Rights, Peace, Justice*, ed. Chris Andrews and Matt McGuire (London: Routledge, 2016), 1.

74. Mireille Rosello, *The Reparative in Narratives: Works of Mourning in Progress* (Liverpool: Liverpool University Press, 2010).

75. Andrews and McGuire, "Introduction," 3.

76. Andrews and McGuire, "Introduction," 1.

77. Névine El Nossery, *Témoignages fictionnels au féminin: une réécriture des blancs de la guerre civile algérienne* (New York: Rodopi, 2012); Benkhaled and Vince, "Performing Algerianness," 243.

78. Belaïd Djefel and Boussad Saïm, "Présentation," *Recherches & Travaux*, no. 76 (2010), 6.

79. Patricia Geesey, "Violent Days: Algerian Women Writers and the Civil Crisis," *The International Fiction Review*, 27, no. 1–2 (2000), https://journals.lib.unb.ca/index.php/IFR/article/view/7658/8715; Mildred Mortimer, *Women Fight, Women Write: Texts on the Algerian War* (Charlottesville: University of Virginia Press, 2018), 10.

80. Danielle Marx-Scouras, "Portraits of Women, Visions of Algeria," in *The Cambridge Companion to Camus*, ed. Edward J. Hughes (Cambridge: Cambridge University Press, 2007), 139.

81. Marx-Scouras, "Portraits of Women," 143.

82. Stora, "Deuxième guerre algérienne?"

83. As Christiane Chaulet-Achour explains, interest in Camus during the 1990s in Algeria begins with coverage in the press, after *El Watan* published a three-page article on a conference held on Camus in Algeria by his French biographer, Olivier Todd. A steady stream of articles followed, including: Arezki Metref's "Camus sera-t-il un jour algérien?," published in 1993 in one of the final issues of *Ruptures*; Abdelkader Djemaï's "Camus à Oran," published in *Algérie Actualité* in 1994, before being republished in Paris as a book the following year; Youcef Zirem invokes Camus's 1945 article, "La contagion," in a full-page spread entitled "Entre l'enfer et la raison," in *La Nation* in 1995. For further references and discussion, see Christiane Chaulet-Achour, "Camus dans la presse algérienne des années 1985-2005," in *Albert Camus: l'exigence morale* ed. Agnès Spiquel & Alain Schaffner, (Paris: Editions Le Manuscrit, 2006), 141–61.

84. Alek Baylee Toumi, "Albert Camus entre la mère et l'injustice," in *Albert Camus et les écritures algériennes: quelles traces* (Aix-en-Provence: Edisud, 2004), 143–78.

85. Albert Camus, "L'Hôte," in *L'Exil et le royaume* (Paris: Gallimard, 1957), 81–99.

86. Alek Baylee Toumi, "Albert Camus, l'algérian(iste): genèse d' Entre la mère et l'injustice," in *Albert Camus et les écritures algériennes: quelles traces* (Aix-en-Provence: Edisud, 2004), 91.

87. In his 1957 Nobel Prize acceptance speech, Camus was interrupted by an Algerian student who asked about his lack of support for the FLN. Camus is widely reported to have responded that he "preferred" his mother to "justice," but Olivier Todd has since noted that Camus's exact words were as follows: "On jette en ce moment des bombes dans les tramways. Ma mère peut se trouver dans un de ces tramways. Si c'est là votre justice, je préfère ma mère à la justice." [At this moment bombs are being planted in the trams in Algiers. My mother could be on one of those trams. If that is justice, I prefer my mother]. Olivier Todd, *Albert Camus: une vie* (Paris: Gallimard, 1996), 699–702.

88. Benkhaled and Vince, "Performing Algerianness," 243.

89. Aziz Chouaki, *Les Oranges* (Paris: Mille et Une Nuits, 1997). For a discussion of the play, see Namaan Kessous and Andy Stafford, "Récit, Monologue et Polémique dans *Les Oranges* d'Aziz Chouaki," *ASCALF Yearbook*, no. 4 (2000), 168–78, http://sfps.org.uk/wp-content/uploads/2018/06/ASCALF-Yearbook-No.-4-28200029.pdf.

90. Chouaki, *Les Oranges*, 31.

91. Chouaki, *Les Oranges*, 48. Albert Camus, *L'Etranger* (Paris: Gallimard, 1942).

92. Aziz Chouaki, "Le Tag et le Royaume," in *Albert Camus et les écritures algériennes: quelles traces* (Aix-en-Provence: Edisud, 2004), 35–40.

93. Chouaki, "Le Tag et le Royaume," 221.

94. For further discussion, see Janice Gross, "Albert Camus and contemporary Algerian playwrights: A shared faith in dialogue," in *Albert Camus, précurseur: Méditerranée d'hier et d'aujourd'hui*, ed. Alek Baylee Toumi (New York: Peter Lang, 2009), 127–40. In other rehabilitations of Camus's ghost, writers such as Assia Djebar developed more complex strategies to restage history in order to interrogate the assumptions upon which historical narrative is written. See Assia Djebar, *Le Blanc de l'Algérie* (Paris: Albin Michel, 1995) and, later, her *La Disparition de la langue française* (Paris: Albin Mihel, 2003). For discussion of Debar and Camus, see Christine Margerrison, "Assia Djebar, Albert Camus et le sang de l'histoire," in *Algérie, vers le cinquantenaire de l'Indépendance*, ed. Naaman Kessous, Christine Margerrison, Andy Stafford and Guy Dugas (Paris: l'Harmattan, 2009), 161–82.

95. Gafaïti, "The Monotheism of the Other," 21. See also Hafid Gafaïti, "Between God and the President: Literature and Censorship in North Africa," *Diacritics*, 27, no. 2 (1997), 59–84.

96. Gafaïti, "The Monotheism of the Other," 21.

97. Andrews and McGuire, "Introduction," 3.

98. Stora, *La guerre invisible*.

99. The French publisher, La Découverte, released two of the most famous nonfiction testimonies to emerge from the Black Decade in 2000 and 2001 respectively: Yous' *Qui a tué à Bentalha?* and Souaïdia's *La sale guerre: le témoignage d'un ancien officier des forces spéciales de l'armée algérienne*. When Souaïdia was sued in a French court for defamation by, Khaled Nezzar, the Algerian general at the center of his claims, the trial attracted widespread media attention. Nezzar lost the trial, but the French courtroom became one of the first places where the events of the 1990s were being played out.

100. El Nossery, *Témoignages fictionnels*; Geesey, "Violent Days." Charles Bonn considers the broader structural dynamics of this body of writing, and the particular focus of publishers on women's writing. He notes how "[c]es témoignages, sans doute autant suscités par une politique des éditeurs friands de drames actuels que par une évolution littéraire 'normale' en rapport avec cette actualité, sont souvent le fait des femmes" [these testimonies, no doubt demanded as much by publishers fond of current dramas as by "normal" literary developments in relation to this news, are often written by women]. See Bonn's entry, "Algérie" in *Littérature francophone. Tome 1: Le Roman*, ed. Charles Bonn and Xavier Garnier (Paris: Hatier, 1997), 208; see also, Farid Laroussi, "When Francophone Means National: The Case of the Maghreb," *Yale French Studies*, no. 103 (2003), 88. For further discussion of the multiple languages of "urgence" circulating in literary criticism and the press during the 1990s, see Joseph Ford, "Rethinking *urgence*: Algerian Francophone literature after the 'décennie noire,'" *Francosphères* 5, no. 1 (2016), 39–57.

101. Bonn, "Algérie"; Yassin Temlali, "Discussion avec Rachid Mokhtari sur la violence dans la littérature algérienne," in *Algérie, Chroniques Ciné-Littéraires de Deux Guerres* (Algiers: Barzakh, 2011), 61; El Nossery, *Témoignages fictionnels*, 19; Fisher, *Ecrire l'urgence*.

102. Fériel Assima, *Une femme à Alger: chronique du désastre* (Paris: Arléa, 1995).

103. Assima, *Une femme à Alger*, back cover.

104. Pamela A. Pears, *Front Cover Iconography and Algerian Women's Writing: Heuristic Implications of the Recto-Verso Effect* (Lanham: Lexington Books, 2015), 2.

105. See Leperlier, *Algérie*, 251; Benkhaled and Vince, "Performing Algerianness," 243; Mundy, *Imaginative Geographies*, 68.

106. This was the case with Malika Boussouf, whose publisher was Calmann-Levy, and Leila Marouane, with Les Editions Julliard. See Leperlier, *Algérie*, 275–76.

107. Leperlier, *Algérie*, 276.

108. Marouane, cited in Leperlier, *Algérie*, 276.

109. For further discussion, see Harrison, *Postcolonial Criticism*, 112–35; see also Jane Hiddleston, *Assia Djebar: Out of Algeria* (Liverpool: Liverpool University Press, 2006).

110. Deepika Bahri, *Native Intelligence: Aesthetics, Politics, and Postcolonial Literature* (Minneapolis: University of Minnesota Press, 2003), 19. Gayatri

Chakravorty Spivak first discusses questions surrounding the "native informant" in her book, *A Critique of Postcolonial Reason* (Cambridge, Mass.: Harvard UP, 1999).

111. Ato Quayson, "Periods versus Concepts: Space Making and the Question of Postcolonial Literary History," *PMLA* 127, no. 2 (2012), 346–47.

112. Harrison, *Postcolonial Criticism*, 95.

113. Gillian Beer, "Representing women, re-presenting the past," *The Feminist Reader: Essays in Gender and the Politics of Literary Criticism*, ed. Catherine Belsey and Jane Moore (Basingstoke: Palgrave, 1989), 19.

114. Jane Hiddleston, *Decolonising the Intellectual: Politics, Culture, and Humanism at the End of the French Empire* (Liverpool: Liverpool University Press, 2014), 205–49; Jane Hiddleston, *Writing After Postcolonialism: Francophone North African Literature in Transition* (London: Bloomsbury, 2017), 14. See also Frantz Fanon, *Les damnés de la terre* (Paris: Maspero, 1968 [1961]) and Jean-Paul Sartre, *Qu'est-ce que la littérature?* (Paris: Gallimard, 1948).

115. Gafaiti, "The Monotheism of the Other."

116. Gafaiti, "The Monotheism of the Other," 20–21; see also Leperlier, *Algérie*, 105–62.

117. See Jane Hiddleston, "'On peut apprendre de la littérature à se méfier': Writing and Doubt in the Contemporary Algerian Novel," *Contemporary French and Francophone Studies* 20, no. 1 (2016), 58–66; see also Hiddleston, *Writing After Postcolonialism*, 22–23.

118. Some of the most prominent publishers include Editions Casbah, Chihab, Apic, Barzakh, and Alpha. For discussion of the shift in focus to peripheral markets in French-language publishing, see Patrick Crowley, "Literatures in French Today: Markets, Centres, Peripheries, Transition," *Australian Journal of French Studies* 50, no. 3 (2013), 410–25.

119. Mary Anne Lewis, "The Maghreb's New Publishing House: *les éditions barzakh* and the Stakes of Localized Publishing," *Contemporary French and Francophone Studies* 20, no. 1 (2016), 88.

120. Corbin Treacy, "Writing in the Aftermath of Two Wars: Algerian Modernism and the *Génération '88*," in *Algeria: Nation, Culture and Transnationalism 1988–2015*, ed. Patrick Crowley (Liverpool: Liverpool University Press), 123–39. Others have referred to the upsurge in the Algerian Francophone publishing industry as a "nahda" [cultural renaissance], "nouveau souffle" [new wind] and "renaissance des mots" [renaissance of words]. See Rachid Mokhtari, *Le nouveau souffle du roman algérien: essai sur la littérature des années 2000* (Algiers: Chihab, 2006); Adlène Meddi and Mélanie Matarese (eds), *Algérie: la nahda des Lettres, la renaissance des mots* (Paris: Riveneuve Editions, 2015).

121. Achille Mbembe, "Provisional Notes on the Postcolony," *Africa: Journal of the International African Institute* 62, no. 1 (1992), 5.

122. "Hirak" is an Arabic term for "movement," and has been used in the past to describe popular uprisings in Morocco. For reflections on the Hirak, see Muriam Haleh Davis, "The Layers of History Beneath Algeria's Protests," *Current History* 118, no. 812 (2019), 337–42.

123. Mbembe, "Provisional Notes," 4.

124. It is important to note that Islam and Islamism are received and understood in very different ways in the Algerian and French contexts. As an Algerian writing and publishing in French, Mimouni was most likely aware of the anxieties around Islamism in France and the way new ideas about Islam in Algeria were leading to increasingly polarized narratives at a time of political crisis. Yet, by lumping together notions of the "Islamic," "religious rule," and "intolerance," Mimouni and others were falling back on long-established tropes around Islam and violence. For a more detailed discussion of definitions of Islamism, see Asef Bayat, "Post-Islamism at Large," in *Post-Islamism: The Many Faces of Political Islam*, ed. Asef Bayat (Oxford: Oxford University Press, 2013), 3–34.

125. Rahal, "1988–1992," 95.

126. Alison Rice, *Polygraphies: Francophone Women Writing Algeria* (Charlottesville: University of Virginia Press, 2012), 1.

127. Benkhaled and Vince, "Performing Algerianness," 265.

128. In her book on disaster narratives and Haïti, Kasia Mika makes the point that it is vital to look to "'less sophisticated' forms of expression" precisely because they can "enrich our understanding of the disaster and its aftermath." See Kasia Mika, *Disasters, Vulnerability, and Narratives: Writing Haïti's Futures* (New York: Routledge, 2019), 17.

129. Benkhaled and Vince, "Performing Algerianness," 265.

130. Said, *The World*, 35.

Chapter 1

Rethinking Testimonial Literature in Rachid Mimouni, Assia Djebar, and Maïssa Bey

Following the cancellation of the January 1992 elections, Rachid Mimouni and Rachid Boudjedra very quickly published political pamphlets on the unfolding crisis. Mimouni's *De la barbarie en générale et de l'intégrisme en particulier* [On Barbarism in general and on fundamentalism in particular] and Boudjedra's *FIS de la haine* [FIS of hate] were both published in 1992.[1] Mimouni followed this political tract with his 1993 novel, *La Malédiction* [The curse], which plots the Islamist siege of a hospital in central Algiers, while Boudjedra's *Timimoun* (1994) and *Lettres algériennes* (1995) also capture the rising violence of the 1990s.[2]

Although already established and highly successful writers of literary fiction, Mimouni and Boudjedra's polemical interventions in effect primed their subsequent literary offerings. Received by French journalists as "engaged" intellectuals, Mimouni and Boudjedra were very quickly consecrated as "spokespeople" for an Algeria in crisis.[3] As the violence intensified, it became almost impossible for Mimouni and Boudjedra to escape being presented through a binary lens, whereby the "enlightened" intellectual was pitted against the "barbarous" and "violent" Islamist or a repressive and censorious State.[4] Critics, publishers, and readers would apprehend nearly all their subsequent literary writing, along with other Algerian writers in exile who adopted a testimonial style, through this polarizing conflict narrative.[5]

In this chapter, I focus on three Algerian writers—Rachid Mimouni, Assia Djebar, and Maïssa Bey—each of whom has been described by commentators as producing testimonial literature. By identifying a set of distinct styles, the chapter explores how the literature of the Black Decade (and, crucially, its publishers and critics) adopted different ways of "telling" the violence of the 1990s. I begin by reading Mimouni's referential style as an example of how testimonial literature of the Black Decade is rooted in the oppositional writing of the political pamphlet. I then show how, in their efforts to develop a stylistically inventive, historically layered, and self-conscious aesthetic, Bey and Djebar challenge the idea that testimonial literature is uniquely assimilable to a referential mode. I argue that, instead of falling into the already gendered "attente de lecture" [horizon of expectation] of the Parisian publishing market, Bey and Djebar revert to a literary mode that, in its inherent ambivalence, interrogates the implications of writing about such a contested period in Algerian history.[6] These women writers can, therefore, be read to challenge both the feminized genre of testimonial literature and the "patriarchal premise" of objectivity in realist literature, which Mimouni's works implicitly invoke.[7]

RACHID MIMOUNI AND THE REFERENTIAL CONFLICT NARRATIVE

Published just three months after the assassination of Tahar Djaout in 1993, *La Malédication* was one of the first and most visible texts of the growing genre of testimonial literature that recounted the mounting violence of the 1990s.[8] Though Djaout was not the first victim of the violence of the Black Decade, his visibility as a writer meant that literature became a privileged site for both recording the events of the 1990s and opposing those responsible for the violence.[9] This privileging of literature and writers as "bearing witness" to the mounting violence was further enhanced due to the lack of access to Algeria by international journalists. For many journalists in France, testimonial literature became a crucial place to access basic information about the unfolding crisis and, as such, fed into their own narratives of the conflict. Newspaper articles written about the Algerian crisis frequently took a piece of "testimony" as their starting point, alluding to the referential style of "écriture de l'urgence" [emergency writing] that was, at least initially, associated with male writers such as Boudjedra and Mimouni.[10] Such readings of Algerian literature through a sociological lens established testimonial literature as the referential genre par excellence.

If, for French newspapers, literary testimonies had the capacity to "tell" the violence as it really was, writers were also active participants in creating an image of themselves as "engaged" intellectual witnesses of the rising violence in Algeria. The case of Boudjedra and Mimouni's political texts is instructive, primarily because of the success of the pamphlets in establishing these writers as "spokespeople" for an Algeria inaccessible to journalists. As Mimouni had admitted during a 1989 interview, the lack of press freedom in Algeria meant it was the writer who became the "porte-parole" [spokesperson].[11] While both Bey and Djebar would later question the capacity of the writer to act as a spokesperson for the entire nation, Mimouni seems unconcerned (at least in 1989) at the prospect of performing this role.[12]

In what follows, I examine how Mimouni's referential style is rooted in the oppositional analysis of *De la barbarie*—a text that, while acknowledging political and economic explanations of the conflict, promotes a binary culturalist critique of Algerian Islamists and political Islam. I argue that by reducing the Algerian crisis to the context of the post–Cold War clash of civilizations, both Mimouni's political and literary texts play on a general anxiety about Islamism around the world and a specific fear around the role of Islam in 1990s Algeria and France.[13]

De la barbarie en générale et de l'intégrisme en particulier (1992)

Published in France in 1992, *De la barbarie* emerges in part from Mimouni's frustration at the lack of response of intellectuals to what he saw as the rising threat of Islamism in Algeria. Though Boudjedra's *FIS de la haine* is more virulent in its condemnation of the FIS, and the multitude of political and media factions that he views to be responsible for giving birth to it, both writers characterize the Islamist movement in Algeria as monolithic.[14] For both intellectuals, the FIS is the main source of the rising violence and, as such, the main target of their attacks.[15]

From the outset, neither Mimouni nor Boudjedra is prepared to entertain the legitimacy of the FIS as a political entity—let alone accept the electoral victory in the first round of legislative elections in December 1991. And indeed, Mimouni makes no distinction between any legitimate strand of political Islam and fundamentalist groups in Algeria; he refers to the FIS as "un mouvement plus qu'un parti" [more a movement than a political party] and pursues a culturalist critique by describing its leaders as inspired by regressive religious models from the Middle Ages.[16] Mimouni conflates his already problematic critique of Islamism with religious practice, as he seems intent on pointing out so-called illogical traditions, such as Ramadan, the growing of beards, the return to a lunar calendar—all part of what he views as the generalized rejection of modernity.[17]

Moreover, the text repeatedly draws an analogy between the "barbus" [bearded Muslims] and "barbarie" [barbarity], placing the figure of the Muslim in stark opposition to that of the "progressive" or "enlightened" artist, writer, or intellectual.[18] This analysis also fed what Vincent Geisser refers to as the construction of an "ideal type" of the "media Muslim" in France, whereby the media regularly seized upon "the image of the fanatical bearded man" to encapsulate the supposed threat Islam posed.[19] In a glossary of terms directed to readers from outside Algeria, Mimouni notes how the "barbus" are, quite simply, "des intégristes" [fundamentalists].[20] While the pamphlet does explore other possible causes of the Algerian political crisis, including social and educational factors, *De la barbarie* is framed by and repeatedly returns to Mimouni's rejection of Islamism as a legitimate political project and, crucially, his setting it in stark opposition to a progressive intellectual culture, which he understands himself to be a part of. For Mimouni, radical Islam is about making a "choice" between art and faith: "Le projet islamique se propose donc explicitement d'étouffer toutes les formes d'expression artistique" [the Islamic project therefore explicitly proposes to stifle all forms of artistic expression].[21]

While this reaction to the initial violence of the 1990s needs to be understood in the context of a growing polarization within Algeria, it is vital to consider the reach Mimouni and Boudjedra's texts have outside Algeria—principally in France. This is important for three reasons: first, because Mimouni invokes the post–Cold War political myth of the "clash of civilizations" that Huntington theorizes in 1992 (Mimouni's vision of a "nouvelle période de rivalités, de divisions et de troubles" [new period of rivalries, divisions and unrest] hints at the "threat" political Islam supposedly poses in the West); second, because both *De la barbarie* and *FIS de la haine* underpin the genre of testimonial literature, as one in which the Algerian writer will perform as "spokesperson" for the population as a whole; and, third, because these texts played into contemporary debates about the role of Islam in 1990s France—especially following the controversial "affair du foulard" [headscarf affair] of 1989.[22] While, of course, Mimouni might not have anticipated all these factors around the reception of his work, the contextual elements directly contributed to the success of the pamphlet and subsequent novel in the French market that, as Charles Bonn writes, actively courted such testimonial texts.[23]

La Malédiction (1993)

Mimouni's announcement in *De la barbarie* of the "real-life" setting of *La Malédiction* (the text recounts the 1991 occupation by Islamists of the Mustapha hospital in Algiers) further encourages the reader to situate this novel within the emerging genre of testimonial literature.[24] It is also important to remember that readers with little access to journalistic accounts of the unfolding violence turned to literary reviews and interviews with Algerian writers to better understand the crisis. Thus, texts published during this period are subject to an intensified level of focus outside of literary circles in journalism that would often reductively package novels as testimonial literature. I show that the novel extends the author's oppositional and culturalist analysis adopted in *De la barbarie*, before examining how the referential style and oppositional stance deployed in the novel feed and reinforce the increasing tendency of critics and publishers to "demand" this particular brand of testimonial literature that attributes the role of "spokesperson" to the author.[25]

Promoted by the publisher, Editions Stock, as "un roman [. . .] d'une dramatique actualité" [a novel (. . .) informed by dramatic current events], the referential style of *La Malédiction* and its setting in the 1990s are not fully evident from the outset. However, groups of characters in the novel do appear to conform to Benkhaled and Vince's "tryptic" of identity types. If El Msili and Hocine represent radical Islam, and Nacer and Saïd are close to the FLN, then the protagonist Kader and his colleague Louisa can be seen to belong to the "pluralists/progressives."[26] Here, gender is also an issue. As one of the few visible women characters in the novel, Louisa (who is also Kader's lover) is rendered firmly in the "progressives" camp, while representatives of the political factions are principally men.

The novel begins by introducing two characters, Abdelkrim and Belkacem, who speak of their participation in the War of Independence. The presence of direct speech foregrounds the testimony of the characters. Closing with the ominous pronouncement, "nous sommes à la veille d'une révolution" [we are on the cusp of a revolution], the first chapter announces the dramatic action to come, but also establishes that action in a longer history of conflict, hinting at the way the FIS wrested control of the revolutionary narrative from the one-party FLN State.[27] The following chapters introduce the protagonist, Kader, a young doctor from Algiers, who is in Paris searching for his missing brother, Hocine. Unable to locate his brother, Kader returns to Algiers where he recommences work.

The main action begins around a third of the way into the novel, as a group of protestors gather in a public square outside the hospital that is Kader's place of work. The reasons for the protest are not immediately evident, but the ideological split which forms the backdrop for the action becomes clear as Nacer and Saïd discuss how God has become the "otage conjoint" [joint hostage] of "le Parti" [the Party—the FLN] and the "Islamistes" [Islamists].[28] Specifically, Mimouni's novel is set during the week-long period between the May 26, 1991, when the FIS began a general strike, and June 4, when the army intervened to break the strike.[29] Like in Mimouni's pamphlet, there is no distinction made between Islamist parties or factions; rather, the term "Islamist" appears as a metonym for the FIS, while "le Parti" is a clear reference to the ruling FLN.

As the story progresses, and the police begin to move in on the occupiers outside the hospital, armed Islamists enter the building to seek medical attention for their injured comrades. Kader is kidnapped and taken to the fundamentalists' hideout after he refuses to hand over patient records. Interrogated by three armed men, Kader soon realizes one of his captors is his missing brother, Hocine, whom he had believed to be dead. Kader is liberated after the intervention of the army, but, in an act that prefigures the unresolved and "tragic" nature of the crisis, Hocine later pronounces his brother's "death sentence" and murders him on an Algiers beach.

An initial interpretation of Mimouni's novel is that it uses the story of the occupation of the hospital as an allegory for the health of the Algerian nation, as it descends into conflict. However, given Walter Benjamin's definition of allegory as "a form of expression" that moves beyond "a mere mode of designation," or Maureen Quilligan's view that "the experience of reading allegory always operates by a gradual revelation," it is questionable whether, strictly speaking, the novel deploys an allegorical figure.[30] Although sustained in the first part of the story and reinforced by the final image—Kader's lover, Louisa, returns to the "grande maison" [great house] of her youth, uncertain of whether she'll have the strength to survive—the allegorical structure is arguably undermined when Kader (via the narrator) makes a direct reference to the political status and history of Algeria outside the hospital space: "Il s'interrogeait sur cette malédiction qui s'acharnait sur le pays [. . .] convaincu que les racines de ce mal plongeait dans un lointain passé." [He reflected on this curse that had been put on the country (. . .) convinced that the roots of this evil delved deep into a distant past.][31] A further reference to Kader's dead father, who fought during the War of Independence, roots the present in the history of the revolution and, as such, invokes an image of Algeria's malediction, or "illness," in a recidivist frame.[32] The absence of this "gradual revelation," that is normally part of the literary figure of allegory, further roots the events of the novel in a referential frame, favoring realist claims to objectivity over a more ambivalent allegorical structure.

While the Muslim characters depicted in Mimouni's novel are by no means homogenous, the general presentation of Islamist characters mimics the oppositional and culturalist analysis of *De la barbarie*. Initially described as "diables malfaisants" [evil devils], Mimouni metamorphoses his Islamist characters into "microbes sournois et ravageurs, agents de maladies capables de malmener le corps et l'esprit" [devious and harmful microbes, agents of diseases capable of mangling body and mind].[33] With frequent descriptions of "barbus" [bearded Muslims] and "barbares" [barbarians], Mimouni's novel mimics the language of his political pamphlet by stressing the near-homophony of these two terms. Whether Mimouni is conscious of it or not, the language of the "barbares" advances a reductive conception of the "other" as inherently prone to an uncivilized, "barbarous," violence.[34] This polarizing conception of the other is further emphasized, as Mimouni's narrator describes the siege in explicitly binary terms: "Il admettait volontiers que les damnés de la Terre réclamassent leur place au soleil, mais il ne pouvait accepter qu'on troquât l'ignorance *contre* le savoir, la haine *contre* la compassion."[35] [He willingly admitted that the wretched of the Earth would claim their place in the sun, but he could not accept that one would swap ignorance for knowledge, hate for compassion.] Here, the conflict narrative relies on the binary oppositions of ignorance and knowledge, hatred and compassion, but, in its reference to "les damnés de la Terre," it also invokes the image of the hijacking of revolutionary legitimacy by the Islamists.[36]

If this culturalist frame has clear implications for the understanding of the Algerian crisis abroad, the novel and political pamphlet might also be seen as remarkable for their ability to predict what would happen after 1993. The fratricidal conclusion to *La Malédiction* prefigures the splits to come in many Algerian families and *De la barbarie* offers a seemingly accurate vision of the "mitraillages dans les rues" [shootings in the street] and a "terreur généralisée" [generalized terror] to come.[37] The author closes his pamphlet by asking a series of what appear to be prophetic questions:

Sera-t-il possible de conjurer les démons de la guerre civile? Nous savons que l'histoire est tragique et que les pays qui y rentrent en payent le pesant de sang et de larmes. Est-ce la condition nécessaire à la formation d'une nation?[38]

[Will it be possible to ward off the demons of civil war? We know that history is tragic and that the countries that suffer such tragedy pay in blood and tears. Is this the necessary condition for the formation of a nation?]

While Mimouni offers no answers here, no suggestions of ways to avoid a seemingly inevitable conflict, he nevertheless frames Algerian history in a theatrical lexis. In so doing, Mimouni not only previews the "tragedy" of the fratricide in *La Malédiction*, he anticipates the dramatic framework of many of the academic readings that emerged on the 1990s, as well as the pronouncements of the Algerian State, which resorted to a language of "national tragedy" in the Charter for Peace and National Reconciliation of 2005.[39]

The difficulty with this language of "tragedy" is not just its apparent portability. Tragedy is also a prescribed mode that proposes a series of mimetic acts through which actors and audience pass in order to reach a moment of catharsis.[40] Mimouni and others' use of the term "tragedy" invokes a narrative that is at once close to a referential (mimetic) form of writing and offers a means of "acting out" a traumatic event in the cathartic retelling of the reality. However, as Jane Hiddleston writes in her discussion of Dominick Lacapra's theory on trauma, "narratives that 'act out' the past are those that pander to the self-fulfilling desires of the narrator, perpetuating fantasies that suit that particular speaker or writer's demands." While "acting out" a violent past might meet a certain demand for meaning, "coherence," and "reassurance," it fails to do genuine "justice to the traumatic moment."[41]

Such "self-fulfilling desire" that one sees in the above process of "acting out" the tragic narrative is also present in Huntington's own conflict narrative of the clash of civilizations, in that this also calls upon predetermined and fixed cultural narratives to plot a set of supposedly inevitable events, while largely ignoring political or economic explanations. Much like Huntington's hypothesis gained traction because of the simplicity of its binary narrative, the language of tragedy (adopted by writers, publishers, critics, and the Algerian State) inaugurated an appealingly simple frame through which to understand the "drama" of the mounting violence. As Benkhaled and Vince write, there is an urgent need for a "post-dramatic" analysis of the 1990s, which would mean "going beyond seeing Algeria as locked in a series of violent confrontations," while at the same time "deconstructing a linear narrative, multiplying perspectives and recognizing that actors are both 'theme and protagonist.'"[42] Mimouni's apparent foresight in the final pages of his text, where he predicts the coming "tragedy" of the "civil war," is not then attributable to some magical ability to see the future, but precisely a result of his dogged determination to "act out" the unfolding present through the lens of a preexisting discursive order. This process of "foreshadowing" echoes Rahal's analysis of the PAGS' radical anti-Islamist stance from the early 1990s, whereby a combative language of war "was forged even before the outbreak of violence."[43]

With the author as "witness" or "spokesperson"—as both "theme and protagonist"—this dominant narrative of "tragedy" permeated the consciousness of those reading about the unfolding crisis through testimonial texts. The unwillingness of Boudjedra, Mimouni, and the journalists that read their work to countenance an alternative discourse—that literary writers were well placed to imagine—meant further entrenching already polarized and polarizing positions. Moreover, while realism is used to establish a more objective viewpoint, there are clear blind spots when it comes to depicting women's experience of and role in the conflict. By resigning themselves to Algeria's "tragic" fate, it could be argued that intellectuals, such as Boudjedra and Mimouni, fail to even attempt to prevent that tragedy from taking place.

ASSIA DJEBAR: ACKNOWLEDGING COMPLICITY

Assia Djebar, who published her first novel, *La Soif*, during the Algerian War in 1957, is widely considered the *doyenne* of Algerian literature, celebrated across the world for her highly original literary aesthetic that breaks with a series of normative classifications and continually unsettles generic and formal categorizations. Between 1967 and 1980, Djebar withdrew from writing because of criticism in Algeria targeting her decision to write in French.[44]

After producing two experimental films, which documented the lives of rural Algerian women in their dialectal Arabic, she returned to writing with the highly original *Femmes d'Alger dans leur appartement* (1980) [*Women of Algiers in their Apartment* (1992)] that took the question of representation as its core focus.[45]

If Mimouni and Boudjedra fall into the trap of perpetuating the self-fulfilling, polarizing, and patriarchal conflict narrative outlined earlier, then Djebar's ten-year hiatus from writing had taught her about the dangers implicit in being a postcolonial writer that often meant being reduced to a "spokesperson" for, or "witness" to events in, one's country of birth.[46] In the opening to her 1980 collection, Djebar writes:

> Ne pas prétendre "parler pour," ou pire "parler sur," à peine parler *près de*, et si possible *tout contre*: première des solidarités à assumer pour les quelques femmes arabes qui obtiennent ou acquièrent la liberté de mouvement, du corps et de l'esprit. Et ne pas oublier que celles qu'on incarcère, de tous âges, de toutes conditions, ont des corps prisonniers, mais des âmes plus que jamais mouvantes.[47]
>
> [Don't claim to "speak for" or, worse, to "speak on," barely speaking next to, and if possible *very close to*: these are the first of the solidarities to be taken on by the few Arabic women who obtain or acquire freedom of movement, of body and of mind. And don't forget that those who are incarcerated, no matter what their age or class, may have imprisoned bodies, but have souls that move more freely than ever before.][48]

In this prefatory passage, Djebar shows a great sense of uncertainty about her efforts to represent the Algerian women who feature in her collection of stories. Keen to distinguish herself from a "porte-parole" [spokesperson] or "specialiste" [expert], the author gives no conclusive vision of how she intends to tackle the problem of not reducing the multiple voices of Algerian women to a "collective voice" of the community. And, because both (community and individual) are important to Djebar, her ambivalence here is central to the work of exploring how the writer will inevitably be implicated in perpetuating a violent or, in the case of *Femmes d'Alger*, an Orientalizing gaze.

Recalling Spivak's discussion of the ambiguity at the heart of the term "representation," and the frequent confusion between political and artistic (or literary) representation—*vertreten* and *darstellen*—Harrison and Hiddleston have separately shown how Djebar is acutely sensitive to the dangers of being reduced to a "representative voice" for the Algerian people.[49] However, it is also crucial to note that Djebar recognizes the inevitability that she will be reduced to a "spokesperson" and that her own work is partly an acknowledgment of this fact.[50] Thus, embedded within Djebar's definition of testimonial literature is the acknowledgment that testimony is itself a potentially reductive and restrictive form of representation.

In her discussion of *Le blanc de l'Algérie* (1995) [*Algerian White* (2000)], Djebar's first text to intervene directly in the violence of the Black Decade, Hiddleston stresses how this "commemorative text" portrays the author's "anxiety towards the written word and her sense of unease towards the capacity of language to testify to recent atrocities," but this does not take account of the possibility that Djebar has also become increasingly wary of the growing genre of testimonial literature published in France and inaugurated by Mimouni and Boudjedra.[51] Echoing her thoughts in the opening of *Femmes d'Alger*, the final part of *Le blanc de l'Algérie* offers a space for Djebar to reflect on the gestation of what Hiddleston calls her "singular testimony":

> D'autres écrivent "sur" l'Algérie, sur son malheur fertile, sur ses monstres réapparus. / Moi, je me suis simplement retrouvée, dans ces pages, avec quelques amis. [. . .] D'autres parlent de l'Algérie qu'ils aiment, qu'ils connaissent, qu'ils fréquentent [. . .] moi, opiniâtre, je les ressuscite, ou je m'imagine le faire. / Oui, tant d'autres parlent de l'Algérie, avec ferveur ou avec colère. Moi, m'adressant à mes disparus et réconfortée par eux, je la rêve.[52]
>
> [Others write "about" Algeria, its prolific misfortune, how its monsters returned. / All I do in these pages is spend time with a few friends. (. . .) Others speak of their beloved Algeria, a place they know and visit (. . .) persistent, I resuscitate them or imagine doing so. / Yes, so many others speak of Algeria fervently or with anger. Directing myself to my departed ones and comforted by them, I dream of it.][53]

Indicating a shift to a more reflective practice, *Le blanc de l'Algérie* is itself a text that hesitates between the forms of fiction and fact. Described as a "récit"—a "tale" or "narrative" in English—the testimony of *Le blanc de l'Algérie* is immediately subject to interrogation. Often viewed alongside the "histoire" [story], the "récit" is similar to what Anglophone readers would understand as the common Aristotelian distinction between story and plot.[54] However, the generic "récit" (used by French writers like Maurice Blanchot, Eugène Fromentin, and André Gide) is distinct from the novel. As Roger Shattuck notes, "During a *récit*, we are conscious of being at one remove from the action; the very act of narration interferes and calls attention to itself."[55] Or, as Daniel Just stresses of Maurice Blanchot's definition, the "récit" is different from the novel in that it draws the reader's attention to the very problems of form, genre, and narrative: "whereas the novel wants to tell a story, the *récit* tries to undermine it."[56]

In her study of testimonial literature during the period of the Black Decade, El Nossery takes Djebar's 1995 text as an example of what she and others name a referential "écriture de l'urgence" [emergency writing].[57] According to El Nossery, Djebar is part of a larger group of Algerian women writers who "se sont armées de leur plume" [armed themselves with their pen] in order to "répond[re] à cette neccessité pressante de témoigner et de dénoncer les intégristes et leur violence brutale et impitoyable, au risque de perdre leur liberté, voire la vie" [respond to this pressing need to testify and denounce the fundamentalists and their brutal and merciless violence, at the risk of losing their freedom, even their lives].[58] However, El Nossery fails to consider the formal instability of the text, as she constructs an image of Djebar's writing as unequivocally oppositional and of the writer's life as being under threat. In fact, Djebar had left Algeria during the 1990s to live in France and then the United States, where she became a professor of literature. To describe her life as being under significant threat, and to reduce Djebar's writing to a form of oppositional discourse, is reflective of the broader tendency among journalists and academic literary critics to make texts fit a theory that is not borne out by the empirical reality. The prescriptive ways in which some commentators understand testimonial literature directly contradict the practice of women writers such as Djebar whose texts are more suggestive of a generic openness that demonstrates an open-mindedness in relation to political events.

Just two years later, Djebar published a further collection directly implicated in the violence of the 1990s. Like in previous texts, Djebar uses the postscript of *Oran, langue morte* (1997) [*The Tongue's Blood Does Not Run Dry* (2006)] to question her practice as a writer and the work of representing Algeria at a time of violence.[59] Beginning with a reference to her 1980 collection, Djebar presents her short stories as a "[r]écit des femmes de la nuit algérienne" [account of women from the Algerian night] and the women she attempts to represent as the "nouvelles femmes d'Alger" [new women of Algiers],[60] the writer asks a series of self-reflexive questions about her new collection of stories:

> Ces nouvelles, présentées ici, sont-elles vraiment nouvelles; ou simplement des *short stories*, fragments d'imaginaire? Sous couvert de tourner le dos à la tragédie et à l'odeur fétide de ses cul-de-sac, me faudrait-il ne rêver qu'au passé où, par-delà les siècles, la violence et les combats représentés ne risquent plus de faire gicler le sang sur mes doigts, sur mes mots?[61]

> [Are the short stories presented here really short stories; or simply *short stories* (i.e. oral tales), imaginary fragments? If I want to turn my back on tragedy and

the fetid odor of its dead ends, do I only need to dream of the past, whose violence and battles across centuries no longer threaten to splash blood onto my fingers, onto my words?][62]

In the above extracts from her 1995 and 1997 texts, Djebar refers to the ongoing conflict, but crucially to the difficulties of capturing the realities of the violence within her writing. In the face of "other" representations of violence that either resort to a negative imagery or don't do justice to those who have lost their lives, Djebar invokes her own form of testimonial commemoration that moves into the space of imagination and dream. The "risk" of blood falling onto the writer's fingers and infiltrating the words Djebar uses to represent the Black Decade in *Oran, langue morte* creates a powerful yet ambivalent image of how the writer might be implicated either in failing to testify to a violence that she wishes to turn away from, or in perpetuating that violence by writing it. The composite image that Djebar presents here conveys an acute sense of complicity, as it "folds together" the layers of actual violence with its literary representation.[63]

Although Djebar was one of the first and most prolific of Algerian writers to adopt this style of self-conscious reflection in her works—a style that would allow her to acknowledge her own complicity in writing a conflict narrative that might itself perpetuate violence—she was not immune from viewing the mounting crisis in polarizing terms. In her postscript to *Le blanc de l'Algérie*, Djebar frames the ongoing conflict in binary terms, as she repeats an oppositional narrative that pitted the Algerian State against fundamentalist Islam.[64] Yet, in continually encouraging her readers (and herself) to question dominant forms of testimony constructed by critics and publishers in France, Djebar goes much further than others in acknowledging the complicity of the writer in forging a potentially reductive and self-fulfilling conflict narrative. Contrary to Mimouni's "acting out" of Algeria's "tragic" fate, Djebar uses her literary texts to "work through," to gain "a critical purchase on," the very narrative by which such tragedy constituted itself in the first place.[65]

MAÏSSA BEY: TOWARD A LAYERED AESTHETIC OF THE BLACK DECADE

One of the many writers compelled to write because of the emerging crisis of the Black Decade, Bey's works were quickly consecrated within the referential frame of testimonial literature.[66] If Bey might initially appear to follow Mimouni's rhetoric of opposition, pitting the writer-as-witness against Islamist violence, a closer examination of her work reveals a self-conscious attention to both the "power of the word" and the increasing tendency for the

Algerian writer to be received as "witness" or "spokesperson" in the context of the ongoing crisis of the Black Decade.[67] What results is a self-aware and layered aesthetic that interrogates the ongoing mediatization of the conflict and situates it in a longer history of representations of Algerian violence.

Maïssa Bey (a pseudonym for Samia Benameur) came to writing aged forty-six. A school teacher of French in her hometown of Sidi Bel Abbès (situated south of the city of Oran, in Western Algeria), Bey was driven to writing by what she describes in an interview as a need to "se mettre au monde" [reveal herself to the world].[68] It is in this sense of personal liberation, and writing on behalf of women in Algeria more generally, that Bey frames her decision to publish her first novel. Speaking of a "nécessité impérieuse, d'urgence" [pressing and urgent need], the author tells of her wish to "donner vraiment la parole aux mots, à tous les mots enfouis au fond de soi depuis si longtemps sans penser à autre chose qu'à rompre le silence et à affronter sa peur" [truly give a voice to words, to all the words long-buried in the depths of oneself, without thinking of anything but breaking the silence and confronting one's fear].[69] While Bey published her first novels and short stories in France, she remained in Algeria throughout the period of the Black Decade. And, indeed, it was this image of the author at increased risk—a teacher of French remaining in an Algeria torn apart by violence—that would, in part, lead to Bey's consecration as a writer of testimonial literature.

In what follows, I examine how Bey's literary texts offer an alternative definition of testimony, similar to that of Djebar—a testimony seeking to distinguish itself from works, such as Mimouni's, that privilege an oppositional and culturalist reading of the emerging crisis. I ague that, rather than capture the mounting violence of the 1990s through a directly referential style, Bey calls on the ambiguity and ambivalence inherent in literary representation to ask a series of questions about the power of literature at a time of conflict and, more specifically, about what it means to write about the contested period of violence that would become known as the Black Decade.

Au commencement était la mer (1996)

Au commencement était la mer [*In the Beginning Was the Sea*] was published in one of the first numbers of the journal *Algérie Littérature/Action* in 1996, a literary review established in the same year, by French academic and critic Marie Virole and the Algerian writer Aissa Khelladi, with the explicit intention to promote a new and pluralistic vision of Algerian literature.[70] Run in association with the French-based publisher Marsa Editions, the journal published articles, reviews, and for several years a novel as part of each issue.[71] The explicit wish of the editors was to establish a new and "autonomous" Algerian literature, removed from the pressures of the French publishing market. And, if Khelladi later admitted that the fictional texts published in the journal were directly rooted in the ongoing crisis, they nevertheless presented more nuanced interpretations of dominant political and media receptions of the mounting violence.[72]

Bey's first novel appears close to Alison Rice's definition of literary testimony, as it fuses fiction, autobiography, and history to "express the experiences of many," while at the same time acknowledging the unreliability of the "truth" it purports to tell.[73] In a story set during the violence of the Black Decade, the protagonist Nadia falls pregnant by Karim, with whom she has fallen in love and has been seeing secretly. In its most explicit scenes, the novel charts how Nadia hides from her family as she aborts the fetus of her unborn child. Readings of the novel by journalists and academic literary critics have interpreted this aborted fetus as an allegorical figure for an aborted or still-born Algerian nation and its descent into the violence of the 1990s.[74] Pursued and ultimately murdered by her brother, Bey's novel also stages a stifling paternalistic society which is shown to determine Nadia's violent fate.

Although the allegorical structure and focus on radical Islam would appear to resonate with Mimouni's novel, Bey's text is distinct because it begins to develop a self-conscious vision of the act of writing itself and the relationship between writing and wider social and political discourse. Throughout, the reader glimpses Nadia's obsession with storytelling and literature. Not only is she the "faiseuse d'histoires" [teller of stories] to her younger siblings, she is herself transfixed by the process of reading: "Elle lit comme on entre en prière, avec la même ferveur mystique, le même respect attentif.[75] Le même oubli de soi et des autres." [She reads as one enters into prayer, with the same mystical fervor, the same attentive respect. The same forgetfulness of oneself and others.][76] This blending of the literary with the religious has the effect of defying their polarization; but the reader is also encouraged to recognize that narrative is at the core of this novel, whether it is the narrative of Nadia's experience, that of the obscure and paternalistic "ordre nouveau" [new order] that appears to be imposing itself upon Algeria, or a meta-narrative that encourages the reader to interrogate the very process of "telling."[77]

As the story of Nadia's love affair and subsequent abortion plays out in the second part of the novel, the limitations of words and language begin to come to the fore. For Nadia, it is through words that she is able to give life to her dreams, but it is at the same time words and language that limit and contain those dreams and desires: "Et ses désirs et ses rêves *ne sont que* des mots dans les livres, des mots dans sa tête." [Her desires and her dreams were *merely* words in books, words inside her head.][78] In a more foreboding passage, the narrator captures a similar anxiety of the dual nature of words: "Mais déjà, déjà dans le mot amour, il y a presque toutes les lettres de la mort." [Yet already, already in the word love, there are almost all the letters of the word death.]⁷⁹ When the story turns to the murder of the father of one of Nadia's school friends who had been working as a journalist, words are seen to be "plus dangereux que des armes" [more dangerous than weapons].⁸⁰ This tension between the liberatory potential of words and their tendency to limit desires and dreams is further brought into focus when the narrator refers to the mythical figure of Antigone, who, much like Nadia, would rather accept a death sentence than renounce her wishes through words. In the case of these killings, it is the sword that is very clearly mightier than the pen. Yet, in refusing to submit to the patriarchal order, Nadia—like Antigone—leaves behind a story, a myth, that survives the death of the individual and thereby offers a lasting testimony that extends well beyond the immediate context of the Algerian crisis.

After Nadia discovers her pregnancy, she is paralyzed by fear; but it is a fear interweaved with the violence in the city around her. The story of the killings is suddenly fused with the anguish of Nadia's decision to have a termination. The following passage can be read both through the lens of Nadia's anxiety about ending her pregnancy and that of the growing gendered body of testimonial literature that seeks to "tell" the violence of the Black Decade:

> Des femmes peuvent raconter cela dans les livres. D'abord avoir le courage de le faire, puis celui de le dire. Non, pas ici. De l'autre côté de la mer. Les femmes ici ne racontent pas. Depuis toujours, elles se taisent. Elles se terrent. / Le sang, la souffrance et les larmes. Un acte de libération disent-elles, ces femmes qui se disent aujourd'hui libérées. / Ici, c'est bien plus. Un acte de survie. Dicté par un instinct sauvage de conservation, rien de plus. Il ne s'agit pas de choisir. Aucune autre alternative n'est envisageable. La mort, peut-être. / C'est ça. Il faut arracher, supprimer cette prolifération de cellules ou mourir. Agir donc. Le plus vite, le plus discrètement possible.⁸¹

> [Women can tell their stories in books. First to have the courage to do it, then the courage to say it. No, not here. On the other side of the sea. The women here do not tell. They have always been silent. They hide themselves away. / The blood, the suffering and the tears. An act of emancipation they say, these women who claim they are now liberated. / Here, it is much more. An act of survival. Nothing more than a primitive instinct for self-preservation. It is not a question of choice. There is no alternative. Death, perhaps. / That's it. It is necessary to tear out, to erase this proliferation of cells, or die. Act then. As fast and as discreetly as possible.]

If this passage is clearly about women's escape from a patriarchal control exerted over their bodies, it is difficult not to interpret the reference to women's testimonies as detached from the emerging genre of testimonial literature that Bey seeks to interrogate. Women may well be able to "raconter" [tell] their stories from the "autre côté" [other side] of the Mediterranean, while those who remain in Algeria "se taisent" [remain silent], despite the blood, the suffering, and the tears. But what use are these testimonies? Do they really make women "free"? Is there really no alternative?

In its allegorical form, the novel resembles Mimouni's *La Malédiction*, but Bey's allegory of the aborted nation is distinct because it reveals the history it invokes in a more subtle and self-conscious way. While the direct reference to Algerian history in *La Malédiction* encourages the reader to interpret the novel within the referential frame of the violence of the Black Decade, Nadia's abortion as an allegorical figure for the failure of Algerian independence to build a stable and peaceful nation-state is a vision the reader must slowly "discover" as they read the novel.[82] Moreover, the fact that Nadia's story is figured within the universal context of the political and social marginalization of women means that the allegorical structure is not limited to a reference to the failure of Algerian nationalism in the context of the 1990s. As an ambiguous and ambivalent figure, the allegory of the aborted child could also refer to an array of possible histories, including the writer's own struggle to "se mettre au monde" [reveal herself to the world].[83]

By moving toward an aesthetic that is increasingly self-aware, Bey refuses to define testimony in merely contestatory or oppositional terms; rather, she situates the genre in the context of the long history of the occlusion of women's voices and outlines a series of questions about whether the gendered genre of testimonial literature is the best means of representing the ongoing crisis. Here, the "patriarchal premise" of objectivity invoked in Mimouni's explicitly realist and referential style meets the more ambivalent modes of allegory and intertextual allusion.[84] As Michael Rothberg writes in his analysis of the Algerian writer Leila Sebbar's use of Antigone, in her novel *La Seine était rouge*, this mythical female figure is both a "monument of cultural memory" and an "ethical subject of multidirectional memory." By invoking Antigone, Bey's novel suggests "the need for an ethics of memory that operates 'beyond good and evil.'"[85]

Nouvelles d'Algérie (1998)

If Bey's first novel could be described as beginning the work of interrogating the testimonial genre emerging in France, then her collection of short stories, *Nouvelles d'Algérie* [Short Stories from Algeria], published just two years later in 1998, deploys the short form to question in more explicit terms the representation of the 1990s crisis.[86] Beginning with an ambiguous reference to the role of the "nouvelle" [news/short story] in "telling" the violence, Bey's collection calls on a layered aesthetic to offer an account of the 1990s that questions and challenges the reductive representations of a genre of testimonial literature which was by then well established in France. Like Djebar, Bey uses the preface to outline her conflicted perspective on the question of representation:

> Voici des nouvelles d'Algérie. Nouvelles écrites en ce temps où le souffle de la mort taillade à vif la lumière de chaque matin. Textes écrits dans l'urgence de dire, la nécessité de donner la parole aux mots, mais qui en même temps, je veux le croire, ne sont pas seulement une litanie de malheurs déclinée au quotidien, parce qu'écrits dans le désir désespéré de croire que tout est encore compréhensible, sans avoir toutefois la prétention de croire que j'ai compris.[87]

> [Here are/is some short stories/news from Algeria. Short stories/news written at a time when the prospect of death sharpens the light of each morning. Texts written with the urgency to speak out, in the need to give a voice to words, but which at the same time, I want to believe, are not only a litany of misfortunes that fade into the everyday, because they are written in the desperate desire to believe that everything is still comprehensible, without, however, pretending to think that I have understood.]

In an interview with the Algerian literary critic Rachid Mokhtari, Bey recounts having three options when coming to writing the *Nouvelles d'Algérie*. The first was to write in a journalistic style, the second was to turn to humor, and the third, which she chose, was to "conferee[r] à la réalité une dimension poétique [où] la beauté du texte transcende l'événement" [confer to the reality a poetic dimension (whereby) the beauty of the text would transcend the event].[88] Although she claims to want to move beyond the event, playing on the French homonym "nouvelle" [short story/news] means making an immediate and self-conscious reference to the representation of the ongoing conflict. These are stories written with a passionate desire to "dire" [tell/speak] the violence of the 1990s, but with a simultaneous acknowledgment of the risk of being reduced to a "witness" or "spokesperson" that is implicit in that "telling." To publish yet another narrative that claims to explain or account for the ongoing violence is to risk being reduced to the "litanie de malheurs déclinée au quotidien" [litany of misfortunes that fade into the everyday]. And yet, by acknowledging this risk, Bey (like Djebar before her) is able to redefine the testimonial genre as one that becomes conscious of its own implicated role in explaining the political and historical causes of the growing crisis.

The short stories (at least in the original collection) proceed in an uninterrupted sequence, without individual titles and with a table of contents at the end of the volume.[89] Interpreting the form of the collection as presenting "des episodes incomplets, privés d'enchainement logique, que la lecture même échouera à ordonner" [incomplete episodes, deprived of a logical sequence, that the reading itself will fail to order], Lila Ibrahim-Ouali argues that Bey's stories use form to capture the fragmented memories of the 1990s—fragments that are unnamable because of the traumatic nature of the original experience.[90] Indeed, according to Cathy Caruth, trauma is defined precisely by the presence of a delayed reaction to an experience that is not "fully grasped" as it occurs, but rather appears later in "repeated flashbacks [and] nightmares."[91] This traumatic lens is adopted by other critics of Bey's work and does offer one possible interpretation of the stories and their referential or formal instability.[92]

However, there is also a danger that reading the fragmented form of the stories through the framework of trauma theory can lead to overly generalized claims about testimonial literature. For instance, El Nossery writes how the referential "écriture de l'urgence" [writing of the emergency] is present in "tous les textes portant sur la décennie noire" [all texts relating to the Black Decade], but such a view neglects to consider how writers deliberately move away from this referential style.[93] In focusing primarily on a traumatic retelling of the 1990s, critics spend less time examining how authors such as Bey have developed a layered aesthetic that seeks to unsettle standard definitions of testimonial literature.[94]

In the analysis that follows, I show how Bey's *Nouvelles d'Algérie* establishes an implicit dialogue with *Au commencement*, in the sense that it continues to develop a self-conscious gaze on an increasingly contested crisis and its literary representations. I argue that, rather than adopt an affirmative or referential style visible in the earlier texts of the decade, Bey employs an interrogative aesthetic that plays a significant role in laying the foundations for the group of experimental writers I explore in the following chapters.[95]

Like in *Au commencement*, Bey is keen to capture the occluded voices of Algerian women. As such, each of the ten stories gives the reader a glimpse into the life of a female narrator or protagonist and those around her. The first story, "Le cri" [The Scream], opens the collection with a "long cri sauvage" [long wild scream] which follows a young girl whose father is taken from his home by unknown assailants.[96] Maintaining a referential ambiguity between the history of the War of Independence and the more recent events of the Black Decade (Bey's own father, whom she knew only as a young girl, was taken and killed by the French army during the 1954–1962 war), the eponymous "cri" has been seen by critics to engulf the whole collection of stories, announcing an incessant and underlying trauma, whose origin is unknown: "[c]'est dans la tête. Dans son corps. C'est quelque chose qui s'écoule d'elle. [. . .] Quelque chose qui la quitte. Et cela fait un vide." [It's in the head. In her body. It's something that flows from the head. (. . .) Something that leaves it.

And that makes a void.]⁹⁷ Citing Gilbert Durand's work on symbolism, Ana Soler argues that the "cri" is representative of an underlying darkness linked to a negative imagery of death, whereas Dominique Le Boucher writes of how the "cri" is both an act of defiance in refusing the imposed silence of dominant history and a founding act of speech which announces the birth of a "parole" [speech] across the stories and is, in turn, a metaphor for the birth of women's voices as a whole.⁹⁸

Other stories oscillate from focusing on a husband killed by Islamists because he worked for the State ("Dans le silence d'un matin" [In the Morning Silence]), to giving a glimpse into the eyes of the terrorist ("Croire, obéir, combattre" [Believe, Obey, Fight]). In "Sofiane B., vingt ans" [Sofiane B., Twenty Years Old], the vision of the so-called terrorist is complicated, as a young man is killed after joining the Islamist *maquis*. Told by Sofiane's aunt, the narrative recalls the family's shock at seeing their son, brother, and nephew described in the newspapers as a "dangereux terroriste" [dangerous terrorist]—a statement taken directly from the communiqué issued by State forces. The family's memories are of a sensitive, thoughtful, and caring young man, but the expectations of an exacting father led Sofiane to rebel, leaving him vulnerable to the growing Islamist movement. The story offers a representation of how prescribed sex/gender roles within Algeria push men to conform to the patriarchal vision society constructs for them and thereby draws a self-conscious attention to the performative role of language and words in defining Sofiane's violent path. Moreover, by describing how the newspaper simply repeats the official narrative issued by the State, the story encourages readers to question both the discursive construction of the "terrorist" and the levels of control exerted over the Algerian press by the State.⁹⁹ The multiple perspectives that the short stories offer constitute a challenge to the single narrative of the crisis adopted in both the local and international news media.

Indeed, as they move from graphic and realist descriptions of violence ("Corps indicible" [Unspeakable Body]) to more dream-like sequences ("La Marieuse" [The Matchmaker]; "Quand il n'est pas là, elle danse" [When he isn't there, she Dances]), the stories do not sit comfortably within an affirmative and referential "écriture de l'urgence" that El Nossery claims to unite testimonies of the Black Decade.¹⁰⁰ As Bey's style begins to shift to a more layered aesthetic—that also characterizes her 2004 collection of short stories, *Sous le jasmin la nuit* [*Beneath the Jasmine the Night*]—the final stories of the *Nouvelles d'Algérie* move away from realist accounts of violence.¹⁰¹ For instance, the seventh story, "Et si on parlait d'autre chose?" [And if We Spoke About Something Else?], underlines the stagnant nature of words which describe the horrors of violence as they become dangerously subsumed into the everyday discursive order:

Elle pensait que *les mots si souvent répétés* ne servent qu'à *essayer* de donner *un semblant d'ordre* à une réalité trop chaotique, et qu'ils s'efforcent ainsi de garder toute leur lucidité pour *essayer de comprendre*, de *prendre du recul*, en parler, au moins pour ne pas perdre pied, et par là même, se convaincre que cela existe vraiment.[102]

[She thought that *words, so often repeated*, serve only as an *attempt* to give *a semblance of order* to a chaotic reality, and that they strive to keep their lucidity to *try to understand*, to *take a step back*, to talk about it, at least so as not to lose one's footing, and at the same time to convince oneself that it really exists.]

Moving through accounts of the violence as reported in the newspapers, the protagonist Hanya questions how she has become so desensitized to the violence that consumes her own country: "elle a lu les articles en entier, sans même frémir" [she read the articles in full, without even shivering].[103] Having anguished over the question of how to "faire front contre la terreur" [stand up against the terror], Hanya recalls the ghostly words of a former teacher and poet assassinated during the violence, whom the narrator describes as searching for words "sous la cendre des jours" [under the ashes of days]. The poet's injunction to "donner la parole aux mots [. . .] et faire comme si demain était possible" [give voice to words and act as if tomorrow were possible] allows Hanya to imagine a freedom beyond the static nature of the text, outside a discourse that contains a restrictive narrative of the violence, and of words that define what the crisis was and how it would continue to develop throughout the 1990s.[104]

Academic literary critics stress how Bey's *Nouvelles d'Algérie* provides a sense of affirmation in the face of negation. For Beate Burtscher-Bechter, Bey's stories are about coming to an understanding of the violence, but they are also framed in terms of "survival," with words themselves deployed in a "lutte ardente contre la tentation du silence" [burning struggle against the temptation to remain silent].[105] Meanwhile, for Soler, Bey's stories initiate "une thérapie collective rendant possible la verbalisation de l'innommable, de l'indicible" [a collective therapy that makes possible the verbalization of the unnameable, the unspeakable].[106] Even Leperlier, in his more recent assessment of Bey's work, classifies *Au commencement* and the *Nouvelles d'Algérie* as forms of "attestation"—in his three-part schematic consisting of "attestation," "evocation," and "interrogation."[107] However, none of these academic critics explain how Bey uses these short stories in particular to interrogate both the process of bearing witness and the genesis of the oppositional frames through which testimonial literature, and the conflict more generally, has been understood. In its very title, the story, "Et si on parlait d'autre chose?" [And if We Spoke About Something Else?], poses a question—suggestive of a broader interrogative stance—around how useful it actually is, or has been, to continue to speak of the violence in a referential mode, or to continually conjure the "ruptures" of the everyday in a traumatic register.[108]

Bey's insight is that it is not enough to simply "attest" or "evoke" the horrors of the everyday. In order to truly capture the complexity of the violence, and the discursive frameworks that perpetuate that violence, the writer must hold up a mirror to their own work, recognizing and anticipating that their status as "spokesperson" or "witness" will mean their writing continually reconstitutes a self-fulfilling narrative of crisis. Bey, like Djebar, redefines testimonial literature as a form of self-conscious writing that, in anticipating its reception by critics and readers and acknowledging the complicity of the writer in forging a conflict narrative, mitigates the risk that it will contribute to an ill-defined, misleading, or patriarchal account of the ongoing conflict. At the very least, Bey's *Nouvelles d'Algérie* sensitizes readers to the question of (and thereby encourages them *to question*) what it means to write at a time of crisis and how testimony will always only offer a partial account of a contested past.

NOTES

1. Rachid Mimouni, *De la barbarie en générale et de l'intégrisme en particulier* (Paris: Le Pré aux Clercs, 1992); Rachid Boudjedra, *FIS de la haine* (Paris: Denoël, 1992). Boudjedra's title plays on the homophone FIS [Algeria's main Islamist party] and "fils" [son] to suggest that the FIS emerged naturally from the FLN—a common idea at the time that reflected the way in which the party emerged from factions within the one-party FLN State. See the introduction for further discussion.

2. Rachid Mimouni, *La Malédiction* (Paris: Stock, 1993); Rachid Boudjedra, *Timimoun* (Paris: Denoël, 1994); Rachid Boudjedra, *Lettres algériennes* (Paris: Grasset, 1995).

3. See, for instance, Jean-Michel Demetz, "Tous les Rushdie du monde," *L'Express*, February 17, 1994, 74, or Gilles Anquetil, "Deux romanciers algériens défient le FIS. Les Voltaire d'Alger," *Le Nouvel Observateur*, June 4–10, 1992, 133–34. See also Leperlier, *Algérie*, 100–02; 180, who notes how Mimouni himself embraced his status as "porte-parole" [spokesperson] in a 1989 interview.

4. Benkhaled and Vince, "Performing Algerianness."

5. As Leperlier underlines, the polarization of the "enlightened" intellectual, on the one hand, and the violent Islamist, on the other, also helped reinforce the myth that the Black Decade was a result of linguistic conflict between Arabic and French speakers. The reality was that both tripartite and binary understandings of the conflict emerged from oversimplifications and myths that fed a false yet ultimately

self-fulfilling narrative of the conflict as founded upon "cultural," rather than social or political, divisions. See Leperlier, *Algérie*, 94–107.

6. See Charles Bonn, "Algérie," 209. For further discussion of the "horizon de lecture," see Gerard Genette, *Fiction et diction* (Paris: Seuil, 1991), 67; see also Hans Robert Jauss, *Toward an Aesthetic of Reception*, trans. Timothy Bahti (Minneapolis: University of Minnesota Press, 1982).

7. On the "patriarchal premise" of objectivity in realist literature, and the way in which this is inherited from sciences and philosophy, see Karin Garlepp Burns, "The Paradox of Objectivity in the Realist Fiction of Edith Wharton and Kate Chopin," *Journal of Narrative Theory*, no. 29 (1999), 29–30.

8. Although Mimouni was one of the first to adopt a referential mode, the testimonial genre was primarily made up of work by women writers, who were seen to be directly threatened by Islamist violence. Notable works include Malika Boussouf's *Vivre traquée* (Paris: Calmann Lévy, 1995); Assima's *Une femme à Alger*; Malika Mokeddem's *L'interdite* (Paris: Grasset, 1993) and *Des rêves et des assassins* (Paris: Grasset, 1995); Leila Marouane's *Ravisseur* (Paris: Julliard, 1998). On the privileged status of women's writing during the Black Decade, see El Nossery, *Témoignages fictionnels* and Geesey, "Violent Days." For discussion of the "feminization" of testimonial literature in the French market, see Leperlier, *Algérie*, 199–200; Laroussi, "When Francophone Means National," 88. See also the introduction for further discussion.

9. Dominique Fisher underlines how Djaout's own literary work gained a mark after his death, whereby the writer's novels were read almost solely in the light of their "condamnation du radicalisme islamiste" [condemnation of radical Islam], when, in reality, Djaout's work was a far more nuanced meditation on the writing of Algerian history over a far longer past. See Fisher, *Ecrire l'urgence*, 21.

10. See, for instance, G.A., "Un écrivain contre la terreur islamiste. Mimouni le valeureux," *Le Nouvel Observateur*, October 7–13, 1993, 118; [No name], "Rachid Boudjedra, 'Dire l'urgence,'" *El Moudjahid*, March 20, 1994, Centre culturel algérien, Paris.

11. Cited in Leperlier, *Algérie*, 180.

12. Djebar had, of course, already posed this question in her preface to the first edition of *Femmes d'Alger dans leur appartement* (Paris: Editions des Femmes, 1980); Gayatri Chakravorty Spivak also took it up in her celebrated essay, "Can the Subaltern Speak?," in *Marxism and the Interpretation of Culture* ed. Cary Nelson and Lawrence Grossberg (London: Macmillan, 1988), 271–313. It is likely that Mimouni's enthusiasm for taking on the role of "spokesperson" is, in part, due to his own concerns over the lack of visibility of intellectuals after the uprisings of October 1988. Mimouni writes of Algerian intellectuals as having "raté le coche de la democratisation" [failed to seize the moment of democratization]. See Mimouni, *De la barbarie*, 98.

13. Huntington, "The Clash of Civilizations?"

14. Carine Bourget, "The Algerian Civil War: Rachid Boudjedra's *Le FIS de la haine*, Rachid Mimouni's *De la barbarie en général et de l'intégrisme en particulier*,

and *Une enfance algérienne*," in *The Star, The Cross, and The Crescent: Religions and Conflicts in Francophone Literature from the Arab World* (Lanham: Lexington Books, 2010), 92.

15. Although it was the FIS that won the most seats in the 1991 elections, it is important to note that (among the sixty or more parties created in 1991) there were multiple different Islamist parties, including the Mouvement pour la Societé et la Paix (MSP) [Movement for Society and Peace], the Mouvement National pour la Renaissance (MNR) [National Movement for Renaissance]. On this, see Benkhaled and Vince, "Performing Algerianness," 249.

16. Mimouni, *De la barbarie*, 17–18.

17. Mimouni, *De la barbarie*, 22.

18. For further discussion of this oppositional image, see Leperlier, *Algérie*, 100–01.

19. Cited in Bottici and Challand, "Rethinking Political Myth," 326.

20. Mimouni, *De la barbarie*, 169.

21. Mimouni, *De la barbarie*, 51.

22. For a detailed account of the affair, see Bourget, *The Star, The Cross, and The Crescent*, Ch. 5.

23. See Bonn, "Algérie"; see also Leperlier, *Algérie*, Ch. 4.

24. Mimouni, *De la barbarie*, 46–48.

25. Bonn, "Algérie," 209.

26. Benkhaled and Vince, "Performing Algerianness," 244.

27. Mimouni, *La Malédiction*, 18.

28. Mimouni, *La Malédiction*, 90.

29. Mimouni, *De la barbarie*, 44.

30. Walter Benjamin, *The Origin of German Tragic Drama* (London: Verso, 1985), 162; Maureen Quilligan, *The Language of Allegory: Defining the Genre* (London: Cornell UP, 1979), 227.

31. Mimouni, *La Malédiction*, 180.

32. For discussion of recidivism, see the introduction.

33. Mimouni, *La Malédiction*, 90.

34. For further discussion see McDougall, "Savage Wars?"

35. Mimouni, *La Malédiction*, 195, my emphasis.

36. Benkhaled and Vince, "Performing Algerianness," 254.

37. Mimouni, *De la barbarie*, 166.

38. Mimouni, *De la barbarie*, 167.

39. See, for instance, Janice Gross, "The Tragedy of Algeria: Slimane Benaïssa's Drama of Terrorism," *Theatre Journal* 54, no. 3 (2002), 369–87; Benjamin Stora, "La tragédie algérienne des années 1990 dans le miroir des films de fiction," *La Pensée du Midi* 3, no. 9 (2002), 32–43; Mohammed Harbi, "La tragédie d'une démocratie sans démocrates," *Le Monde*, April 1, 1994. Malik Aït-Aoudia and Séverine Labat's 2003 documentary on the Black Decade was entitled, *Algérie 1988–2000, autopsie d'une tragédie*. See also Ministère de l'Intérieur et des Collectivités Locales, *Charte pour la Paix et la Réconciliation Nationale*.

40. Malcolm Heath underlines Aristotle's definition of tragedy as "an imitation [. . .] of events that evoke fear and pity." See Malcolm Heath, "Introduction," in Aristotle, *Poetics* (London: Penguin, 1996), xxi.

41. Hiddleston, *Assia Djebar*, 134–35.

42. Lehmann, cited in Benkhaled and Vince, "Performing Algerianness," 266.

43. As discussed in the introduction, Rahal shows how the leadership of the PAGS pursued a language of "radical suppression" that sought not only to construct the Islamist enemy as a clear threat, but attacked its own members for not being "aggressive enough towards Islamists." Rahal, "1988–1992," 95.

44. This is despite Djebar's inability to master modern Arabic, because of her French colonial education in Algeria. For further discussion of this decade-long hiatus, see Mireille Calle-Gruber, "Eléments pour un portrait d'écrivain dans l'entrelangues," in *Assia Djebar ou la résistance de l'écriture* (Paris: Maisonneuve et Larose, 2001), 7–17.

45. Assia Djebar, *Femmes d'Alger*; Assia Djebar, *Women of Algiers in their Apartment*, trans. Marjolijn de Jager (Charlottesville: University of Virginia Press, 1992).

46. For further discussion of postcolonial writers being subsumed in the postcolonial marketplace, see Graham Huggan, *The Postcolonial Exotic: Marketing the Margins* (London: Routledge, 2001) and Sarah Brouillette, *Postcolonial Writers in the Global Literary Marketplace* (Basingstoke: Palgrave, 2007).

47. Assia Djebar, *Femmes d'Alger*, 8, emphasis in original.

48. Djebar, *Women of Algiers*, 2.

49. Spivak, "Can the Subaltern Speak?," 275. See also Harrison, *Postcolonial Criticism*, 95, and Hiddleston, *Assia Djebar*, 55.

50. As Hiddleston underlines, the critique of Delacroix offered by Djebar in the postscript to *Femmes d'Alger* "is not a straightforward affirmation of her own successful representation, as some critics have argued, but the trigger for an exploration of her own struggle." Hiddleston, *Assia Djebar*, 67.

51. Assia Djebar, *Le blanc*; Assia Djebar, *Algerian White*, trans. David Kelley and Marjolijn de Jager (New York: Seven Stories Press, 2000); Hiddleston, *Assia Djebar*, 122.

52. Djebar, *Le blanc*, 232–33.

53. Djebar, *Algerian White*, 217–18.

54. Aristotle, *Poetics* (London: Penguin, 1996).

55. Roger Shattuck, "The Doubting of Fiction," *Yale French Studies*, no. 6 (1950), 101.

56. Daniel Just, "The Politics of the Novel and Maurice Blanchot's Theory of the Récit, 1954–1964," *French Forum* 33, no. 1–2 (2008), 137.

57. El Nossery, *Témoignages*, 18.

58. El Nossery, *Témoignages*, 18.

59. Assia Djebar, *Oran, langue morte* (Paris: Actes Sud, 1997); Assia Djebar, *The Tongue's Blood Does Not Run Dry: Algerian Stories*, trans. Tegan Raleigh (New York: Seven Stories Press, 2006).

60. Djebar, *Oran*, 367.

61. Djebar, *Oran*, 367.

62. Djebar, *The Tongue's Blood*, 212. I adapt the published translation here, because Djebar appears to make a distinction between the tradition of oral story telling ("fragments d'imaginaire") and the prose form of the short story (the "nouvelle"), which, as Johnnie Gratton and Brigitte Le Juez note, is a more "tightly structured" modern form than more traditional oral accounts. See Johnnie Gratton and Brigitte Le Juez, "Introduction," in *Modern French Short Fiction: An Anthology* (Manchester: Manchester University Press, 1994), 14.

63. Debarati Sanyal stresses the Latin root of complicity, *complicare*, meaning "to fold together"; see her book, *Memory and Complicity: Migrations of Holocaust Remembrance* (New York: Formham University Press, 2015), 1.

64. Djebar, *Le blanc*, 241. According to Benkhaled and Vince, Djebar has also regularly repeated "mutually exclusive versions of Algerianness" that tend to promote a reductive vision of Algerian history. See Benkhaled and Vince, pp. 252–53.

65. Hiddleston, *Assia Djebar*, 134–35. See also Dominick Lacapra, *Representing the Holocaust: History, Theory, Trauma* (Ithaca: Cornell University Press, 1994), 209.

66. See, for instance, Farid Mellal, "La violence de la réalité ne cède que très peu de place à la fiction dans ces récits," *La Tribune Culture*, September 23, 1998, 16–17. See also Beate Burtscher-Bechter, "'Donner la parole aux mots, et faire comme si demain était possible.' Mutisme et prise de parole dans les *Nouvelles d'Algérie* de Maïssa Bey," in *Subversion du réel: Stratégies esthétiques dans la littérature algérienne* ed. Beate Burtscher-Bechter and Birgit Mertz-Baumgartner (Paris: L'Harmattan, 2001), 203; Nicole Buffard-O'Shea, "*Les Agneaux du Seigneur* de Yasmina Khadra et *Nouvelles d'Algérie* de Maïssa Bey: écrutures sans appel?," in *Subversion du réel: Stratégies esthétiques dans la littérature algérienne* ed. Beate Burtscher-Bechter and Birgit Mertz-Baumgartner (Paris: L'Harmattan, 2001), 103; Ana Soler, "Un espace littéraire empreint de violence: *Nouvelles d'Algérie* de Maïssa Bey," in *Diversité littéraire en Algérie* ed. Najib Redouane (Paris: L'Harmattan, 2009), 98.

67. As Abdelkébir Khatibi has written, "the power of the word" is to be understood as part of a discourse that can be traced back to imperial domination. Cited in Barbara Harlow, "Introduction," in Malek Alloula, *The Colonial Harem* trans. Myrna Godzich and Wlad Godzich (Minneapolis: University of Minnesota Press, 1986), xxii.

68. Maïssa Bey and Martine Marzloff, *A Contre-silence* (Grigny: Parole de L'Aube, 1998), 29.

69. Bey and Marzloff, *A Contre-silence*, 29.

70. Bey's novel is published in the fifth number of *Algérie Littérature/Action*.

71. Further works published within the 1996 journal issues include Amine Touati's *Peurs et mensonges*, no. 1 (May 1996); Arezki Métref's *Quartiers consignés*, no. 2 (June 1996); Waciny Laredj's *La gardienne des ombres*, no. 3–4 (September–October 1996); Alek Baylee's *Maddah-Sartre*, no. 6 (December 1996). The journal continued to publish novels, plays, and short stories alongside reviews and articles until the end of 2001.

72. Though its editors professed a certain level of "autonomy" from French publishing houses, the journal was supported by mainly left-wing figures in France,

including Pierre Bourdieu, Jacques Derrida, and Etienne Balibar, and was strongly anti-FIS. For further discussion of the journal, see Leperlier, *Algérie*, 280–93.

73. Rice, *Polygraphies*, 1.

74. Claire Etcherelli, "Postface," in Maïssa Bey, *Au commencement était la mer* (La Tour-d'Aigues: L'Aube, 2003 [1996]), 153–55. See also Lila Ibrahim-Ouali, "Maïssa Bey: 'des mots sous la cendre des jours': *Au commencement était la mer . . . et Nouvelles d'Algérie*," *L'Esprit Créateur* 40, no. 2 (2000), 75–85.

75. Bey, *Au commencement*, 31.

76. Bey, *Au commencement*, 43.

77. Bey, *Au commencement*, 90.

78. Bey, *Au commencement*, 51, my emphasis.

79. Bey, *Au commencement*, 60. This observation is not captured in the English translation of "amour" and "mort" as "love" and "death."

80. Bey, *Au commencement*, 108.

81. Bey, *Au commencement*, 115–16.

82. Quilligan, *The Language of Allegory*, 227.

83. Bey and Marzloff, *A contre-silence*, 29.

84. Burns, "The Paradox of Objectivity," 29–30.

85. Michael Rothberg, *Multidirectional Memory: Remembering the Holocaust in the Age of Decolonization* (Stanford: Stanford University Press, 2009), 306.

86. Maïssa Bey, *Nouvelles d'Algérie* (Paris: Grasset, 1998).

87. Bey, *Nouvelles d'Algérie*, 11.

88. Maissa Bey and Rachid Mokhtari, "Maïssa Bey: 'J'écris pour éviter les hurlements,'" in *La Graphie de l'horreur: essai sur la littérature algérienne (1990-2000)* (Algiers: Chihab, 2002), 149.

89. Subsequent editions of *Nouvelles d'Algérie* print the individual titles of the stories before each story.

90. Lila Ibrahim-Ouali, "Maïssa Bey," 82.

91. Cathy Caruth, *Unclaimed Experience: Trauma, Narrative, and History* (Baltimore: Johns Hopkins University Press, 1996), 91.

92. See, for instance, Soler, "Un espace littéraire" and Burtscher-Bechter, "Mutisme et prise de parole."

93. El Nossery, *Témoignages*, 19.

94. It is likely that, because produced so soon after the publication of the *Nouvelles d'Algérie* and near to the end of the Algerian crisis, critical reflections lacked sufficient distance from the Black Decade and so were, in effect, unable to clearly apprehend the author's relationship to the contested period.

95. In his three-part classification (attestation, evocation, and interrogation), Leperlier places Bey's *Au commencement* and *Nouvelles d'Algérie* in the categories of "attestation" and "evocation." However, he does not acknowledge how Bey continually *interrogates* her own place in the genre of testimonial literature. See Leperlier, *Algérie*, 197.

96. "Le cri" was first published in *Algérie Littérature/Action* no. 9 (1997), 131–32. Bey, *Nouvelles d'Algérie*, 15.

97. Bey, *Nouvelles d'Algérie*, 20. For Burtscher-Bechter, the "cri" is a "fil conducteur" [central thread] throughout the ten stories. Burtscher-Bechter, "Mutisme et prise de parole," 206.

98. Dominique Le Boucher, "Un corps qui dance," in Bey and Marzloff, *A Contre-silence*, 98–101.

99. As Hafid Gafaïti has written, "Until recently, journalists were relatively well-paid civil servants and were therefore expected to reflect and promote the official discourse of the government. Like most Algerians in the various professions, the press generally complied with the state's ideological orientations and worked to the satisfaction of the so-called Revolution leaders for nearly three decades." See Hafid Gafaïti, "Power, Censorship and the Press: The Case of Postcolonial Algeria," *Research in African Literature* 30, no. 3 (1999), 52.

100. El Nossery, *Témoignages*, 19.

101. Maïssa Bey, *Sous le jasmin la nuit* (La Tour-d'Aigues: L'Aube/Algiers: Barzakh, 2004).

102. Bey, *Nouvelles d'Algérie*, 114, my emphasis.

103. Bey, *Nouvelles d'Algérie*, 122.

104. Bey, *Nouvelles d'Algérie*, 125.

105. Burtscher-Bechter, "Mutisme et prise de parole," 204.

106. Soler, "Un espace littéraire," 102.

107. Leperlier, *Algérie*, 197.

108. Soler, "Un espace littéraire," 102.

Chapter 2

Exploring Complicity in Salim Bachi

Je ne suis pas un écrivain-témoin au sens traditionnel du terme. Je pense avoir décrit l'esprit plus que la lettre d'une époque. Ma contribution est, en somme, le portrait spirituel d'une période historique à travers les destins de quelques personnages éminemment romanesques.[1]

[I am not a writer-witness in the traditional meaning of the term. I think of myself as having described the spirit more than the letter of the period. My contribution is, in short, the spiritual portrait of a historical period told through the fate of a few eminently fictional characters.]

—Salim Bachi

In a 2007 interview with the journalist and critic Yassin Temlali, Salim Bachi is asked to comment on the link between his novel, *Tuez-les tous* (2006), which stages the final days of one of the perpetrators of the September 2001 attacks in New York, and Samuel Huntington's thesis that the post–Cold War order will engender a clash of civilizations along the lines of religious and cultural identity. In his response, Bachi dismisses Huntington's theory as "une escroquerie" [a swindle/fraud] that, while it may have taken hold as a myth in the minds of certain commentators, does not exist in reality: "Il n'y a pas de choc de civilisations qui tienne. Les conflits actuels sont des conflits d'intérêts et de puissance. [. . .] C'est terrible, mais c'est le mouvement du monde" [there is no clash of civilizations. Current conflicts are conflicts of interest and power. (. . .) It's terrible, but it's the way of the world].[2]

Emphasizing that the space of the novel is essential for unveiling such myths, Bachi asserts his desire to "réinventer une perspective romanesque" [reinvent a novelistic perspective]—a perspective he says "manquait à la littérature de témoignage des années 90" [was lacking from the testimonial literature of the 1990s].³ But, Bachi also wishes to ask a question about the critical reception of Algerian literature in France during and after the years of the Black Decade:

> Pourquoi un livre mettant en scène les massacres en Algérie provoque-t-il un intérêt soudain de la critique? Pourquoi un livre mettant en scène un autre massacre, le 11 septembre, ne soulève-t-il plus le même intérêt?⁴
>
> [Why does a book about the massacres in Algeria provoke such a sudden interest among critics? And why does a book about another massacre, the September 11 attacks, not give rise to the same interest?]

Here, Bachi implicitly repeats suggestions of an "attente" [expectation] among French readers for depictions of Algerian violence.⁵ Distinct from the testimonial genre, Bachi seeks a form of distance in the novel, not just a distance from any claim to give a direct account of the events of the Black Decade but a critical distance in which he can "faire œuvre d'écrivain" [do the work of a writer].⁶ For Bachi, the task of the novelist is to deploy formal experimentation to test the limits of what literature can do in the political realm and its capacity to unveil how existing cultural and historical myths reinforce the interests of the powerful.⁷

In this chapter, I examine how Bachi's works move across multiple geographical and historical settings—from 1990s Algeria to more distant Algerian history before moving to more recent terrorist attacks in the United States and Europe—in an attempt to reveal the myths upon which dominant binary narratives have been written. I show how, although Bachi attempts to create a composite account that implicates writers and critics in the process of "naturalizing" dominant conflict narratives, the writer still falls into the traps of reductive and polarizing narratives.⁸ I argue that the success of the riposte Bachi sets out to issue to the political myth of the clash of civilizations will depend on the writer's ability to acknowledge his own complicity in perpetuating other reductive myths about Algerian history and the role of literature in telling that history.

THE CYRTHA TRILOGY

Born in 1971, Bachi grew up in the city of Annaba and came to prominence after the publication of his first novel *Le Chien d'Ulysse* [*Ulysses' Dog*] (2001), which was awarded the prestigious Prix Goncourt du Premier Roman that same year.⁹ He is one of only a handful of Algerian writers writing today to be published by the highly regarded French publisher Editions Gallimard and has, since 1996, lived in Paris. Bachi has published some twelve works to date, including, in the "Cyrtha trilogy," *Le Chien d'Ulysse*, *La Kahéna* [*Kahina*] (2003), and a collection of short stories, *Les Douze contes de minuit* [*The Twelve Tales of Midnight*] (2006).[10] In 2006, the author published *Tuez-les tous* and a further terrorism-related novel, *Moi, Khaled Kelkal* [*I, Khaled Kelkal*] in 2012, both to a controversial reception.[11] Given Bachi's position at the center of the Parisian publishing market, the author has been well placed to challenge the dominant myths about terrorist violence in Algeria, Europe, and beyond.[12]

In his early twenties during the first years of the Black Decade, the political crisis Bachi saw emerging around him did not demand immediate testimony, but rather allegory.[13] His first published work, "Le vent brûle" [The Wind Burns], was released as a short story by *Le monde diplomatique* in 1995 after the author won the newspaper's annual competition for young writers.[14] Presenting the initial events of the 1990s through an allegorical lens, as seemingly innocuous insects metamorphose into bees, wasps, and mosquitos, Bachi's first act as a published author was to offer the distanced and layered perspective of a writer, rather than fall into a preexisting testimonial genre. In this regard, Bachi can be seen to echo Djebar and Bey's anxieties about how Algerian writers were increasingly being read and received by commentators as "witnesses" or "spokespeople." However, though he examines the complicity of his characters in perpetuating reductive myths about Algerian history, the writer himself risks failing to account for his own complicity in forging a narrative of conflict that reproduces these same binary visions of the past.

Le Chien D'Ulysse (2001)

Charting twenty-four hours in the lives of the first-person narrator Hocine and his friends, *Le Chien d'Ulysse* is set at the heart of the violence of the 1990s. The day is June 29, 1996, exactly four years after the assassination of President Mohamed Boudiaf, and the setting is the mythological city of Cyrtha which at least obliquely resembles modern-day Algiers. The violence of the 1990s is approaching its height, as we see from press reports voiced from within the novel. Though, on the surface, this description might appear to place this novel firmly in the realm of testimony, Bachi's mythological style—and the way he employs the mythologized city of Cyrtha—means the novel is both reminiscent of realist narrative and a rejoinder to it. Zoubida Belaghoueg stresses that there are two underlying vagabond forms of *Le Chien d'Ulysse*: the first is related to the space of the city, while the second revolves around writing itself.[15] One might, therefore, as Patrick Crowley has done, describe Bachi's style as a kind of composite "mythological realism."[16]

The novel introduces the city of Cyrtha, the setting for Bachi's broader trilogy, as a sometimes living and breathing character of its own. It is described as a contradictory space: a "cité en construction et pourtant ruinée" [city under construction and yet in ruins], a "rocher" [rock] whose inhabitants are "captifs, emmurés dans le dédale de ses rues" [captive, imprisoned in the maze of its streets] and a space which produces "émanations délétères" [deleterious smells].[17] Cyrtha is a hybrid figuration of the historical and geographical metropolises of the ancient Numidian capital of Cirta (now Constantine), Annaba, the city in which Bachi spent his childhood, and modern-day Algiers, where Bachi was born.[18] The composite space that hesitates between reality and myth makes Cyrtha a blank slate, sitting at once inside and outside the Algerian cities it purports to describe.[19] If writers such as Mimouni and Boudjedra understand the crisis of the Black Decade firmly within an Algerian locale, Bachi's mythological style forces the reader to consider the amorphous city of Cyrtha outside the referential constraints of the testimonial genre.

Within the novel, Cyrtha is both setting and living character—the home and nemesis of Hocine and his friends, Mourad, Rachid Hchicha, Poisson, and Seyf—and at one point Hocine's lover who becomes pregnant and gives birth to his degenerate children. Cyrtha is also a distinct part of the imagination of each character. As intruders attack the journalist and aspiring writer Hamid Kaïm in his home and destroy his works, the city disappears with them: "Cyrtha bâtie de mes mains, sortie de ma cervelle, me fuyait et mourait sous les coups répétés" [Cyrtha built by my own hands, from my brain, fled and died in the face of repeated blows].[20] The city is, moreover, a cradle of corruption with its police station described as a "vaste prison [. . .] confondant bourreaux et victimes" [vast prison (. . .) confusing executioner and victim].[21] It is a city in which the threat of being "disappeared" by the military looms large. Referring to the assassination of Boudiaf—the focal point both produced by and which continues to produce the deleterious space—Hocine announces that "[t]out finissait mal à Cyrtha. C'était écrit" [Everything ended badly in Cyrtha. It was written], and continues, "[d]ans notre croyance, l'homme, avant même de vivre, lit le compte rendu exact de son existence future. Quelle dérision! Pourquoi ne déchiffrais-je pas mes errances dans le ciel?" [In our belief, man reads the exact account of his future existence, even before living it. How ridiculous! Why not return to deciphering my wanderings in the sky?][22] If Hocine's critique of "croyance" [belief] appears to refer to a religion and national culture that violently clash in their efforts to shape Algeria of the 1990s, the mythological city still frustrates the referential narrative that produces these binary visions, or myths of clash and division.[23] Here, Cyrtha unsettles the polarizing logics introduced by characters who are embedded in the conflict.

In its paradoxical status, as both "written" and indeterminate, Cyrtha encapsulates the double meaning of myth as, on the one hand, stories that tell the long and celebrated history of modern civilization and, on the other, widely held but ultimately idealized conceptions or false beliefs that lead to disappointment and polarization. Early in the novel, the city is described as both writing its own illustrious history and yet also engendering the downfall of its inhabitants:

> Par une sorte de charme, Cyrtha écrit son histoire, érige ses tourelles, ouvre ses ruelles, creuse ses échoppes où des légions de vieillards prennent place, assis les jambes croisées sur une natte ou une peau de mouton, et commencent à marteler le cuivre, à polir une pièce de bois, à assouplir un cuir. Pourtant, depuis des décennies déjà, les dinandiers ont fermé boutique, les tanneurs ont fini de sécher leurs peaux au soleil, les vieillards blanchis par les vapeurs nocives de l'argent sont morts, anéantis par la ville, enterrés dans ses combles.[24]

> [By a kind of charm, Cyrtha writes its own story, erects its turrets, opens its passages, creates the market stalls where crowds of old men sit, cross-legged on a mat or sheepskin, and begin to hammer copper, polish a piece of wood, soften some leather. However, for decades now, the metalworkers have closed shop, the tanners no longer dry their skins in the sun, and the old men corrupted by the harmful scent of money are dead, destroyed by the city, buried in the recesses of its attic.]

This depiction of Cyrtha as a place that produces both hope and despair captures how the writing of history as a series of myths is an always double-edged endeavor. Cyrtha may well author an illustrious version of its own history, but in propelling that mythological vision, it establishes that same history upon a set of shaky foundations.

Reminiscent of Djebar and Bey's consideration of the dangers of testimonial writing, attention to the processes of writing history, and the inevitable challenges this presents, is a theme that runs throughout Bachi's work. However, *Le Chien d'Ulysse* does not assume the same interrogative stance adopted by Djebar and Bey. While Bachi is clearly interested to examine the mythical roots of the binary and polarizing discourses that configure narratives of conflict—whether that be during the period of the Numidian king, Jugurtha, the Berber warrior queen, Kahina, or the rise and fall of Mohammed Boudiaf during the 1990s—the author still repeats recidivist tropes about "la permanence de la violence" [the permanence of violence] throughout Algerian history.[25] Thus, in his attempts to reject one myth, Bachi risks perpetuating another.

La Kahéna (2003)

Whereas *Le Chien d'Ulysse* mythologizes the city to draw attention to the roots of the binary narratives that constitute the Black Decade, *La Kahéna* tells a set of longer interweaved histories. At once an account of a house inhabited by the colonial explorer, Louis Bergagna, and named after the eponymous Berber queen who had resisted the Arab invasion of Algeria in the seventh century, *La Kahéna* presents a complex web of inextricable stories. Occupied, in its most recent iteration, by the journalist Hamid Kaïm and Bergagna's granddaughter—the sometimes-slippery narrator of the novel and Kaïm's lover—the house is a point of entry into Algeria's multilayered history.

Structured around three "nuits" [nights] (spent between Kaïm and his lover), the main intrigue of the novel is in the discovery of the diaries belonging to Louis Bergagna and Kaïm's father, which had been kept within the walls of the house and which Kaïm reads throughout the novel. The stories of the father and the son become inextricable, as both in turn experience the violence of independence and October 1988, as well as its immediate aftermath; Bergagna's diaries also trace a longer history prior to independence, making *La Kahéna* a story of modern-day Algeria told through the lens of a far broader political and historical context.

In engaging with a set of fused and indeterminate metaphorical figures, the narrative complicates and unsettles the telling of Algerian history. References to Bachi's mythical Cyrtha are placed alongside references to Algeria and Algiers (Hamid Kaïm travels by plane from Cyrtha to Algiers, for instance), meaning the reader is never quite sure of how to read diegetic references within the novel—or indeed any extra-diegetic "reality" to which the novel might refer—especially because Cyrtha is itself a hybrid figuration of the cites of Annaba, Constantine, and modern-day Algiers.[26] Later imagining Cyrtha and Algeria as amalgamated, one living within the other, Bergagna further adds to the confusion: "Cyrtha et l'Algérie, l'une incluse dans l'autre, en s'embrassant" [Cyrtha and Algeria, one included within the other, encompassing each other].[27] The unsettled status of *La Kahéna* (it is at once a house, a historical and mythical reference and novel) creates a sense of doubt about the reliability of written accounts and, like *Le Chien d'Ulysse*, disrupts the "naturalization" of the myths contained within its pages.[28] As Hiddleston writes of this novel, Kaïm's "confused apprehension of the various narrative threads betrays the inability of any single historical discourse to claim to own the past."[29] Indeed, Hiddleston understands the narrative of *La Kahéna* as staging a broader "struggle for coherence" we all must endure as we live our own lives through dreams and illusions.[30]

The link to *Le Chien d'Ulysse* is established by the novel's setting in the city of Cyrtha, but also in maintaining several characters from the previous novel. Hamid Kaïm is now the central character of *La Kahéna*, while Mourad and Rachid are also present. Kateb Yacine's iconic *Nedjma* is prominent in both the presence of characters and in several analogous scenes.[31] Rachid and Mourad are characters in both Kateb and Bachi's stories; Rachid, traumatized by his torture after the October 1988 riots, murders a hotel manager on a beach before turning the knife on himself. The allusion to the pivotal scene of Camus's *L'Etranger* is clear, as Kaïm describes Rachid as the "jeune homme sur une plage que le soleil incendiait" [young man on the beach being burned by the sun].[32] The life of Camus and some of his other major works are alluded to, perhaps especially in relation to the posthumous reading of Kaïm's father's diaries.[33] If these intertextual elements offer interesting subtexts to Bachi's novel, they also serve a function within the narrative structure itself, as they bring into focus the process of writing, as well as ask questions surrounding the originality of the text and its ability to tell a single story at one time or in one place. In this regard, the novel collapses the historical boundaries constructed between the generations who have lived within the walls of Bergagna's house and, as such, interrogates the reliability of the historical narrative written within the book's pages.

If *Le Chien d'Ulysse* moves away from Bey and Djebar's self-conscious attention to the problem of testimony, *La Kahéna* deploys the enquiring journalist, Kaïm, to reflect—albeit obliquely—on the abundance of testimonial narratives during and since the end of the Black Decade. Asked for a "témoignage" of Rachid's downfall, Kaïm expresses anxiety about the ability of the testimonial form to capture the facts:

> Le mélange des genres ne le séduisait pas, lui qui sa vie durant cherchait à lever les voiles successifs qui masquaient le réel, dont la quête, fictive parfois, visait à pourfendre l'illusion et le mensonge. Un journaliste devait rendre compte des faits et non ajouter de l'obscurité aux ténèbres. Il refusa.[34]

> [The mixture of genres did not seduce him, he who for his whole life had sought to lift the veils that masked reality, and in whose quest, sometimes fictitious, had intended to defeat illusion and lies. A journalist had to report facts, not add further obscurity to darkness. He refused.]

Kaïm's recognition of the "sometimes fictitious" pursuit of "reality" recalls Derrida's understanding of testimony as always implying "the possibility of fiction, simulacra, dissimulation, lie and perjury."[35] In other words, myth (as possible deception) is present within all forms of testimony. Moreover, as a journalist who refuses to act as a spokesperson, Kaïm is perhaps representative of the writer himself, his words recalling those of Bachi who rejects the label of the "écrivain-témoin" [writer-witness]. What the author calls the mythological "filtre" [filter] of the city of Cyrtha is Bachi's principal means "pour *ne pas* tomber dans le témoignage" [of *not* falling into the trap of testimony].[36] Yet, while in this same interview Bachi distances *La Kahéna* from the other two texts in the Cyrtha trilogy, the novel still foregrounds the events of October 1988 as pivotal for the onset of the violence of the 1990s.

Indeed, in discussing the events of October 1988, Bachi's novel invokes further recidivist images of the violence that would culminate in the Black Decade. The narrator repeats a common trope in noting how the same weapons would be used against those who rebelled against the independent State as those who had resisted colonialism. Kaïm's lover underlines how the events of October 1988 are inscribed in a long line of Algerian violence: "Les massacres d'octobre 1988 étaient dans la lignée de cette violence obscure, réfléchie depuis des millénaires sur les miroirs de la haine" [the October 1988 massacres were in the tradition of this obscure violence that had been reflected for millennia in the mirrors of hate].[37] The narrator continues to stress how the violence is written in the "origines" [origins] of a people: "Personne ne pensait plus à ses actes avant de les commettre. La connaissance venait toujours après le crime. Cela aussi était inscrit aux origines." [Nobody thought of their actions before committing them. Knowledge only came after the crime. That too was inscribed in our origins.][38] Therefore, while apparently committed to questioning dominant mythologies of history, *La Kahéna* is by no means immune from repeating reductive myths, or perpetuating falsehoods, about the nature of Algerian violence.[39]

If the mythological surface of Bachi's novels allow readers to explore their own complicity in the process of constructing conflict narratives like those adopted in the French newspapers and by writers like Mimouni, it also risks giving way to a form of normative critique that fails to interrogate its own presuppositions. It is essential here to ask about what Bachi means when he speaks of the "*œuvre* d'écrivain" [the *work* of a writer] as an injunction to reject the testimonial genre.[40] The danger of taking Bachi's claim at face value is that we mistake an idea he has about literature for its actual function in society. In some ways, then, myth offers distance, but it can also be a somewhat thin veil for just another form of testimonial.

Les Douze contes de minuit (2006)

The short stories that make up *Les Douze contes de minuit* constitute the third text in the Cyrtha trilogy. If, like *Le Chien d'Ulysse* and *La Kahéna*, these stories remain rooted in the mythological realm, the violence of the stories might lead the reader to situate them as more direct representations of the events of the 1990s. While each short story stands alone in terms of plot, the characters survive across them. Cyrtha makes its appearance from the first story "Le vent brûle," a redrafted version of Bachi's 1995 story from *Le Monde diplomatique*; many other characters, including Seyf, Rachid, and Hamid Kaïm, survive from *Le Chien d'Ulysse*.

The crossover with the previous two novels suggests that some of Bachi's short stories (in addition to "Le vent brûle") precede the publication of *Le Chien d'Ulysse* and *La Kahéna*—suggesting they were authored during the period of the Black Decade itself. Bachi's return to the central and guiding myth of Cyrtha, evident in many of the short stories published here, parallels a return to the history of the Black Decade. While *La Kahéna* runs only to the rupture of the riots of October 1988, *Les Douze contes de minuit* offers fragmented and yet often realist depictions of the tumultuous years that follow.

"Le vent brûle" maintains a quasi-allegorical form, when the inhabitants of Cyrtha lose their way in a city where the sole means of escape is to join a plague of insects transformed into increasingly violent wasps, bees, and mosquitos. The story also offers a realist account of dead bodies populating the streets, left unburied because of the fear of reprisals. Meanwhile, the fragmented form of "Le naufrage" [The Drowning] captures the traumatic narrative of children drowning at sea. Written in verse, the lines of text delineated only by blank space are absent of punctuation and regurgitate the story through a violent imagery: "c'est comme si on m'arrachait les entrailles et que les vers qui me rongent de l'intérieur me ressortaient par la bouche" [it was as if my intestines were being torn out and the worms/verses that were gnawing at me from the inside came out through my mouth].[41] If recounting the violent experience of drowning, the double meaning of "vers" [worms/verses] also emphasizes the urgency of voicing the lines of verse that spill out on the pages before us. In this way, Bachi's stories might be read in similar terms to Bey's *Nouvelles d'Algérie*. As academic critics of Bey's stories stress, the short story is particularly suited to this fragmentation that captures the traumatic experience of the violence of the Black Decade through formal experimentation, as well as through content.[42] By drawing self-conscious attention to the double meaning of "vers," Bachi explores the complicity of the writer as he or she brings the violent reality into existence for readers. Like Bey, the short form offers Bachi the possibility of a self-conscious register when it comes to writing testimony.

Indeed, toward the end of the collection, the testimonial function of the stories becomes even more visible. In "Icare et le Minotaure" [Icarus and the Minotaur], journalist Hamid Kaïm recounts the death of intellectuals and writers, who are killed by what he calls a "horde barbare" [barbarous horde].[43] In "Nuée ardente" [Pyroclastic Flow], the "disappeared" of the 1990s are represented as the victims of the so-called "grand moudjahid" [great mujaheddin—celebrated Algerian independence fighters], recalling the image that Algeria's liberation fighters were now implicated in a new period of resurgent violence.⁴⁴ At the same time, Kaïm uses irony to call out the tautology and cliché used by journalists and writers to depict the mounting violence: "Un intellectuel est mort, 'sauvagement assassiné' titreront les journaux demain [. . .] 'Sauvagement assassiné.' Y a-t-il une autre manière de l'être?" [An intellectual has died, "savagely murdered" so tomorrow's headlines will read (. . .) "Savagely murdered." Is there any other way of being murdered?]⁴⁵ As Kaïm's own writings are discovered and laid out by two armed figures who come to assassinate him, it is the existence of Cyrtha—the city Kaïm has himself been trying to imagine—that is threatened. As he stares down at the fragments of his work, Kaïm sees "Cyrtha en ruines" [Cyrtha in ruins] as "[l]es pages craquaient et se tordaient, la proie des flammes" [the pages creaked and twisted, the prey of the flames].⁴⁶ As the dream of Cyrtha is destroyed, Bachi's characters are framed increasingly within the referential setting of Algeria of the 1990s, but the testimonial mode through which they communicate their experience is also present for readers to see.

By alluding to the tropes used in the dominant news media narrative—and in clearly figuring Cyrtha as an imagined and written account of the city—Bachi draws further attention to the ways writers are implicated in the process of writing conflict. However, Bachi's concern around the processes of narrative and myth-making in each of the texts of the Cyrtha trilogy does not make his works immune from falling into the traps laid by preexisting binary narratives. Kaïm is also presented as threatened by violence, enacted by obscure figures around him, as Bachi's narrative moves away from myth and toward an increasingly referential style.

Ultimately, though, Cyrtha is itself continually staged within the novels and stories as a written and imagined thing. And, as the final lines of the final story of *Les Douze contes de minuit* attest, narrative is the sole medium through which we can gain access to historical truth: "Le manuscit entre les mains de ses lecteurs constitue la seule garantie d'authenticité" [the manuscript between our hands is the sole guaranty of authenticity].⁴⁷ As Cyrtha disappears "sous les strates sucessives de la terre et de l'histoire" [under the successive layers of the earth and of the story], Bachi's final words in the cycle assert that access to truth is always mediated by mythologized accounts.⁴⁸ By drawing attention to this paradoxical image, and by deploying his own unsettled depiction of Algeria at a time of conflict, Bachi's Cyrtha trilogy recalls Derrida's notion of literary "suspense," as it cautions journalist, historian, and literary critic alike.⁴⁹ Literature can never be fully attached or detached from the circumstances in which it is produced or received. Indeed, those circumstances are themselves always produced by and are thereby potentially alterable by successive interpretations.

THE POST-9/11 NOVELS AND THE "MYTHE AGISSANT"

The hesitation between historical reference and the mythological city evident in *Les Douze contes de minuit* is also present in Bachi's 2006 novel, *Tuez-les tous*. Although Cyrtha remains present, it is pushed to the background of the novel, mentioned only as the birthplace of the protagonist. However, myth reappears here in the form of what Bachi calls the "mythe agissant" [active myth] or "mythe contemporain" [contemporary myth] that surrounds events such as the attacks of September 11, 2001:

> Je m'intéresse aussi au mythe agissant, au mythe contemporain comme le 11 septembre par exemple. [. . .] Je me suis intéressé à la violence en Algérie en tant que mythe moteur de son Histoire [. . .] La figure du terroriste est pour moi une figure mythique, un mythe violent qui me fascine.[50]
>
> [I'm also interested in active myth, in contemporary myth, like 11 September for instance. (. . .) I became interested in the violence in Algeria as the driving myth of its history. (. . .) The figure of the terrorist is a mythical figure, a violent myth that fascinates me.]

If violence has been a "mythe moteur" in Algeria, Bachi also examines how this can be seen to be the case in the wake of so-called "global" terrorism events of the 1990s and 2000s. Although recalling another recidivist trope in his focus on violence as "mythe moteur," Bachi nevertheless widens his perspective to the Unites States and Europe, exploring how the myth of the terrorist has been established in these contexts.[51] At the same time, Bachi's two novels, *Tuez-les tous* and *Moi, Khaled Kelkal*, which take up the voices of the accused perpetrators of terrorist attacks, also show how myth has been used to brainwash vulnerable young men and inspire them to carry out such acts of terrorism. Here, myth works from both "sides" to further entrench an already dangerously polarized narrative of a clash of civilizations and cultures. Again, myth must be understood as double-edged: it helps the reader see the histories of modern civilization as only partial narratives, while at the same time acting upon and taking hold of characters as it further entrenches false beliefs.

Tuez-les tous (2006)

Despite its short length, Bachi's third novel, *Tuez-les tous*, is richly intertextual and poetic. As Carine Bourget has shown, the title of the novel is an expression which can be traced back to several historical moments of terror. "Tuez-les tous" finds its root in the thirteenth-century Albigensian Crusade, specifically from a command given by the abbot of Citeaux, Arnaud Amaury, at the massacre at Béziers in 1209. In response to the question of how to distinguish Cathars from others in the town, the abbot apparently answered: "Tuez-les tous, Dieu reconnaitra les siens" ["kill them all, let God sort them out"].[52] Bourget goes on to note how the expression was also used by American soldiers in Vietnam and in Alfred Hitchcock's *The Birds*, when one of the film's characters proposes destroying a whole species of bird in response to the attacks.[53] The image of "the birds" as a figure for the planes, and the subsequent "kill them all" reference, also functions as a broader metaphorical narrative of the September 11 attacks and the hardline response from the US military.

The story, which plays back the experience of one of the hijacker-pilots in the twenty-four-hour period leading up to the attack on the World Trade Centre towers, is told through a variety of third-person narration and direct speech.[54] The identity of the protagonist remains unstable: he has no fixed name for the practical purpose of avoiding capture (described variously as San Juan, Seyf el Islam, "Personne" [Nobody] or, simply, "Pilote" [Pilot]), but this also allows for the uprooting of the main character ready for his identity to be mythologized once more, drawn into Bachi's "mythe agissant" of the terrorist.[55]

The immediate narrative describes the night before the attack is carried out, taking as its setting a hotel room in the US city of Portland where the protagonist is staying. Within the early lines of the novel, we learn of the life of the protagonist as he takes a bath, sipping from a glass of champagne delivered by room service, paid for on his MasterCard, before launching into a violent, anti-Semitic, diatribe against Israel and the West. The third-person narrative, mixed with a significant degree of free indirect speech, both adds to the ambiguity of the narrative identity and gives a caricatured account of the protagonist's entrenched political beliefs, which are drawn in extreme binary opposition to the supposed values of the West and particularly those of the United States.

One early example of this binary thinking is evidenced in the protagonist's view of the film *Hiroshima mon amour* [*Hiroshima My Love*], a recurrent reference throughout the novel.[56] Alain Resnais's 1959 film explores the event of the atomic bomb at Hiroshima, staging the problem of seeing horror from insider and outsider perspectives in a multilayered manner, and thus questions viewer complicity in the violence depicted. It is repeatedly described by Bachi's protagonist as a "sale titre de film vu dans une salle obscure à Paris" [dirty movie title seen in a dark room in Paris].[57] The protagonist has apparently seen the film, "quand il se civilisait" [when he was civilizing himself], fitting into the Paris he moved to after he left his native Cyrtha.[58] Paris is staged here, early in the novel, as the place where the "sale type sans histoires et sans Histoire" [dirty type without stories nor History] became "intégré en voie de désintégration" [integrated in the process of disintegration] and who preferred "intégrisme" [fundamentalism] over being "intégré" [integrated— i.e., a *fundamental* part of French civilization].[59]

As he continues to sip champagne in his hotel room, the protagonist learns of yet another "attentat [qui] avait secoué sa ville" [attack which had rocked his hometown] on the television news.[60] In Cyrtha, the general perception is that women and children are killed and raped, and throats are regularly cut.[61] The population of the city is described as having been reduced to "miettes" [crumbs], where now official amnesty reigns and where "la mémoire appartient aux vainqueurs" [memory belongs to the victors].[62] Since he left Cyrtha, the protagonist's life in the West is described as a pursuit, in opposition to religious doctrine, of the material objects and experiences of the MasterCard, champagne, nightclubbing, and women. Indeed, the figure of a scantily clad woman attempting to hail a taxi in the street is described as a symbol for the United States; the protagonist is described as wanting to "[tuer] l'Amérique à travers elle" [kill America through her]—the narrator gives a brutal account of how the protagonist would rape her and cut her up into pieces.[63] Though disturbing, it is important to understand these images as caricatures of the terrorist constructed in the popular imagination.

In a further reference to Resnais's *Hiroshima mon amour*, Hiroshima begins to affect the protagonist. Still described as a "sale titre de film" [dirty movie title], the city of Hiroshima is substituted for New York in an image that at once prefigures the destruction and horror to come and transfigures Resnais's palimpsest. In an image which also recalls the hidden trauma of the violence in Cyrtha, the reader is introduced to a memory of the protagonist as a child, hiding in a dark cupboard—"un placard sombre et noir, derrière une porte close, sous laquelle filtrait parfois un rai de lumière" [a dark, black closet behind a closed door, under which sometimes filtered a ray of light]; here, the child invents the "histoire absurde d'oiseaux" [absurd story of the birds], which will function later as a metaphor for the planes flying into the Twin Towers.[64] This foundational trauma is described as one of the "gamin forcé d'imaginer pour meubler son existence" [child forced to imagine in order to furnish his own existence].[65] In the final scenes evoked before the event itself, the protagonist, sitting in the heat of the bath, recalls the images of children at Hiroshima he had been shown at a terrorist training camp in Afghanistan and is likened, in an image which recalls the disfigured bodies of Hiroshima, to a "foetus de six ans qui l'appelait Papa, sauve-moi" [a six-year-old fetus crying out: Dad, Dad, save me].[66] He checks in for his flight, makes a final call to his handlers, and boards the plane, fully realizing the absurdity of the action he is about to take.

The event of the plane hitting one of the towers is evoked in the final paragraph of the novel, where the doors of the dark cupboard of the protagonist's childhood are morphed into the door of the plane's cockpit, and where he no longer knows his name.[67] Just before the plane hits, there is a literal inversion of the self-other binary, where the protagonist flying the plane, who becomes the Nietzschean "dernier homme" [last man], sees multiple reflections of his own image in the kaleidoscope of mirrored glass of the tower. This moment is suddenly lost as the plane hits the glass, taking the protagonist into "la nuit noire et aveugle" [dark and blind night].[68] This is the darkness and blindness of death, a blindness in the face of extreme violence committed against a perceived other, but it is also a sudden vision—a realization. In the kaleidoscope, the pilot is presented with an infinite number of mirror images of himself—"[il] pénétra dans la salle du trône où il vit des milliers de miroirs qui l'entourent et reflétaient à l'infini ses multiples et effrayants visages" [he entered the throne room where he saw that thousands of mirrors surrounded him, covered with the endless reflections of his various terrifying faces]—where the singular (reference to a single God, a single text, a single self) is pluralized, liquefied, universalized, and preserved in the image of the face of horror—in the endless faces of the *self-as-other*.[69] The novel ends here, but the reader already knows the iconic images that follow. The tower falls, the kaleidoscope of mirrors—once symbolic of a Western arrogance, vanity, imperialism, and which for a single moment offered an image of a human caught between the binary—collapses, forming pile upon pile of wreckage.[70] This image both obliterates the different "sides" of the binary and returns us to an understanding of complicity as a "folding together [. . .] of subject positions, histories, and memories."[71]

In his reading of the novel, the academic critic Bruno Chaouat accuses Bachi of writing an "apology," "eulogy," and "literary cenotaph to Islamic terrorists."[72] For Chaouat, Bachi's novel, at best, portrays these characters as "victims"; at worst, they are depicted as "heroes."[73] However, Chaouat does not consider how Bachi deconstructs the popular mythologization of the terrorist in social and political discourse—nor does he accept Bachi's representation of the terrorist as caricature. To claim that the terrorist is not representable in human form, or is a figure whose "monstrous" qualities exclude him from literary representation, not only fails to understand the roots of the violence Bachi depicts but actively promotes an overly simplified image of the terrorist that further entrenches an already polarized narrative. Rather, in this final image of the novel, where the unstable, fluid identity of our protagonist also returns—San Juan, Seyf el Islam, "Personne" [nobody], "Pilote" [pilot]—the reader perhaps sees themselves in the mirror reflection, as they recognize their own "entanglement" in the production of the catastrophe.[74] The focus for Bachi is to understand how polarized discourses, that abound in historical, political, and media narratives of the terrorist, produce characters such as those depicted in the post-9/11 novels. The terrorist is perhaps a "nobody," but he is at the same time a product of the media myth we collectively imagine and perpetuate.

Moi, Khaled Kelkal (2012)

Bachi's shift toward a referential style in *Tuez-les tous* is repeated in his 2012 novel, *Moi, Khaled Kelkal*. Invited to write for the Grasset series, "ceci n'est pas un fait divers" [this is not news], Bachi turns more explicitly to the myth of the terrorist cultivated and staged in a media spectacle. By fictionalizing the "fait divers" [news item], Bachi's post-9/11 novels draw attention to the spectacle of violence at work within media organizations, where predetermined narratives and generic tropes or modes are regularly deployed alongside images which purport to describe a dispassionate "reality."[75]

In an article on the theater of terror, communications theorist Gabriel Weimann examines how terrorist organizations have increasingly manipulated the mass media to advance a form of "psychological warfare" on citizens.[76] For Weimann:

> Modern terrorism can be understood in terms of the production requirements of theatrical engagements. Terrorists pay attention to script preparation, cast selection, sets, props, role playing, and minute-by-minute stage management. Just like compelling stage plays or ballet performances, the media orientation in terrorism requires full attention to detail in order to be effective.[77]

Weimann's understanding of the production of a theater of terror aligns with Michael Rothberg's important insight about the need to distinguish between individual acts of "terrorism" and the idea of "terror," which draws its power from an "affective level of politics."[78] However, while he acknowledges the threat posed to the imposition of limits on freedom of expression in the wake of terrorist attacks, Weimann does not consider how media organizations themselves benefit from, and thereby perhaps encourage, the theatricalization of terror in the mass media. It is this perspective on the theater of terror that Bachi pursues in his 2012 novel.

Moi, Khaled Kelkal follows the eponymous real-life protagonist, a twenty-four-year-old Algerian who moved to France as a child with his family and who was suspected of planting a bomb in the Paris RER which exploded at Saint-Michel on July 25, 1995. Kelkal was subsequently shot dead by police in an ensuing man-hunt.[79] It is thought that the attack and a series of other attempted attacks that same year were orchestrated by the GIA, whose strategy was to internationalize the fundamentalist cause in Algeria.[80] Kelkal's killing, which had been filmed by a news crew, was later broadcast on French television and gave rise to a heated debate in the French media. Shortly after the publication of Bachi's novel, the Franco-Algerian Mohammed Merah—another so-called "radicalised" young Muslim—shot dead seven people in the city of Toulouse; in scenes resembling the Kelkal case, the police launched a manhunt and finally caught up with Merah and he was shot dead. In the days following Merah's death, the French newspaper *Le Monde* commissioned Bachi to write an article, entitled "Moi, Mohammed Merah" [I, Mohammed Merah], which, like the novel, reimagined the voice of the terrorist from beyond the grave.[81] The author in effect asks the same questions he asks in his novel on Kelkal, in a text which, again, gave rise to fierce debate in France.[82]

While *Le Chien d'Ulysse* and *Tuez-les tous* unfold within a twenty-four hour period, this later novel is *staged* in five sections (five *acts*) as if a Shakespearean tragedy, with each act split into shorter scenes. Indeed, Kelkal returns as a Hamletian ghost as he recounts his story from beyond the grave. The tragic frame follows the Freytag pyramid of dramatic action: in the exposition, Kelkal describes the initial aftermath of the explosion of a bomb and his childhood growing up in the *banlieues* of Lyon. The rising action occurs as Kelkal commits the "crime impardonnable" [unforgivable crime] of stealing the BMW belonging to the chairman of the Olympique Lyonnais football club and Kelkal finds himself in prison.[83] At the climax, Kelkal plants the bomb, which explodes at the beginning of the fourth section. In the falling action, Kelkal retreats into his inner thoughts as he takes refuge in the woods from the gendarmes who hunt him down "comme un animal" [like an animal]. In the denouement, Kelkal is shot dead by gendarmes, who can apparently be heard to shout "Finis-le! Finis-le" [Finish him! Finish him!].[84] Kelkal's violent act is redeemed by the action of the gendarmes and life returns to normal.[85]

However, the tragic frame is subverted when, captured by camera crews, Kelkal's extrajudicial killing is shown on the television news that same evening. As Kelkal's ghost recounts, "[j]e m'attendais donc à mourir comme j'ai vécu, ni simplement, ni tragiquement, mais sur scène, face aux caméras, sous les coups d'une mauvaise fortune. A-t-elle jamais été clémente pour moi et les miens?" [I expected therefore to die as I had lived, neither simply nor tragically, but on stage, in front of the cameras, under the blows of bad luck. Have we ever been lucky, me and my kind?].[86] The media spectacle of "terror," killing Kelkal before any legal trial has been allowed to take place, is played out as an acceptable catharsis, but also one that was inevitable, predetermined, and prewritten.

In responding to an invitation to write *Moi, Khaled Kelkal*, Bachi stresses how the mainstream media relies on classic narrative structures, such as tragedy, to portray events and characters. If this is understandable—journalists are given very little time by editors to properly communicate the structural complexity of events—it is nevertheless part of a broader critique Bachi seeks to make of reductive narrativizations of conflict. By bringing the tragic spectacle under a spotlight, Bachi seeks to expose how media narratives morph moments of terrorism into an affective "theater of terror" that plays on the fears of an audience and perpetuates the myth that the terrorist is only comprehensible within existing narrative tropes and stereotypes.

Explicit in the argument of this book is the suggestion that literature might have effects its authors do not, or are unable to, anticipate. Bachi is clearly aware of this important pillar of literary reception, as he deploys the mythological figure of Cyrtha to distinguish his work from the testimonial genre described in the first part of chapter 1.[87] It is important, however, that we do not take at face value Bachi's own idea of what testimonial literature was or could be. As I show in my analysis of the "Cyrtha trilogy," it is possible to read Bachi's works as testimonial texts. As such, looking back to Djebar and Bey is clearly useful when thinking about how to contextualize what Bachi thinks of as the "work" of writers and literature during and after the Black Decade.

Another reason we might want to be wary of Bachi's earlier literary works, and the ideas he has about their ability to rewrite history, is that Bachi and his characters repeat many of the reductive tropes about Algeria that the author claims in interviews to want to avoid. And, while of course it is not desirable to simply impute the voice of an author to his characters, Bachi repeats the recidivist language of the fictional narrator of *La Kahéna* in his interview with Temlali. Echoing the words of Aziz Chouaki, whose recidivist take we discussed in the introduction, Bachi states: "On sortait à peine la guerre d'Algérie, la première, et voilà qu'on s'engouffrait dans un 'remake,' une réplique." [We had barely emerged from the first Algerian War and now we were engulfed in a "remake."][88] As Benkhaled and Vince note in their own commentary on Bachi's language here, the act of juxtaposing the War of Independence and the 1990s conflict risks perpetuating "the essentializing view of Algeria as condemned to cycle upon cycle of atavistic violence."[89]

It is intriguing that Bachi is able to avoid these kinds of reductive characterizations when it comes to his post-9/11 novels, set in Europe and the United States. In *Tuez-les tous* and *Moi, Khaled Kelkal*, the author deploys a referential style not as a means of testifying to violence but in order to unpick the way contemporary narratives of conflict reproduce political myths, such as Huntington's clash of civilizations. Though Bachi has lived in Paris since 1996, it is perhaps his "proximity" to the early years of the Black Decade, and the testimonial writing of figures such as Mimouni and Boudjedra, that has led him to reproduce these recidivist stereotypes regarding Algerian violence.

In the way Bachi repeatedly presents Cyrtha as a written and imagined figure, there is an implicit suggestion that the writer seeks to explore his own complicity in reproducing reductive narratives of the Black Decade. And yet, paradoxically, it is in a turn to a referential style that the writer appears most able to advance a clear understanding of how writers, critics, and journalists might begin to acknowledge the ways they are complicit in the reproduction of the self-fulfilling polarizing narratives of conflict. Bachi's movement away from the myth of Cyrtha, and toward the "mythe agissant" of 9/11, is perhaps suggestive that all myths are based on "selective elision"—that is, myths fail to capture a story in all its complexity.[90] While the "Cyrtha trilogy" clearly marks a significant shift in interest from testimonial narrative to literary experimentation, it is Bachi's later novels that more effectively tackle questions around the clash of civilizations and the complicity of journalists, academic critics, and writers in repeating that reductive logic. Indeed, the controversy that has surrounded the reception of *Tuez-les tous*, *Moi, Khaled Kelkal*, and Bachi's *Le Monde* article on Merah has undoubtedly led to intensified debate both about Huntington's hypothesis and regarding the role of the novelist in contemporary France. What is curious—and perhaps somewhat contradictory—is that those commentators who might once have celebrated Algerian writers for adopting a referential or testimonial mode during the Black Decade would later come to insist that literature was emphatically *not* the place to explore terrorist attacks in France.[91] The dual edges of myth, it would appear, cede to a kind of double standard among French journalists who are happy to embrace representations of Algerian violence but reluctant to offer the same treatment when that violence is closer to home.

NOTES

1. Yassin Temlali, "Salim Bachi: «un romancier et non un témoin»," in *Algérie: Chroniques Ciné-Littéraires de Deux Guerres* (Algiers: Barzakh, 2011), 92.
2. Temlali, "Salim Bachi," 97.
3. Temlali, "Salim Bachi," 97.
4. Temlali, "Salim Bachi," 95–96.
5. Bonn, "Algérie," 209; Laroussi, "When Francophone Means National," 88.
6. Ali Remzi, "Salim Bachi: Les quêtes fertiles d'un écrivain," *La Dépêche de Kabylie*, July 20, 2010, http://www.depechedekabylie.com/cuture/84737-salim-bachi-les-quetes-fertiles-dun-ecrivain.html.
7. Temlali, "Salim Bachi," 95.
8. See Patrick Crowley, "Mythologizing the City, Rethinking the Nation: Salim Bachi's Cyrtha Trilogy," in *Mediterranean Cities: Real and/or Imaginary*, ed. Federica Frediani (Florence: Nerbini Editore, 2014), 267.

9. Salim Bachi, *Le Chien d'Ulysse* (Paris: Gallimard, 2001). The novel was also awarded the Prix littéraire de la Vocation and the Bourse Prince Pierre de Monaco de La Découverte. See Patrick Crowley's introduction to his interview with Bachi, which includes biographical information, some of which I repeat here. Patrick Crowley, "Myth, Modernism, Violence and Form: An Interview with Salim Bachi," *Bulletin of Francophone Postcolonial Studies* 4, no. 1 (2013), 2–11.

10. Salim Bachi, *La Kahéna* (Paris: Gallimard, 2003); Salim Bachi, *Les Douze contes de minuit* (Paris: Gallimard, 2006). Aside from Bachi's major works under study here, he has published *Autoportrait avec Grenade* (Paris: Editions du Rocher, 2005), a "récit" which is an autobiographical, turned dream-like account of his travel to Grenada; *Le silence de Mohamet* (Paris: Gallimard, 2008), a novel that reimagines the life of the prophet Mohammed; *Le grand frère* (Paris: Editions du Moteur, 2010), which tells of the young naive inhabitant of the Paris "banlieues," Rachid, who is recruited to the fundamentalist cause by the eponymous "Grand frère." Bachi has also published *Amour et aventures de Sinbad le Marin* (Paris: Gallimard, 2010), a novel which charts the travels and adventures of the newly imagined Sinbad, inspired by the initial stories of *Les Mille et Une Nuits*, but here morphed into a contemporary setting. Sinbad is also a modern-day *harraga* in this story, crisscrossing the Mediterranean. In 2013, Bachi published *Le dernier été d'un jeune homme* (Paris: Flammarion), which imagines a portion of the life of Albert Camus and fits alongside a number of other Algerian works published in the centenary year of Camus's birth. Further novels include, *Le consul* (Paris: Gallimard, 2014) and *Un jeune homme en colère* (Paris: Gallimard, 2018).

11. Salim Bachi, *Tuez-les tous* (Paris: Gallimard, 2006); Salim Bachi, *Moi, Khaled Kelkal* (Paris: Grasset, 2012).

12. As Pascale Casanova writes, Paris is the "universal homeland" for literature, the so-called world republic of letters. See Pascale Casanova, *The World Republic of Letters* (Cambridge: Harvard University Press, 2007), 29.

13. As discussed in chapter 1, Walter Benjamin understands allegory to go beyond "a mere mode of designation." Walter Benjamin, *The Origin of German Tragic Drama*, 162.

14. Salim Bachi, "Le vent brûle," *Le Monde diplomatique*, January, 1995, https://www.monde-diplomatique.fr/1995/01/BACHI/6009.

15. Zoubida Belaghoueg, "Algérianisation du mythe de *l'Odyssée* et parodie de *Nedjma* dans *Le Chien d'Ulysse* de Salim Bachi," *Synergies Algérie*, no. 3 (2008), 134; see also Valerie Orlando, "The Truncated memories and fragmented pasts of contemporary Algeria: Salim Bachi's *Le Chien d'Ulysse*," *International Journal of Francophone Studies* 6, no. 2 (2003), 106.

16. Crowley, "Mythologizing the City," 275.

17. Bachi, *Le Chien d'Ulysse*, 13, 17, 72.

18. Bernard Aresu offers a whole range of possible interpretations of Cyrtha. See "Arcanes algériens entés d'ajours helléniques: *Le Chien d'Ulysse*, de Salim Bachi," in *Echanges et mutations des modèles littéraires entre Europe et Algérie* vol. 2 (Paris: L'Harmattan, 2004), 178.

19. See Crowley, "Mythologizing the City," 271–72.

20. Bachi, *Le Chien d'Ulysse*, 143.
21. Bachi, *Le Chien d'Ulysse*, 219.
22. Bachi, *Le Chien d'Ulysse*, 271.
23. See introduction for further discussion of the myth of the clash of civilizations.
24. Bachi, *Le Chien d'Ulysse*, 21–22.
25. See Temlali, "Salim Bachi," 93.
26. Bachi, *La Kahéna*, 237.
27. Bachi, *La Kahéna*, 261.
28. Crowley, "Mythologizing the City," 267.
29. Hiddleston, *Writing After Postcolonialism*, 133.
30. Hiddleston, *Writing After Postcolonialism*, 135.
31. Kateb Yacine, *Nedjma* (Paris: Seuil, 1956).
32. Bachi, *La Kahéna*, 298.
33. There appear to be allusions to several of Camus's major works: the question of the relation to the father and the reading of the posthumously discovered manuscript resonates both with the plot and with the event of the discovery of Camus's posthumously published unfinished work *Le premier homme*; the story of Hamid Kaïm's education—the "bon Arabe" who gets into the Grand Lycée de Cyrtha—and his encouraging teacher M. Germain, is a reference to Camus's education under Louis Germain. Finally, there are increasing references to rats toward the end of *La Kahéna*, which brings to mind Camus's *La Peste*. This reference is also present at the beginning of *Le Chien d'Ulysse* where the narrator announces the memory of the "grande peste" of the "seconde hécatombe" of the century. Bachi, *Le Chien d'Ulysse*, 14.
34. Bachi, *La Kahéna*, 302.
35. Derrida cited in Rice, *Polygraphies*, 4.
36. Temlali, "Salim Bachi," 92, my emphasis.
37. Bachi, *La Kahéna*, 299.
38. Bachi, *La Kahéna*, 300.
39. This kind of language resembles that described by James McDougall in his article, "Savage Wars?," and is also highlighted by Benkhaled and Vince in "Performing Algerianness."
40. Remzi, "Salim Bachi," my emphasis.
41. Bachi, *Les Douze contes de minuit*, 33.
42. See, Soler, "Un espace littéraire"; Burtscher-Bechter, "Mutisme et prise de parole"; Lila Ibrahim-Ouali, "Maïssa Bey."
43. Bachi, *Les Douze contes de minuit*, 159.
44. Bachi, *Les Douze contes de minuit*, 148.
45. Bachi, *Les Douze contes de minuit*, 159.
46. Bachi, *Les Douze contes de minuit*, 168.
47. Bachi, *Les Douze contes de minuit*, 190.
48. Bachi, *Les Douze contes de minuit*, 190.
49. Harrison, "Who Needs an Idea of the Literary?," 12.
50. Crowley, "Myth, Modernism, Violence and Form," 8.

51. Benkhaled and Vince discuss Bachi's use of the recidivist trope. See "Performing Algerianness," 256.

52. Carine Bourget, "Portrait of a Terrorist: Slimane Benaïssa and Salim Bachi's 9/11 Novels," in *The Star, The Cross, and The Crescent: Religions and Conflicts in Francophone Literature from the Arab World* (Lanham: Lexington Books, 2010), 150–51.

53. Bourget, "Portrait of a Terrorist," 150–51. More recently, in 2004 (still before the publication of Bachi's novel), "Tuez-les tous" was the title of a French documentary on the Rwandan genocide. See *Tuez-les tous! Rwanda: histoire d'un génocide sans importance*, dir. Raphael Glucksmann, David Hazan & Pierre Mezerette (Dum Dum Films, 2004).

54. Martin Amis also published, in 2006, a short story, which in a similar manner charts the final days of the supposed leader of the terrorist cell responsible for the September 11 attacks, Muhammad Atta. See: "The Last Days of Muhammad Atta," *The Observer*, August 31, 2006, http://www.martinamisweb.com/documents/lastdays_one.pdf.

55. Crowley, "Myth, Modernism, Violence and Form," 8.

56. Alain Resnais (dir.), *Hiroshima mon amour* (Argos Films, 1959).

57. Bachi, *Tuez-les tous*, 14, 41–42, 56.

58. Bachi, *Tuez-les tous*, 14.

59. Bachi, *Tuez-les tous*, 15. Bachi seems to make an ironic comment here on the legacy of the history of the cultural assimilation of Algerians, where they were historically required to ascend to citizenship in the *métropole*, despite the fact that colonial Algeria was considered to be an *integral* part of France.

60. Bachi, *Tuez-les tous*, 16.

61. Bachi, *Tuez-les tous*, 17–18.

62. Bachi, *Tuez-les tous*, 23.

63. Bachi, *Tuez-les tous*, 34.

64. Bachi, *Tuez-les tous*, 87.

65. Bachi, *Tuez-les tous*, 88.

66. Bachi, *Tuez-les tous*, 110.

67. Bachi, *Tuez-les tous*, 153.

68. Bachi, *Tuez-les tous*, 153.

69. Bachi, *Tuez-les tous*, 153. This final scene recalls Judith Butler's discussion of Emmanuel Levinas and his inscribing of "the face as the extreme precariousness of the other." Butler cites Levinas: "The face of the other in its precariousness and defencelessness, is for me at once the temptation to kill and the call to peace, the 'You shall not kill.'" The face, for Butler, is the site of an ethical "struggle" whereby our recognition of the precariousness of the other—and the ability to relate peacefully to the other on this basis—is dependent on the recognition that the other can be eliminated. See Judith Butler, "Precarious Life," *Precarious Life: The Powers of Mourning and Violence* (London: Verso, 2004), 134–35.

70. This image recalls Walter Benjamin's "Angelus Novus" in the ninth of the "Theses on the Philosophy of History." And, indeed, thereafter the United States might be seen to be "propelled into the future to which its back is turned." Walter

Benjamin, "Theses on the Philosophy of History," in *Illuminations* (New York: Schocken Books, 1969), 257–58 (quotation adapted).

71. Sanyal, *Memory and Complicity*, 1.

72. Bruno Chaouat, *Is Theory Good for the Jews? French Thought and the Challenge of the New Antisemitism* (Liverpool: Liverpool University Press, 2016), 109.

73. Chaouat, *Is Theory Good for the Jews?*, 109.

74. Sanyal, *Memory and Complicity*, 38.

75. Vincent Geisser has noted how, throughout the 1990s, the French media developed what he calls a "mise en ordre mediatique du sens commun" [common sense media order] around the trope of the "media Muslim." See Bottici and Challand, "Rethinking Political Myth," 325.

76. Gabriel Weimann, "The Theater of Terror: The Psychology of Terrorism and the Mass Media," in *The Trauma of Terrorism: Sharing Knowledge and Shared Care, An International Handbook*, ed. Yael Danieli, Danny Brom and Joe Sills (Binghamton, N.Y.: Haworth Maltreatment and Trauma Press: 2005), 379–90.

77. Weimann, "The Theater of Terror," 381.

78. Michael Rothberg, "Seeing Terror, Feeling Art: Public and Private in Post-9/11 Literature," in *Literature after 9/11*, ed. Ann Keniston and Jeanne Quinn (New York: Routledge, 2008), 124.

79. "Moi, Khaled Kelkal" was initially the title given to an interview, published after Kelkal's death in October 1995, by a German sociologist who had been conducting doctoral research on the Lyon *banlieues* in 1992. Dietmar Loch had interviewed Kelkal as part of a wider research project studying young people of North African origin living in the Lyon suburb of Vaulx-en-Velin. His study is published in German as *Jugendliche maghrebinischer Herkunft zwischen Stadtpolitik und Lebenswelt. Eine Fallstudie in der französischen Vorstadt Vaulx-en-Velin* (Weisbaden: VS-Verlag für Sozialwissenschaften, 2005). After the events of 1995, Loch's interview with Kelkal was published in *Le Monde*, October 7, 1995, 10.

80. This is seen to have been effective, but not in the interests of the GIA. After these attacks, a poll conducted in France revealed that 91 percent of French citizens supported the Algerian government policy of "eradication." See Evans and Phillips, *Algeria*, 213.

81. Salim Bachi, "Moi, Mohamed Merah," *Le Monde des livres*, March 30, 2012, http://www.paperblog.fr/5477915/317-moi-mohamed-merah-article-de-salim-bachi-et-les-reactions/.

82. In his interview with Bachi, Crowley helpfully points us toward a selection of articles which appeared at the time. See Crowley, "Myth, Modernism, Violence and Form," 4–5.

83. Bachi, *Moi, Khaled Kelkal*, 55.

84. Bachi, *Moi, Khaled Kelkal*, 84.

85. On the Freytag pyramid, see Gustav Freytag and Elias J. MacEwan, *Freytag's Technique of the Drama: An Exposition of Dramatic Composition and Art* (Amsterdam: Nabu Public Domain Reprints, 2013).

86. Bachi, *Moi, Khaled Kelkal*, 128.

87. See Temlali, "Salim Bachi," 92.

88. Temlali, "Salim Bachi," 98–99.
89. Benkhaled and Vince, "Performing Algerianness," 256.
90. Priyamvada Gopal, *Insurgent Empire: Anticolonial Resistance and British Dissent* (London: Verso, 2019), 4.
91. See, for instance, Jacques Tarnero, "Merah n'est pas un héros de roman," *Causeur*, April 2, 2012, http://www.causeur.fr/merah-n%e2%80%99est-pas-un-heros-de-roman-16861; Edith Ochs, "Un lapsus dans la tête de Merah?," *The Huffington Post*, February 4, 2012, https://www.huffingtonpost.fr/edith-ochs/bachi-mohamed-merah_b_1399787.html; see also the mixed responses in the letters, "Dire l'indicible, nommer l'innommable . . . Mission impossible?," *Le Monde*, April 6, 2012, https://www.lemonde.fr/le-monde/article/2012/04/06/dire-l-indicible-nommer-l-innommable-mission-impossible_5984777_4586753.html.

Chapter 3

Beyond a Grotesque Aesthetics of the Black Decade in Habib Ayyoub

"Ayyoub" est le nom du prophète le plus misérable et le plus patient, "Job" en français; "Habib" en arabe c'est "l'ami." L'ami du pauvre, c'est ce que je veux être.[1]

["Ayyoub" is the name of the most miserable and long-suffering prophet, "Job"; "Habib" means "friend" in Arabic. The friend of the poor, that's what I wish to be.]

—Habib Ayyoub

Unlike the previous writers examined in this study, Habib Ayyoub, whose real name is Abdelaziz Benmahdjoub, is little-known outside his native Algeria and has, thereby, been read largely within local literary circles and by commentators residing in contemporary Algeria. Working initially as a journalist and cinematographer, Ayyoub (like Maïssa Bey) came to writing later in life, prompted by the crisis years of October 1988 and the onset of the Black Decade.[2] Published by the newly established Algiers-based independent publisher, Editions Barzakh, Ayyoub's works develop a self-conscious, humorous, and ironic take on the idea of "telling" the period of the 1990s and the processes of writing Algerian history.

As a master of the allegorical fable, Ayyoub maintains a level of proximity to the crisis years of the Black Decade, but his works also disrupt dominant historical narratives associated with the third-worldist national allegory adopted by writers and theorists such as Sartre, Fanon, and Kateb Yacine in the wake of Algerian independence.[3] Ayyoub styles himself as defending the downtrodden masses against the worst excesses of the powerful. In so doing, the author sets out to *speak truth to power* in a different way to the testimonial or mythological modes adopted by writers such as Djebar, Bey, and Bachi, examined in chapters

1 and 2. What is brought to the fore in Ayyoub's early works and interviews is an exploration of literature as a form of "combat" or "dissenting force," in line with Sartrean and Fanonian ideas of literature as part of the writer's revolutionary toolbox.⁴ For Ayyoub, the self-professed "ami du pauvre," a literary "engagement" is at least initially one that embodies a form of opposition to the ideological discourse of the "regime." In this respect, Ayyoub's oppositional aesthetic is distinct from Mimouni or Boudjedra's in that it targets the obscure figures of power within the Algerian State, rather than the FIS.

However, this understanding of literature as pitted in opposition to political or ideological discourse is a problematic one. As Achille Mbembe has noted, classic images of resistance that imagine the masses in binary opposition to the State ignore the more complex reality of the entangled relationships of power in the postcolony.⁵ Here, the "regime" itself deploys forms of grotesque representation in order to draw writers and artists into a "convivial" discursive space, where "opposition" is co-opted into an overarching spectacle of power.⁶ In other words, the grotesque acts of the president or his backstage manipulators that Ayyoub allegorizes are actively welcomed by the State apparatus because they fall within anticipated forms of opposition that allow citizens to use humor to perform a kind of collective catharsis. As Hiddleston notes of the neighboring Moroccan context, writers and critics have increasingly warned of the ways in which cultural production can be subsumed within a preexisting "political programme" that leads to a kind of collective "indoctrination."⁷ Even if Hiddleston (after Rancière) stresses that literature should be seen as "distinct from" politics insofar as it "throws into question the relationship between language and meaning," Ayyoub's works present a more uneven picture.⁸

In this chapter, I explore how shifting ideas of the power of literature are captured in three of Ayyoub's most prominent texts. Examining representations of power—and of the language of power—in *Le Gardien* [*The Guardian*] (2001), *Le Palestinien* [*The Palestinian*] (2003), and *Le Remonteur de l'horloge* [*The Clock Winder*] (2012), I argue that Ayyoub moves from a reliance on the oppositional aesthetics of the grotesque to a mode that stages and unveils the way citizens and commentators unknowingly participate in the ratification of a dominant spectacle of power.⁹ In this way, Ayyoub begins to unpick how writers, citizens, and commentators alike have been complicit in obscuring the multilayered and complex realties of recent Algerian history.¹⁰

LE GARDIEN (2001)

As several historians have recently outlined, the Algerian context is a privileged site for understanding the dialectical entanglement between "ruler" and "ruled"—a structure that replicates the language of resistance inherited from the War of Independence. Here, Islamist groups claimed to represent the "true" freedom fighters of the Algerian nation, denouncing the other "side" as *hizb fransa* [the party of France], whereas those opposed to the Islamist groups labeled them "sons of harkis."[11] As James McDougall highlights, writers such as Yasmina Khadra deliberately repeated these tropes in their fictional works.[12]

Others have been more circumspect about the relation between literature and political discourse. As Charles Bonn had already noted in the late 1980s,

> La littérature [. . .] n'affirme rien: affirmer est le rôle du discours idéologique, nécessaire à l'édification nationale, mais qui ne peut être efficace que s'il accepte sa perpétuelle mise en question par le texte littéraire et ce qu'on peut appeler son carnaval.[13]

> [Literature (. . .) affirms nothing: to affirm is the job of ideological discourse, necessary for national edification, but which can only be effective if it accepts that it will be perpetually questioned by the literary text and what one can call its carnival.]

Bonn's use of the term "carnaval" [carnival] to describe the role of literature will immediately remind the reader of Mikhail Bakhtin, whose theory of literature attributes a clearer contestatory power to the carnival—and to the use of grotesque caricature it encapsulates.[14] Bakhtin nuances his account of the grotesque by stressing the ambivalence at the heart of the carnival.[15] Yet, it is the prevalence of humor, irony, and grotesque bodies across Ayyoub's literary work—coupled with the stance the author adopts in interviews—that, at least initially, suggests the author pursues a form of grotesque caricature in a binary or contestatory mode. By highlighting how ideological discourse that brings the nation-State into existence is reliant on its literary or carnivalesque counterpart, Bonn appears to question how effective such caricatures might be at undermining prevailing manifestations of power.

Described on its front cover as a "récit" [narrative], *Le Gardien* is set in a traditional Maghrebi village, complete with a castle, war monument, and a "mer intérieure" [internal sea]—an abandoned desert harbor created to house the pleasure boats of rich and corrupt army generals whose base was once located in the village. Ayyoub presents an apocalyptic vision of the end of civilization in a comical allegorical fable that obliquely resembles a critique of Algerian society's obsessive valorization of monuments to the War of Independence.

While, like Djebar, Ayyoub does not draw explicit attention to the classification of the text, its status as a "récit" is of interest, especially when considering the extent to which the reader might map Ayyoub's fictional tale onto the crisis years of the 1990s or view it as disrupting the "telling" of those events. To recall Shattuck and Just's definitions, the "récit" makes readers more acutely aware of the problem of narrative, when "the very act of narration interferes and calls attention to itself."[16] This unsettling effect, produced by the categorization of the text alongside the use of the allegorical fable, makes it tempting to interpret Ayyoub's text as part of a more generalized bid to disrupt the dominant conflict narrative of the Black Decade, as examined in chapter 1. Yet, it is not clear that Ayyoub targets any specific narrative here. In continually hesitating between the referential and the fictional, and the different temporalities of narration that come with the "récit" and novel, Ayyoub prompts the reader to pause and think more carefully about the text they see before them.

The main plot of *Le Gardien* charts the final days of the "Chef suprême de la guerre" [Supreme leader of war], whose soldiers have constructed an army base and monument overlooking the desert harbor and the old castle. The inhabitants of the unnamed village flee because of a lack of freshwater and the refusal of the army to provide for their basic survival. Yet, a mysterious sleeping child, the eponymous "gardien" of the old village and keeper of a sacred text, remains within the heart of the castle. After being abandoned by his soldiers, the general tries to destroy the monument they have built, before being buried in a deluge of rain and salt. Meanwhile, the child awakens from his long sleep and is named as the "premier gardien" [first guardian]—defender of the ravaged land.

The significance of the child in this story is twofold: an allusion to the collective of believers who act as a "gardien" of the sacred text of the Qur'an, the child is portrayed as a symbol of hope for the future.[17] In addition, the description of the child as "quelqu'un sans armes et les mains nues [qui] n'affirmerait que des vérités" [a person without weapons whose bare hands affirm only truths], coupled with the fact that he is the holder of a text, makes it possible to interpret him as a figure for the writer himself.[18] Much like Ayyoub fashions his own writerly identity in solidarity with the downtrodden masses, the defenseless child symbolizes the remnants of the oppressed villagers who had been forced to flee their homes. The image of the oppressive "chef suprême" set against the heroic figure of the child, or writer, and their embodiment of "truth," offers an image of the writer and his text as a "dissenting force."[19]

As the story comes to an end, revenge for the grotesque general's self-interested pursuits comes not just from the oppressed masses, represented in the figure of the child or writer, but from the land itself. Depicted as a clear imposition on the natural desert landscape, the "mer intérieure" summons the elements that, at the end of this story, bring about the dictator's end. After a "vulgaire orage" [vulgar storm] from the south floods the land on which the general has constructed his monument, he is drowned in mud and salt.[20] Buried alongside his victims, the once "supreme" leader is reduced to "the body's depths" and the "subterranean passages" of the grotesque, evoking both a sense of divine retribution and solitude in death.[21] The exploited land is mapped onto the suffering masses in an image that recalls once more the oppositional discourse of the War of Independence. Figured as a "vulgaire orage" the storm is marshaled in the service of the ordinary people it embodies in the etymological roots of its name.

And indeed, it is these scenes that appear to evoke most clearly Bakhtin's account of the grotesque. As he underlines, in the system of grotesque imagery, "death is not a negation of life [. . .] but part of life as a whole—its indispensable component, the condition of its constant renewal and rejuvenation."[22] The failure of the general to become aware that life and death are part of a cycle of renewal—that death should not be figured in *opposition* to life—results in the grotesque. Or, as Bakhtin puts it, "The struggle of life and death in the individual body is conceived by grotesque imagery as the struggle of the old life stubbornly resisting the new life about to be born, as the crisis of change."[23] In his dogged resistance to the "new life" beyond the tired status quo, Ayyoub's fictional dictator is pitted firmly against a body of a land, and by implication a "people," both of which have suffered under his rule.

By celebrating the heroic nature of the opposition between the oppressed masses and the grotesque body of the supreme leader, and invoking the cathartic images that come with his gruesome end, Ayyoub runs the risk that his story falls into a preexisting spectacle of power whereby a recidivist understanding of history stages the FLN State as the new "oppressor." By no means salutary, this dissent is tolerated within the realm of art and literature because the oppositional discourse it advances "ratifies" the hegemonic idea of the "regime," thereby permitting the authorities to maintain a level of control over a shared narrative of accommodation and resistance.[24] Thus, there is a need to be cautious of celebratory narratives that understand the rise of independent publishers, such as Editions Barzakh, as liberating writers aesthetically and politically from the control or surveillance of the Algerian authorities.[25] Academic literary critics who have written of a revival of Algerian publishing after the end of the Black Decade risk rehabilitating a revolutionary image associated with the previous generation of writers who had lived through the War of Independence.[26]

LE PALESTINEN (2003)

In an essay that seeks to move beyond understanding postcolonial Algeria through the lens of French colonialism, Olivia Harrison stresses how, in the novels of Ahlem Mosteghanemi, Algerian national allegory is supplanted by a transnational allegory of Palestine.[27] For Mosteghanemi, who underlines how the occupied territory inhabits the place Algeria once did as the "nation that exported revolution and dreams to the world," Palestine is "a vehicle for anti-neocolonial critique"—a comment on what the author sees as the "failed revolution" in Algeria which led to the political instability of the Black Decade.[28] While it might not initially appear as an overt critique of the one-party State, Ayyoub's use of the transnational figure of Palestine in his 2003 novel, *Le Palestinien*, is significant because Algerians understand the Palestinian as an enduring rebel, persistently oppressed by violent State power. By making his protagonist both "Palestinian" and Algerian, Ayyoub plays on popular narratives of Palestine, offering a vision of the Algerian as suffering at the hands of a neocolonial oppressor.

Doubling as an "écrivain public" [public writer], Ayyoub's protagonist also draws readers' attention to the crucial question of narrative. As Hiddleston writes of other North African works featuring public writers, "writing for others is associated with a persistent sense of ambivalence and serves as an indication of the contemporary writer's doubt towards his craft."[29] One task of the novel seems to be to unmask and disrupt dominant ideologies by disfiguring and destabilizing the very narrative they employ. By figuring writing and the writer as central to the plot, Ayyoub highlights how the narrative will always to some degree obscure the truth. However, in pitting the "engaged" public writer against grotesque figures of power, Ayyoub still deploys oppositional tropes that risk reinforcing a dominant discourse of opposition in a similar way to *Le Gardien*.

The story, told in an unbroken stream of text by an omniscient third-person narrator, follows the life of the eponymous Palestinian, who has returned to his desert village, Sidi Bounekhla, from the Israel-Palestine conflict of 1948. Led by the corrupt "chef du village" [village leader], named Si Messaoud, the central plot of the novel reflects the oppositional narrative of *Le Gardien*. As one of the few villagers able to write, the Palestinian takes on the role of the public writer. He is given a desk at the local post office, where villagers queue to see him every day, each revealing their private squabbles over land, family disputes, and administrative grievances. The public writer produces official letters for the villagers, promising discretion as part of his service. At least initially, then, the Palestinian's revolutionary credentials mean he is trusted by his clients.

As we learn that Si Messaoud has been stealing from Leila and Samed— the widow and son of the Palestinian's friend, Rabah, killed during the Israel-Palestine conflict—the Palestinian faces the ethical dilemma of whether to unveil the village leader's illicit activities. By never revealing what he writes for others, the Palestinian hopes to keep himself out of the local squabbles which consume his clients' lives, but this wish to remain ignorant propels the public writer into a confrontation with both Si Messaoud and the villagers who end up turning against him. In his role as the public writer, the Palestinian is not only aware of his clients' deepest secrets but also privy to the largely corrupt workings of power and the efforts of figures such as Si Messaoud to maintain an image of respectability. In his commitment to discretion, the Palestinian fails to see how Si Messaoud manipulates the language of power for his own benefit, as he spreads rumors that call into question the Palestinian's revolutionary credentials. When he eventually reveals the village leader's corruption, the Palestinian merely feeds the narrative trap that has been laid for him: disenfranchised after the loss of his job, he is painted as a traitor seeking revenge.

With the whole village turned against the Palestinian, the novel culminates in a mythic but somewhat comical battle fought between the two antagonists. Transformed from the corrupt village leader into an Islamist "cheikh," Si Messaoud rallies the villagers behind him and chases the Palestinian from his home. As the Palestinian flees into the desert, Si Messaoud follows, fresh from his wedding celebrations, but the village leader becomes disoriented as he has been drinking alcohol. He falls from his horse and is killed by his own sword in a violent beheading. A comical and explicit description ensues: "Sous la violence du coup, la tête tranchée net roula sur le sable puis s'arrêta d'aplomb, conservant le même regard suppliant, avec la bouche qui continuait silencieusement d'invoquer un impossible pardon." [Under the violence of the blow, the decapitated head rolled across the sand and then stopped upright, maintaining the same pleading look, with the mouth silently continuing to invoke an impossible forgiveness.][30] Triggering an ambivalent identification, which Bakhtin argues is a key tenet of the grotesque image, the beseeching expression of the amputated head invites the reader to feel empathy for the defeated "Chef du village" at the same time as evoking a sense of retributive justice.

This ambivalence, along with Si Messaoud's transformation from corrupt leader to Islamist "cheikh," is reflective of the way narrative tropes and binary "types" were deployed throughout the Black Decade. Depicted as one and the same character, Ayyoub stresses how both "chef du village" and "cheikh" abuse power to attack their political enemies and advance their own personal agendas. By depicting the changing allegiance of the villagers, Ayyoub demonstrates the complicity of the popular masses in upholding dominant or oppressive structures of power, whatever the political "side" or faction they identify with. Understood by Bakhtin in terms of an "ambivalent laughter" that stems from "the people," the tension between empathy and retribution prompts a more self-conscious and inward-looking gaze on Ayyoub's grotesque caricatures.[31] The reader is asked to recognize that the target of

Ayyoub's satire is the same world in which they themselves also live. Thus, rather than elevate the satirist "above the object of his mockery"—in what Bakhtin posits would constitute a relationship of "negative laughter"—the ambivalent identification triggered in the final scene of Ayyoub's novel evokes the possible complicity of the satirist or writer in the production of the spectacle they seek to attack.[32] Here, Ayyoub writes for more than comic effect and, instead, seeks to unveil the universally corrupting nature of excessive power by moving toward Mbembe's vision of the grotesque as "intrinsic to all systems of domination."[33] In figuring the downfall of leaders in an empathetic (rather than merely pathetic) register, Ayyoub's novel functions as a forewarning to all those who would consider abusing their positions of power.

However, in continuing to advance an understanding of grotesque power affixed to one "side" of a universal binary between "ruler" and "ruled," Ayyoub's oppositional aesthetic doesn't fully address how the writer, reader, or commentator is a participant in the construction and actualization of a theater of grotesque power, thereby only hinting at the way characters fetishize the *commandement*, State, or *le pouvoir* as an unimpeachable and untouchable elite. Because of its fiercely oppositional surface, this is an aesthetic that risks further ratifying a State that relies upon a "shared language" of resistance forged during the War of Independence.[34] In other words, texts such as *Le Gardien* and *Le Palestinien* might be understood to maintain the dominant "fantasy" or "mythology" of power that keeps the masses in check.[35] It is precisely this "fantasy" that Ayyoub explores in further detail in *Le Remonteur de l'horloge*, as the writer shifts form once more—this time from novel back to the "récit."

LE REMONTEUR DE L'HORLOGE (2012)

In his return to the "récit," Ayyoub plays more explicitly with notions of teleological history and narrative. Offering a self-conscious reflection on the role of narrative in constructing and maintaining an absurd spectacle of power, *Le Remonteur de l'horloge* uses the figure of the clock—and the clock time it embodies—to make both a specific commentary on the function of historical narratives and their tropes and a critique of the ideology of modernity that deploys time to maintain order and control. Ayyoub's tale charts the story of a broken village clock, which the inhabitants of Sidi Ben Tayeb rush to repair before the visit of a government official. If the story inevitably flags questions of the malleability of time and narrative for the reader, the stopped clock prompts the villagers of Sidi Ben Tayeb to uncover a whole history of oppression and corruption that lurks beneath the clock face.

In this final text, Ayyoub appears to move beyond the Sartrean notion of "littérature engagée" [committed literature] and toward a more intricate understanding of the role of literary and cultural discourse conceived by the likes of Mbembe and Rancière. If, as Davis and Serres write, "the state is the locus of competition where different groups cooperate and struggle to obtain a specific form of capital," then power is clearly attained and distributed in more slippery ways.[36] Here, absolutist visions of the oppressive State or "regime" are revealed to be fetishes—products of the ideas writers, critics, and citizens have of power, rather than an acknowledgment of the performative reality in which we all live.[37] As Rancière underlines, the "verité cachée" [hidden truth] of literature is in its ability to "déchiffrer les témoignages que la société elle-même donne à lire" [decipher the testimonies society offers us to read].[38] Moving away from the grotesque caricatures of his previous works, Ayyoub offers his readers what Rancière refers to as a "voyage dans les souterrains" [journey through the subterranean passages]—a means of unveiling the shared performance of power in which citizen and State are pitted against one another.[39]

The full title of Ayyoub's tale is *Le Remonteur de l'horloge, ou le manuscrit de Sidi Ben Tayeb (découvert en l'an de grâce 2050, par la section Archéologie du ministère des Finances et de l'Histoire intelligente)* [*The Clock Winder, or the Manuscript of Sidi Ben Tayeb (discovered in 2050AD by the Archeology Department of the Ministry of Finance and Intelligent History)*]. By creating a meta-narrative of the manuscript the reader has before them, Ayyoub draws attention to the act of recording history and rendering the story of the inhabitants of the small desert village. The fact that the text is a *historical* artifact supposedly discovered by government officials *in the future* is at once a satire of the way the postindependence State imagined itself being propelled into the future through the rational processes of economic planning and a temporality of the machine and a comment on the fact that the "end" of history, or historical narrative, is always a posited or imagined thing—never fully realized.[40] Here, the obstacle of the malfunctioning clock is both a symbol and literal embodiment of the failure of the machine and of the narrative of progress that leads the villagers to place so much importance upon having a working clock in the first place, but it is also a seeming commentary on the way historical narratives—especially ones that invoke ideas of progress—must posit factitious "ends" to their stories.

As the villagers of Sidi Ben Tayeb desperately attempt to fix the clock, they accidentally delve into the history of the colonial era, which in turn reveals how their current leaders have obtained power through corrupt means. When crowds assemble in the streets and erupt into rioting, it is difficult not to draw parallels between Ayyoub's fable and the lead up to the events of October 1988 in Algeria. Sidi Ben Tayeb's clock becomes a microcosm for the suspended time of the 1988 uprisings. As Davis and Serres write of the period between the early 1970s and the protests of October 1988, the failure of the developmentalist project led leaders to lose hold of a "coherent narrative of authority" they had hitherto imposed upon the country.[41] As in the late 1980s Algeria, so for the fictional village of Sidi Ben Tayeb, the future is suddenly blown wide open, as the historical narrative, symbolized by the ticking clock, is placed in abeyance. As the former street sweeper, Si Kaddour, underlines, "[s]i ce n'était pas pour cette histoire de l'horloge, on ne se serait surement jamais aventuré dans les souterrains de notre histoire" [had it not been for this matter of the clock, we would have probably never ventured into the subterranean passages of our history].[42] Although, on the surface, a negative comment made by a character exhausted by the obsession with the clock, Si Kaddour reveals a level of self-understanding among some of the inhabitants of Sidi Ben Tayeb, as well as recalling Rancière's notion of the capacity of the "voyage dans les souterrains" to reveal "hidden truths" about the spectacle of power.

Despite the discontent, however, the protesters soon return home to their everyday lives, resigned to their fate of continual yet seemingly ineffective uprisings:

> Au village, les choses étaient rentrés dans l'ordre. Tout le monde vaquait à ses occupations dans le calme le plus total. Le Peuple, c'est connu, après avoir assouvi ne serait-ce qu'à moitié sa colère, rentre toujours se coucher, hiberner pour ainsi dire, pour un temps que les gouvernants mettent toujours à profit pour reprendre leurs jeux imbéciles, tirant des plans sur la comète pour ne jamais les appliquer jusqu'au soulèvement suivant.[43]
>
> [In the village, things were back to normal. Everyone went about their business in complete calm. As is well known, having satisfied even half their anger, the people always go to bed, hibernate so to speak, for a time; meanwhile, the rulers take advantage to resume their foolish games, forging ambitious plans, to only ever apply them at the next uprising.]

Depicted throughout as a largely homogenous group—captured in the use of the descriptors, "villageois," "la population," "le Peuple," or "la foule," the majority of those living in Sidi Ben Tayeb return to a state of "convivialité," ultimately failing to deconstruct the teleological narrative of history, whose constructed status is captured in the town's stopped clock.[44] Thus, despite the momentary insight the inhabitants were granted of the underlying truths of their history, they remain caught up in a deception of their own making. It is at this point that Ayyoub shifts his focus from a satire directly attacking those in positions of authority and toward the villagers themselves. If, as Amine Aït Hadi underlines, the caricatured portraits of the powerful are indeed "clownesque," Ayyoub's critique now also encompasses the general population, including individuals such as Si Kaddour, as they too participate in the quest to repair the broken clock.[45] Figured early on as "des fourmis aveugles" [blind ants] or "[des] poissons rouges enfermés dans un bocal trop étroit" [goldfish trapped in too small a bowl], the villagers are framed both as a mass of citizens set to explode and as an obedient army ready to perform their role as participants in the continued ratification of a theater of grotesque power.[46]

In *Le Remonteur de l'horloge*, Ayyoub shows how a teleological narrative embodied in clock time captures citizens in an "intimate tyranny," whereby they perpetuate their own oppression.[47] By continuing to accept the clock at face value, the villagers fail to break free of the discursive constraints within which clock time prevails. As Mbembe has stressed, it is not enough to grasp that citizens "collaborate in their own oppression" by a hegemonic power; rather, it is vital to understand that in leading the "fight against" that oppression, citizens risk reinforcing the very discourse of power that entraps them in the first place. For Mbembe, "The substance of what one might call 'resistance' is inseparable from the texture of servitude."[48]

For historians of Algeria, Mbembe's insights on the performance of power have become increasingly important for framing notions of accommodation and resistance, as well as for the way citizens imagine their own interactions with the State. According to Benkhaled and Vince, scholarly accounts of post-1988 Algeria are replete with the "black and white language of perpetrators versus victims and totalizing, mutually exclusive identities."[49] Meanwhile, for Davis and Serres, critics and citizens alike have deployed "nebulous" notions such as *le pouvoir* and the "regime" to describe the State in contemporary Algeria. Not only does the use of such "floating" terminology serve to obscure the *actual* configuration of State power, it also reinforces the very strategy of indeterminacy pursued by State actors who have had little desire to build democratically accountable political institutions.[50]

This understanding of power matters for the kind of work writers imagine their fictional narratives to do in the political realm. While Ayyoub in no way commits to giving a referential account of the violence of the 1990s, he does fashion himself as a voice for the downtrodden—as the "ami du pauvre"—and, at least initially, defines the figure of the "engaged" writer in opposition to a mystifying and powerful elite. In so doing, Ayyoub risks making the same mistake as citizens and commentators who reduce complicated structures of power to the floating signifier of the "regime," thereby ratifying a performance of power already sanctioned by the obscure system we pretend to oppose.[51]

If *Le Gardien* stages the hubristic downfall of the grotesque leader and the revenge of the popular masses, *Le Palestinien* introduces an ambivalent identification, where character and reader alike can begin to acknowledge their complicity in enacting a dominant spectacle of power. In its explicit attention to time and narrative, Ayyoub's *Le Remonteur de l'horloge* is at a remove from these previous narratives that seek to more directly satirize grotesque figures of power. In this final text, the author stages the play of collaboration and resistance as always contained within an overarching "regime"—that is, a *discursive* regime in which "ruler" and "ruled" alike compete for power. The seemingly innocuous clock face serves here as a symbol for the way citizens entrap themselves in oppressive structures they take at face value. In the discursive framework that emerges after the Black Decade—whose "end" was mandated in the naming of the period a "national tragedy"—Ayyoub draws attention to the way citizens themselves perform and perpetuate a preapproved conflict narrative.

In the ambivalent and allegorical language these fictional stories deploy, they risk remaining part of the theater of grotesque power they ultimately seek to contest. However, by simultaneously staging and unveiling the performance of a "shared language of power" and the kinds of narrative tropes that perpetuate a reductive vision of history in contemporary Algeria, Ayyoub's texts envision a way out of the ossified discourse that traps citizens in a state of "mutual zombification."[52] The way in which "engaged" writers have always been at the core of the political debate in Algeria means they have a particular stake in the way power is maintained or contested. Like the secret truths that lie hidden beneath the surface of Sidi Ben Tayeb's clock face, Ayyoub's stories remain a potentially powerful space for revealing how citizens are themselves complicit in the passive maintenance of a dominant clock time—a discursive "regime" that maintains the myth of a coherent and cohesive hierarchy of power.

NOTES

1. Habib Ayyoub and Amina Bekkat, "Entretien avec Habib Ayyoub," *Algérie Littérature/Action* no. 57–58 (2002), 81. http://www.revues-plurielles.org/_uploads/pdf/4_57_12.pdf

2. In a personal interview in 2014, Ayyoub noted he had written many of his works in notebooks kept throughout the 1990s, only publishing his texts after the emergence of new independent publishing houses in Algeria.

3. Sartre, *Qu-est-ce que la littérature?*; Fanon, *Les damnés*. Kateb Yacine's *Nedjma* is frequently cited as *the* national allegory for Algerian independence; though, this understanding has been interrogated by critics. See, for instance, Jane Hiddleston, "Kateb Yacine: Poetry and Revolution," in *Decolonising the Intellectual: Politics, Culture, and Humanism at the End of the French Empire* (Liverpool: Liverpool University Press, 2014), 205–49. On national allegory and the Third World, see Fredric Jameson, "Third-World Literature in the Era of Multinational Capitalism," *Social Text* no. 15 (1986), 65–88.

4. Hiddleston, *Writing After Postcolonialism*, 18. Hiddleston cites several other critics and writers, including Abdellatif Laâbi, Khalid Zekri, and Benoît Denis, who embrace Sartre and Fanon's vision of literature as "engaged." See also Sartre, *Qu'est-ce que la littérature?*; Fanon, *Les damnés*.

5. Mbembe, "Provisional Notes"; see also Achille Mbembe, "Prosaics of Servitude and Authoritarian Civilities," *Public Culture* 5, no. 1 (1992), 123–45.

6. Mbembe, "Provisional Notes," 10.

7. Hiddleston, *Writing After Postcolonialism*, 19.

8. Hiddleston, *Writing After Postcolonialism*, 22–23.

9. Habib Ayyoub, *Le Gardien* (Algiers : Editions Barzakh, 2001); I refer to a later edition, *Le désert, et après: suivi de le gardien* (Algiers: Editions Barzakh, 2007). Habib Ayyoub, *Le Palestinien* (Algiers: Editions Barzakh, 2003); Habib Ayyoub, *Le Remonteur de l'horloge* (Algiers: Barzakh, 2012).

10. Mbembe, "Provisional Notes."

11. McDougall, *A History of Algeria*, 313. See also Benkhaled and Vince, "Performing Algerianness," 265.

12. McDougall, *A History of Algeria*, 389, n. 60.

13. Bonn, "Littérature algérienne," 37.

14. Mikhail Bakhtin, *Rabelais and his World*, trans. Hélène Iswolsky (Bloomington: Indiana University Press, 1984).

15. Bakhtin, *Rabelais*, 12.

16. Shattuck, "The Doubting of Fiction," 101.

17. "C'est nous qui avons fait descendre le Coran et qui en sommes les gardiens." See *Le Coran*, trans. O. Pesle and Ahmed Tidjani (Paris: Editions Larose, 1948), 162, 15:9.

18. Ayyoub, *Le Gardien*, 129.

19. Hiddleston, *Writing After Postcolonialism*, 18.

20. Ayyoub, *Le Gardien*, 131.

21. Bakhtin, *Rabelais*, 137–38.

22. Bakhtin, *Rabelais*, 50.

23. Bakhtin, *Rabelais*, 50.

24. Mbembe, "Provisional Notes," 26.

25. It is notable, for instance, that many independent Algerian publishers still rely on funds from the Algerian State. Moreover, major cultural events, such as the Salon international du livre [International Book Fair] or SILA, are organized and controlled by the Ministry of Culture. Less official networks exist (as I explore in chapter 5), but the SILA is one of the principal venues where publishers can sell works and bring readers into contact with authors. For two recent studies of the role of independent publishers in Algeria, see Corbin Treacy, "L'Effet Barzakh," *Contemporary French and Francophone Studies* 20, no. 1 (2016), 76–83; Lewis, "The Maghreb's New Publishing House."

26. See Hervé Sanson, "Moins qu'une nahda, plus qu'un 'air de flute'," in *Algérie: la nahda des Lettres, la renaissance des mots*, ed. Adlène Meddi and Mélanie Matarese (Paris: Riveneuve Editions, 2015), 14–21.

27. Olivia Harrison, "Beyond France-Algeria: The Algerian Novel and the Transcolonial Imagination," in *Algeria: Nation, Culture and Transnationalism: 1988-2015* ed. Patrick Crowley (Liverpool: Liverpool University Press), 228.
28. Harrison, "Beyond France-Algeria," 227.
29. Hiddleston, *Writing After Postcolonialism*, 97.
30. Ayyoub, *Le Palestinien*, 251–52.
31. Bakhtin, *Rabelais*, 12.
32. Bakhtin, *Rabelais*, 12.
33. Mbembe, "Provisional Notes," 3.
34. Benkhaled and Vince, "Performing Algerianness," 265.
35. Mbembe, "Provisional Notes," 8.
36. Davis and Serres, "Political Contestation," 105.
37. Mbembe, "Provisional Notes," 3–4.
38. Rancière, cited in Hiddleston, *Writing After Postcolonialism*, 23.
39. Rancière, cited in Hiddleston, *Writing After Postcolonialism*, 23.
40. Davis and Serres, "Political Contestation," 103.
41. Davis and Serres, "Political Contestation," 103.
42. Ayyoub, *Le Remonteur*, 47.
43. Ayyoub, *Le Remonteur*, 113.
44. Ayyoub, *Le Remonteur*, 7, *passim*. See also Mbembe, "Provisional Notes," 10.
45. Amine Aït Hadi, "Carnaval à Sidi Bentayeb ou l'horloge de la discorde: Le Remonteur d'horloge de Habib Ayyoub," *L'Expression*, November 12, 2012. https://www.djazairess.com/fr/lexpression/163600.
46. Ayyoub, *Le Remonteur*, 7; Benkhaled and Vince, "Performing Algerianness," 265; Mbembe, "Provisional Notes."
47. Mbembe, "Provisional Notes," 25.
48. Mbembe, "Prosaics of Servitude," 133.
49. Benkhaled and Vince, "Performing Algerianness," 243.
50. Davis and Serres, "Political Contestation," 107.
51. Mbembe, "Provisional Notes," 5.
52. Benkhaled and Vince, "Performing Algerianness," 265; Mbembe, "Provisional Notes," 4.

Chapter 4

Specters of the Black Decade in Kamel Daoud's *Meursault, contre-enquête*

Recent academic criticism on the Algerian novel has highlighted how a generation of writers sought to both partake in and register the Algerian revolution of 1954–1962. In her 2015 book, *Decolonising the Intellectual*, Hiddleston shows how writers such as Kateb Yacine conceived of their writing as part of a revolutionary poetics of decolonization.[1] And, in *The Algerian New Novel* (2017), Valérie Orlando focuses on a generation of writers whose texts offered experimental yet nevertheless deeply "committed" mediations of Algerian identity in the aftermath of 1962.[2] While these scholars understand the next generation of Algerian writers in a slightly different light, they nevertheless stress the importance of the contestatory beginnings of Algerian literature for writers like Kamel Daoud. Thus, for Hiddleston, Daoud's *Meursault, contre-enquête* is a means for the author to "express his dissent towards the contemporary regime," while, for Orlando, the book is part of an effort to "guarantee civil rights and freedom."[3] Hiddleston further notes that Daoud's text requires more "careful attention on the ways in which literary texts can refer to the world," but both scholars show the difficulty—near impossibility, even—of separating Daoud's literary or fictional voice from his political persona.[4]

A response to Camus's world-renowned *L'Etranger*, Daoud's novel was hardly noticed when it was published in Algiers in 2013. It was not until it was released by the French publisher Actes Sud in 2014 that the text quickly garnered worldwide attention. The story, which retells the tale of the nameless Arab murdered by Camus's protagonist, won numerous accolades, including the prestigious Prix Goncourt du Premier Roman, which Bachi had won in 2001. It was swiftly translated into several languages and distributed around the globe.[5] Camus, whose trajectory and success Daoud and his publishers might understandably seek to imitate, encountered the not dissimilar issue of separating an author's political writings from their literary texts, especially when that writing takes place at a time of conflict. Even if, as critic Kevin Newmark underlines, Camus understood the respective realms of fiction and nonfiction as distinct, his works were nevertheless taken together to construct an image of the writer's "engagement" (or *lack* thereof) in the political debates of the time.[6] As the renowned Algerian journalist and writer Sid Ahmed Semiane writes in his preface to Daoud's collected journalism,

> Ses chroniques n'étaient pas seulement une analyse politique, un coup de gueule éditorialiste, comme le sont souvent les chroniques dans le monde de la presse, plus aptes à créer de la proximité avec l'idéologie qu'avec l'art. Non. Ses chroniques alliaient l'esprit à l'humour, la noblesse des lettres à la vulgarité morbide de l'actualité, la colère à la légèreté, la réflexion littéraire à la prise de parole politique.[7]

> [His columns were not just a political analysis, or ranting editorials, as are many other columns, closer in proximity to ideology than art. No. His columns combined wit with humor, the grandeur of literature with the morbid vulgarity of the everyday, anger with frivolity, literary reflection with political speech.]

For Semiane, Daoud's journalism is crucial for his development as a writer, just as his literary imagination was at the core of his politics. In line with the legacy of his key interlocutor, Camus, Daoud's journalistic and literary discourse are crucially entwined. As such, much of the journalistic reception of *Meursault* has noted its *oppositional* nature, often describing the writer as using the novel as a means of resisting more extreme political and religious ideologies, and violence, associated with the Black Decade. Supposedly critical accounts have perpetuated reductive explanations of contemporary Algerian politics and society, as commentators pit the authoritarian "regime" against the "oppressed masses," Francophone writers against those writing in Arabic, or Islam against secularism.[8] Since the publication of *Meursault*, Daoud has also been co-opted by (and indeed frequently adopted) some of the more extreme positions of intellectuals and journalists on the French right, who have sought to frame the author and his literary work as a "challenge" to contemporary Islamism (and Islam in general) in Algeria and France.

In this chapter, I ask how we might read Daoud's literary production in light of his status as an outspoken public intellectual. How might we resolve, or at the very least begin to explain, some of the abovementioned contradictions? Has the fusion between literary and journalistic discourse led critics to overstate the writer as an oppositional figure? If so, what are the implications for the way we think about literature at a time of conflict? In responding to these questions, I argue that the ambivalent space of literature allows the author to explore acts of reading and writing Algeria's recent history in more drawn-out and self-conscious ways, while noting that the affirmative discourse of journalism runs the risk of curtailing more nuanced discussion of politics, religion, and conflict. I show that, despite his claims to the contrary, Daoud might be understood to deliberately play upon the (con)fusion between his literary and political writings, with the aim of fashioning himself as an embattled public intellectual. In so doing, I suggest that the resemblance between Daoud and Camus's contested relationship with Algeria should not be understood as merely coincidental, but rather as part of an attempt to fashion the writer in oppositional terms.

READING AND WRITING IN *MEURSAULT: CONTRE-ENQUÊTE* (2013)

Although it is regularly labeled as Daoud's debut, *Meursault: contre-enquête* was in fact the third in a cycle of literary texts written by Daoud, beginning with *Ô Pharaon* [*O Pharaoh*], published in Oran in 2004.[9] His little known, *La Préface du nègre* [*The Ghost-Writer's Preface*] (2008)—rereleased in France with the title *Le Minotaure 504* [*The Minotaur 504*] (2011)—is a collection of four short stories that offer self-reflexive accounts of the writing of postindependence Algerian history.[10] Distinct from the popular narrative that stresses Daoud was working only as an Algerian journalist before writing *Meursault*, it is important to note here that he was a writer of status within the Algerian literary field prior to the appearance of his most famous novel and, as such, was very much aware of the way writers and literary writing in particular could be mobilized for political or ideological purposes.

In the eponymous short story of Daoud's collection, *La Préface du nègre*, the decision of the author to self-consciously stage the figure of the ghostwriter prompts the reader to reflect on "the potentially obstructive or obfuscatory effects of literary writing and its attempt to record and reflect experience in contemporary [. . .] Algeria."[11] Asked to transcribe a memoir of a former fighter during the War of Independence, Daoud's ghostwriter (the "nègre") tries to subvert the text he has been asked to write with the aim of breaking the repetitive and clichéd narrative of the former soldier. Left only with a "preface," the ghostwriter's incomplete rendition is presented to the reader in Daoud's story. As Hiddleston has noted, Daoud's tale is a cautionary one, conscious as it is of the restrictions placed on creative writing—both in terms of the possibility of moving beyond dominant accounts of history and the lack of material spaces in which writers can publish.[12] This self-conscious vision of the writer and literature as "constrained" by competing narratives is also present in Daoud's *Meursault*.[13] If the overarching aim of the novel is to stage an act of (re)writing of a text the narrator views as fundamentally flawed, the attention soon shifts to a self-conscious examination of the practices of reading in contemporary Algeria and how such practices place interpretative restrictions on the literary text.

In *Meursault*, the story of the Arab's murder is told by the brother of the victim, Haroun, from a bar in Oran. Camus's original text is incorporated when the narrator notes that Meursault was not just the murderer of his brother, named here as Moussa, but the famous author of a novelized *account* of the killing. For Haroun, the text (a novel written by Meursault *about* Meursault) is unjustly focused on the murderer and is, as such, presented as a chronicle of the author's life:[14]

> C'est le Français qui y joue le mort et disserte sur la façon dont il a perdu sa mère, puis comment il a perdu son corps sous le soleil, puis comment il a perdu le corps d'une amante, puis comment il est parti à l'église pour constater que son Dieu avait déserté le corps de l'homme, puis comment il a veillé le cadavre de sa mère et le sien, etc.[15]

> [So the Frenchman plays the dead man and goes on and on about how he lost his mother, and then about how he lost his body in the sun, and then about how he lost a girlfriend's body, and then about how he went to church and discovered that his God had deserted the human body, and then about how he sat up with his mother's corpse and his own, et cetera.][16]

Outraged by the fact nobody has come to ask about the victim of the brutal murder—"[c]'est mon frère qui a reçu la balle, pas lui!" ["my brother was the one who got shot, not him!"]—the narrator then clearly confuses Camus's fiction with autobiographical events, blending the fictional Meursault with the real-life Camus: "Qui sait si Moussa avait un revolver, une philosophie, une tuberculose, des idées ou une mère et une justice?" ["Who knows whether Musa had a gun, a philosophy, tuberculosis, ideas or a mother and a sense of justice?"][17] In the final part of the novel, Meriem—a young researcher who has been studying the offending text—helps Haroun read Meursault's novel, and he begins to appreciate the greater nuances of the work.

There are several points to raise here about Haroun's reading and the didactic process imagined by Daoud in relation to Algerian reading practices. Clearly, Daoud is reflecting ironically on how Algerians read novels such as Camus's *L'Etranger*. As an unreliable narrator, Haroun is ridiculed for his excessive drinking and painted as an unsophisticated reader and a confounding author narrator. As Alice Kaplan writes, to stage Meursault as the writer of a text in which he also appears makes a mockery of the situation whereby readers mistake the author for a fictional narrator.[18] However, Daoud's use of Meriem as a reader who sees a more ambivalent relationship between the author and the narrator is clear evidence that not *all* Algerians read in this way.

Later, Haroun reveals that he has committed a murder in revenge for his brother's death. With his mother's encouragement—she is present at the scene of the crime—Haroun shoots dead a French settler, named Joseph Larquais, on a beach one day after Algerian independence in 1962; when interrogated at his local Gendarmerie, the murder is rather quickly glossed over, and Haroun is instead quizzed for not signing up to the *maquis* during the War of Independence. The interrogating colonel repeatedly asks why Haroun could not have committed the murder just one day prior, before the ceasefire was announced on July 5, 1962; the implication is that Haroun would have been considered a participant in the fight for independence if only he had paid closer attention to the time. This part of the narrative is a particularly playful inversion of the story of Meursault's trial in Camus's *L'Etranger*. Ironically inverted, the story now tells of how Haroun, rather than being investigated for the murder he has admitted committing, is judged on his nonparticipation in the *maquis*. Just as the court in Meursault's case is distracted by the moral question of his behavior at his mother's funeral, the colonel in Haroun's case is obsessed with the revolutionary narrative of independence.

Concerned with the need for lineage and filiation throughout the novel, Haroun is shown to be a victim of the postindependence obsession with telling a teleological narrative of history. The empty grave of Moussa, which his mother is said to fill with "une fausse biographie" ["an invented biography"], haunts the story and becomes a symbolic vessel for the tale Haroun will tell.[19] In contrast to Kateb's famous claim that the French language had been for Algeria a "butin de guerre" [spoils of war], Haroun describes it as a "bien vacant" ["unclaimed goods"] into which he steps, as if occupying the former home of a departed French settler.[20] In many ways the figure of Moussa, the now named Arab, performs a similar role. The two characters (Moussa and Meursault) might be read as metonyms for the Arabic and French languages. The attempted State erasure of the French language after independence is embodied by Haroun's need to avenge his brother's killing, while the Arabic language is symbolized by an empty hole in the ground. But both also reflect the monolingual policies adopted under French colonialism and seemingly replicated after independence by the Algerian State. Moussa and Meursault are continually spoken of alongside each other, and the narrator negotiates the question of naming, and the potential confusion of these names in particular, throughout the novel. As Lia Brozgal suggests, spoken out loud, there is a near-homophony between the two names.[21]

While concerned with the details of his brother's tale, Haroun on more than one occasion claims to know nothing of the geography of the story: "sache que si je connais l'histoire, et pas qu'un peu, je ne sais presque rien de sa géographie" ["be aware that even though I know the story—all too well—I know virtually nothing about its geography"].[22] Later, Haroun affirms: "Je ne cherche pas du côté de la géographie, je te dis." ["Don't do any geographical searching—that's the point I'm trying to make."][23] In this way, the narrator resists the novel being read and placed in a referential time or space. Time appears important once more when Haroun describes the killing of the Frenchman, Joseph Larquais, where the justice of the "restitution" is reliant on the murder taking place at the exact point when Meursault killed the Arab in 1942.[24] Only, Moussa was killed at 2 o'clock in the afternoon, in the heat and blinding light of the Algiers sun, whereas Joseph is killed at 2 o'clock in the morning, by moonlight. Haroun winds back his watch, and hence manipulates time, noting how his mother will now be able to grow old naturally, "et non plus par rancune" ["no longer preserved by spite"].[25] On one level, this temporal ambiguity reinforces Haroun's obsession with filiation and time, but it is perhaps also a reference to the temporal ambiguity exhibited by Camus. As Harrison notes of *L'Etranger*, Meursault's account of time is ambiguous, captured most strikingly in the first lines of the novel—"Aujourd'hui, maman est morte. Ou peut-être hier, je ne sais pas" ["My mother died today. Or maybe yesterday, I don't know"].[26] By turning back the clock, Haroun alters time to fit his mother's need to mourn her son after the killing of Joseph has supposedly taken place at the exact time as her son's murder some twenty years earlier. Later, Haroun will say that he killed Joseph, "parce qu'il fallait faire contrepoids à l'absurde de notre situation" ["because (he) had to counterbalance the absurdity of our situation"].[27] Yet, given it cannot be subjected to any dialectical resolution, any attempt to "counterbalance" the absurd would surely mean reproducing another absurd set of events.

As Haroun reads Meursault's text as a chronicle of the events of the life of both the author and his brother, the vexed question of understanding contemporary Algeria through literature is brought to the fore. However, rather than encourage a stable identification between the novel and its setting, the literary *contre-enquête* parodies the idea that literature could be used as a lens through which to perceive contemporary Algeria. In Haroun's words, the reader is "piégé" ["hooked"] in the pursuit of facts that no literary text can reliably provide.[28] In this way, Daoud appears to use his novel to engage in a form of criticism not just of those Algerian readers who would too easily confuse author and fictional narrator, but of even more renowned academic literary critics, such as Edward Said and Conor Cruise O'Brien, who had questioned Camus's representation of native "Arabs" and their treatment by the narrator, Meursault.[29] As Harrison has shown, these criticisms of Camus allowed little space for the possibility that the author was deploying a mode of literary realism, whereby his fictional colonial settler characters embodied precisely the kinds of reductive classification that Said and O'Brien single out for criticism.[30] As Harrison goes on to underline, Said and O'Brien further assume that the French reader will automatically identify, through a stable realist *vraisemblance*, with the character of Meursault. What is not broached in their respective critiques is the possibility that Camus's text in fact disrupts "realist modes of reading" such that Camus himself performs a level of "criticism" within the fictional text.[31] If Daoud's novel could be said to engage Said's practice of contrapuntal reading, reinserting glossed over elements of a story back into the narrative, it also draws attention to the potential flaws of this mode of critical engagement which resulted, in the case of Camus's novel, in an assumption of the reader's straightforward and unproblematic identification with the (anti)hero of the story.[32]

Daoud's novel presents a remarkably nuanced account of reading and writing as they are practiced in and beyond Algeria. As Brozgal stresses, the text develops "a praxis that has been a mainstay of the North African novel for as long as it has existed in French, that is, the relentless interrogation of literature itself."[33] Yet, the image created at the juncture between Daoud's journalism and the cultural commentary on his text is one of a far more self-assured and controversial public intellectual. In both the stances adopted by the author and in the readings of his literary text made by several journalists and academic literary critics, the publication of *Meursault* served a catalyst for the consecration of Daoud as a "dissident" writer-journalist.[34] For many commentators, the novel becomes less a text that is worthy of close reading, more a milestone in the consecration of the public intellectual at a time of crisis or conflict. As I will show, this process of constructing the writer as an embattled public intellectual is very much like the way Mimouni and Boudjedra were fashioned as firm opponents to Islamism, and Islam more generally, during the 1990s.[35]

THE WRITER AS EMBATTLED PUBLIC INTELLECTUAL

In December 2014, the leader of the unofficial "Front de l'Eveil islamique salafiste" [the Salafist Islamic Awakening], Abdelfatah Hamadache, called on his Facebook page for the Algerian State to sentence Daoud to death after the author made comments on television which Hamadache deemed insulting to Islam. His words, reported by *Le Monde*, read as follows: "Le Front de la Sahwa, écrit-il, 'considère que si la charia islamique était appliquée en Algérie, le châtiment contre lui aurait été la mort pour apostasie et hérésie'" [the Sahwa Front, he writes, "considers that if Islamic sharia law were applied in Algeria, the punishment against him would have been death for apostasy and heresy"].[36] A report published on the website Algeria-Watch, which repeats claims that Hamadache was embedded as an agent in the Algerian security services during the 1990s and that the self-styled "imam" was still operating with the approval of the Algerian security apparatus, cites the statement further: "Nous appelons le régime algérien à appliquer la charia et à le condamner à mort en le tuant publiquement pour la guerre qu'il mène contre Dieu et le Prophète" [we call on the Algerian regime to apply Sharia and condemn him to death in a public execution for the war he is waging against God and the Prophet].[37] Despite the dispute centering on comments made on television, Hamadache is also reported to have implicitly recalled the targeting of writers during the Black Decade when he wrote: "ceux qui nous combattent par la plume doivent périr par l'épée" [those who fight us by the pen, must perish by the sword].[38]

This call for the Algerian State to sentence Daoud to death was widely reported in the French press as a "fatwa," despite the fact that Hamadache apparently had no authority to declare any fatwa.[39] Daoud himself referred to the call as a fatwa on his own Facebook and Twitter pages and, in an article published on the website of *Le Point*, speaks (no doubt with more than a hint of irony) about the "fatwaisation" of his life.[40] In March 2016, Hamadache was sentenced by a court in Oran to pay a fine and to serve six months in prison.[41] Whatever Hamadache's intent, his intervention served to draw further attention to Daoud's novel as journalists, academic critics, and publishers explicitly noted the threat to Daoud's life. If, during the 1990s, Boudjedra and Mimouni were held up in an "enlightened" opposition to "barbarous" and violent elements of Islam or the Algerian State, the "fatwaisation" of Daoud's life placed him in a renewed antagonism with Islam and the State.

In his own journalism, Daoud had almost always been outspoken on the question of radical Islam, especially in his famous columns written for *Le Quotidien d'Oran* throughout the period of the Black Decade.[42] In his articles written since the end of the Black Decade, Daoud continues to speak of "le tabou maladif du réligieux" ["the sick taboo of religion"], describing Islamists as "les enfants hysteriques" ["the hysterical children"] of Arab dictators, as "remont[ant] le temps" ["going back in time"] and "comme origine de ce mal du siècle" ["as the origin of this century's evil"].[43] In a not dissimilar way to Mimouni and Boudjedra, Daoud stood in firm opposition to a violence he saw as principally carried out by extremists. While Daoud also seeks to challenge historical narratives advanced by the Algerian State, his nonliterary writing—like that of Mimouni and Boudjedra—still advances a mythologized image of power as drawn along oppositional lines, pitting "the people" against a violence he sees as being largely carried out by Islamists.

Though Daoud remains living in Algeria, he has shifted his journalistic activities to Paris, as well as to the United States, where he has been welcomed not just by the political right but by supposedly "leftist" writers and intellectuals who fear what they see as an encroaching Islamist threat. From the French context, philosophers, such as the right-wing thinker Alain Finkielkraut, promote Daoud's image as that of the "courageous" intellectual pitted against an "oppressive" Islam.⁴⁴ Whereas Daoud's anti-Islamist sentiment could be quickly explained in the polarized context of the Black Decade, it did not easily "translate" to the European setting, where an escalating refugee crisis had led to Islam being polarized in more malevolent ways, principally along the lines of race and ethnicity.⁴⁵

The "Affaire Daoud" and the Specter of the Black Decade

On January 31, 2016, Daoud authored an article for *Le Monde*, entitled "Cologne, lieu de fantasmes" [Cologne, place of fantasies].⁴⁶ Focused on the events of New Year's Eve 2015 in the German city of Cologne, when reports emerged that several women had been sexually assaulted by men of North African or Arab appearance, the article pretends to delve into the minds of two sets of actors: "des agresseurs" [aggressors], those who (supposedly) committed the acts, and "des Occidentaux" [Westerners].⁴⁷ Daoud argues that what happened on New Year's Eve in Cologne was caused by the clash of a set of "fantasmes" [fantasies]. The first fantasy was that belonging to members of the European Right: "Des immigrés accueillis s'attaquent à 'nos' femmes, les agressent et les violent" [immigrants welcomed into our communities attack "our" women, assaulting and raping them]; a second emanated from the left who had fallen victim to a "surdose de naïveté" [overdose of naivety], privileging refugees' "rights" and not their "culture," while the third fantasy concerned the position of women in the Islamic world, where, for him, "[l]a femme est niée, refusée, tuée, voilée, enfermée ou possédée" [woman is denied, rejected, killed, veiled, locked up or possessed].⁴⁸ If he continues to support giving asylum to refugees in Europe ("il faut offrir l'asile au corps" [we must offer asylum to the body]), Daoud adopts a provocatively reductive language in his call for the need to "convaincre l'âme de changer" [convince the soul to change]. Here, he claims, "l'Autre vient de ce vaste univers douloureux et affreux que sont la misère sexuelle dans le monde arabo-musulman, le rapport malade à la femme, au corps et au désir" [the Other comes from this vast, painful and awful universe of the Arab-Muslim world, replete with sexual misery and which has a sick relationship with women, the body and desire]. Extending an invitation to this cultural other, Daoud continues, "n'est pas le guérir" [is not to cure him].⁴⁹

In the days that followed, a collective of nineteen historians, political scientists, and literary scholars responded to Daoud's article in a letter to *Le Monde*.⁵⁰ They accused Daoud of psychologizing the violence reported in Cologne and of recycling obvious and well-worn Orientalist clichés.

For the collective of academics, Daoud had reductively read all refugees to be "[c]ulturellement inadaptés et psychologiquement déviants" [culturally maladapted and psychologically deviant] and was calling for their collective reeducation and cultural assimilation. According to the scholars, Daoud's analysis had been misplaced; his point of reference was rather Algeria during the 1990s where he had been "marqué par son expérience" [marked by his experience]. Here, he was intervening "en tant qu'intellectuel laïque minoritaire dans son pays" [as a minority secular intellectual in his country], while in Europe Daoud risked espousing an increasingly mainstream Islamophobia. On February 11, *The New York Times* published a contribution from Daoud, entitled "The Sexual Misery of the Arab World."[51] Apparently drafted before the academics had published their letter, the article nevertheless looked as if Daoud were responding to the collective of scholars.[52] The tone and language of the article were far more direct than his previous piece in *Le Monde*; Daoud explicitly links Cologne to similar incidents reported in Tahrir Square in Cairo at the time of the "Arab Spring" in 2011 and goes on to speak of how the Arab and Muslim world is plagued by what he calls its "sick relationship with women." Daoud's point seemed to be that the fact that sex remains taboo and marginalized in the Arab and Muslim world, and which he speaks of as a "disease," meant it was now "bursting onto the scene in Europe."[53]

Meanwhile, the journalist Adam Shatz, who had become friends with the author having reviewed *Meursault* in *The New York Times*, wrote to Daoud to challenge what he called the "mountain of hyperbole" the author was climbing.[54] In response to Shatz's suggestion that he explore these complex questions of identity and sexuality in his fiction, Daoud claimed he would give up journalism and devote himself solely to literature. As Shatz has written since, the publication of the exchange of letters between him and Daoud sparked polemics on both sides of the Mediterranean.[55] Yet, despite Shatz being at the root of Daoud's apparent commitment to give up journalism, the ensuing flood of defenses of the author doubled as attacks against the group of academics that had first challenged Daoud in their letter to *Le Monde*. The Franco-Tunisian writer Fawzia Zouari, for instance, turns on the group of academics accusing them of trying to silence Daoud in the same way he had been threatened by the "barbus de son pays" [bearded Muslims of his own country]. If Daoud lacked nuance, she argued, this was precisely his aim, belonging as she claimed to "une autre tradition de l'islam, celle des poètes rebelles" [another tradition of Islam, that of the rebel poets].[56] By implicitly invoking Hamadache's "fatwa" alongside the image of the rebellious poet, Zouari reinforces the contestatory frame in which writers are celebrated for their heroic opposition to supposedly "backwards" or "barbaric" Islamic traditions. In her analysis, Zouari reinforces two reductive "types" of a prevailing "identity crisis" in Algeria: Islam versus secularism and tradition versus modernity.⁵⁷ As Shatz reflects, responses like Zouari's miss the crucial point (made in the academics' letter) that, given this debate occurs in the distinct political, cultural, and religious contexts of Europe *and* North Africa, nuance is required in each respective setting.

In a bizarre turn of events, the then French prime minister, Manuel Valls intervened in the "affair," publishing a defense of Daoud on March 2, 2016. In a familiar refrain, Valls attacks the academics for *their* lack of nuance and directly links Daoud's decision to give up journalism to the apparently censorious letter: "un romancier de talent—et sur qui pèse déjà une 'fatwa' dans son pays—décide, face à la violence et la puissance de la vindicte, de renoncer à son métier de journaliste" [a talented novelist—already threatened by a "fatwa" in his own country—has decided, in the face of the violence and force of public persecution, to give up his job as a journalist]. Valls goes on to defend Daoud's personal interventions as not in need of proof, given the writer "nous parle du réel, de ce qu'il voit, de ce qu'il ressent, de ce qu'il vit aussi" [tells us about reality, what he sees, how he feels, what he experiences].⁵⁸ Not only does Valls equate the threat of a "fatwa" with a letter signed by nineteen academics, he defends Daoud on the basis that he is a novelist. The "romancier de talent" [talented novelist] need not present us with proof of the views espoused in his journalism, because he is to be treated as a "witness," speaking directly of a "reality" he himself has seen, felt, and lived. Of course, Daoud was not in Cologne on New Year's Eve of 2015, so this most talented novelist saw nothing of the actual events he claims to be able to report. The specter of the Black Decade looms large as Valls reveals an implicit association between the writer's Algerian identity and his enduring capacity to serve as a witness to Islamist violence. As Gayatri Spivak remarked in the early days of the *Satanic Verses* "affair," making a literary reading of Rushdie's novel quickly became an impossibility.⁵⁹ Though admittedly on a smaller scale, the same, perhaps, can be said of *Meursault*.

Those commentators reading, promoting, and thereby consecrating Daoud's work in France and beyond make selective readings of his literary and nonliterary production. If Daoud's views on Islam have created a polarized and polarizing debate around the status of the Algerian writer, as well as bringing into focus his experiences of the events of the Black Decade, it has also obscured the author and journalist's clearer insights into the way oppositional discourse is part of a preexisting spectacle of power in Algeria. Though Daoud does clearly reproduce reductive and racist stereotypes about Muslims and the "Arab" world, it is equally the case that his articles exhibit levels of nuance that are echoed in his literary writing. For instance, in a 2012 column entitled "Le peuple est-il coupable ou victime?" ["Are the People Culprits or Victims?"], Daoud asks whether "the people" are subjected to a power that they themselves possess and reproduce: "Le peuple est-il donc victime du pouvoir qui émane du peuple?" ["Are the people victims of this power, which in fact comes from the people?"][60] For Daoud, in this "jeu de soumission, le peuple est aussi coupable" ["game of submission, the people are also guilty"].[61] Yet, these more nuanced articles have largely fallen between the gaps of the international media coverage of Daoud's writing. Thus, while Daoud's actual persona is highly contradictory, what is captured in the French and international image of the writer is his oppositional nature, and embattled status, ready to bear witness to a violent past that many critics view to have forged his intellectual trajectory.

"Illuminating" the Black Decade

The figure of the witness and a reductive conflict narrative of the Black Decade are two common points of reference around which the reception of Daoud's novel has revolved. Indeed, much of the supposedly "literary" criticism of Daoud's text is characterized by a concern for identifying a set of external historical factors that can help critics frame the novel as an "explanation" of the events of the Black Decade. In what follows, I show that by replicating many of the binary "types" associated with reductive conceptions of contemporary Algerian identity, literary critics working for journalistic outlets bolster the simplistic image of the writer qua secular intellectual pitted against a violent Islamist threat.[62] If, in his own journalism, Daoud was beginning to comprehend the complexities of the "shared language of power" in contemporary Algeria, the French and international media had little real interest in comprehending the conflict of the 1990s and its impact on the present.[63]

Reviews of Daoud's novel in the French press frequently draw attention to the Raïna Raïkoum [Our opinion, your opinion]: columns Daoud wrote for *Le Quotidien d'Oran* throughout the 1990s, but none refers explicitly to them. Elsewhere, the figure of the novelist is fused with that of a journalistic commentary on a set of violent events, including those of the Black Decade and the *Charlie Hebdo* killings of January 2015.[64] Indeed, it is difficult to find reviews of *Meursault* that do not in some way link its author to the conflict of the Black Decade or more recent moments of crisis in France or Europe.

As one might expect, after the announcement of Hamadache's "fatwa," journalists regularly refer to this threat in accounts of Daoud's novel. A series of reports in *Le Figaro* is illustrative. Mohammed Aïssaoui, writing about the award of the Goncourt du Premier Roman, focuses on how the author is flanked by two bodyguards at the prize ceremony after being "menacé par la fatwa d'un fou dangereux, imam salafiste" [threatened by the fatwa of a dangerous madman, Salafist imam].[65] In another article, Armelle Héliot confuses Daoud the columnist with Daoud the novelist, as *Meursault* is viewed to emerge from the journalistic "esprit" [wit] and establish a lens on contemporary Algeria:

> Un imam salafiste a lancé contre lui [Daoud] une fatwa demandant au gouvernement algérien la peine de mort pour cet homme qui défend depuis toujours la laïcité et qui n'a pas peur. *Meursault, contre-enquête* est le premier roman de cet esprit caustique qui pose sur son pays, mais sur la France aussi, un regard très sévère.[66]
>
> [A Salafist imam has pronounced a fatwa against him [Daoud], demanding the Algerian government sentence to death a man who has always defended secularism and who is not afraid. *The Meursault Investigation* is the first novel from this caustic wit, who is seriously critical of his country, and of France too.]

By stressing the notion of the secular—and Daoud's apparent pursuit of it—Héliot summons a familiar image of the intellectual pitted in opposition to a regressive Islam. For *Le Nouveau Marianne*, the Black Decade is formative for Daoud in his writing of *Meursault*. Reported to have been aged just twenty when "les djihadistes des GIA, les groupes islamiques armés, égorgeaient l'espérance" [the jihadists of the GIA, the armed Islamic groups, slaughtered hope], Daoud is described here as "le témoin et le survivant" [the witness and survivor] and as having written the novel "dans le sillage de ses chroniques rebelles au *Quotidien d'Oran*" [in the wake of his rebellious columns at *Le Quotidien d'Oran*].[67] Meanwhile, the literary magazine *Lire* introduces Daoud's novel, describing it as painting the portrait of "une Algérie encore marquée au fer rouge par l'héritage colonial, mais aussi prise en étau entre l'armée et la religion" [an Algeria still branded by its colonial legacy, but also caught between the army and religion].[68] The arbitrary construction of two distinct "sides" feeds the myth that the violence of the Black Decade was the outcome of a clear split between the army and dissenting Islamist groups. Not only do these commentators continue to (con)fuse Daoud's fiction with his journalistic writing, using fiction to suggest a sociological commentary, they perpetuate the reductive notion of a crisis of identity and culture, linked to Algeria's unresolved history of violence.[69]

Of course, Daoud cannot be held responsible for journalists who use his novel to make a sociological reading of Algeria's recent history. As the author affirms in response to Hamadache's "fatwa," "Il ne faut pas mélanger entre les idées d'un personnage fictif et les positions de l'écrivain" [one must not confuse the ideas of a fictional character with the positions adopted by the writer].[70] And yet, in his own journalistic writing and interviews, Daoud advances a binary vision of the "identity crisis" he sees as being at the heart of the Arab and Muslim world.[71] In an interview with Marc Voinchet, broadcast in the days following the *Charlie Hebdo* attacks of January 2015, Daoud makes clear his wish for Muslims around the world to "sortir de la victimisation" [stop feeling victimized] and to do more to "affirmer leur position face au terrorisme" [affirm their opposition to terrorism].[72] In another interview, published two weeks later in *Le Figaro*, Daoud makes an explicit link between the *Charlie Hebdo* attacks and the violence of the Black Decade, as he speaks of the "bataille culturelle" [cultural battle] necessitated by the increase in terrorist attacks:

> Les attentats contre *Charlie Hebdo* ou contre la communauté juive me rappellent la décennie noire avec le groupe islamique armé (GIA) en Algérie. Les islamistes ont au commencement visé l'armée et la police, mais certains groupes s'attaquèrent rapidement aux civils. Depuis, l'islamisme a été vaincu militairement, mais il l'a emporté culturellement. On le voit bien aujourd'hui dans la société algérienne. Il a vaincu également dans l'ensemble du monde musulman. Et tente maintenant de s'imposer en Occident.[73]
>
> [The attacks against *Charlie Hebdo* or against the Jewish community remind me of the Black Decade with the Armed Islamic Group (GIA) in Algeria. Islamists initially targeted the army and police, but some groups quickly attacked civilians. Since then, Islamism has been defeated militarily, but it has prevailed culturally. We can see it today in Algerian society. It has also spread throughout the Muslim world. And it is now trying to impose itself in the West.]

In placing the blame for the attacks unambiguously with Muslims, Daoud advances a simplistic reading that does not even begin to take into account the range of factors leading to the killings. Daoud, once again, evokes an anti-Islamist sentiment that is not easily translated from the Algerian to the European context, thereby risking further entrenching divisions along lines of race and ethnicity. Furthermore, by advancing a language of "cultural war," Daoud's comments recall the way in which the Black Decade was framed by figures such as Mimouni and Boudjedra as a simple polarization between the culture of the secularist intellectual and that of "barbaric" Islamists.[74] Daoud's belief that "culture" can be mobilized in the "fight" against Islamism helps to explain why critics have been so keen to stress his status as a writer. Regardless of whether *Meursault* stages this "battle" within its pages, commentators use the novel to establish Daoud's cultural capital as a writer engaged in a struggle against the regressive forces of Islam. The prevailing discourse of a clash of cultures or civilizations visible in the work of writers like Mimouni and Boudjedra in the early 1990s had not abated by 2015, but was alive and well at the heart of Europe.

Playing more explicitly on the "local" context in which *Meursault* was written, the international press goes even further in constructing what Mundy calls the "imaginative geography of violence" of the Black Decade that, once more, stresses culturalist notions of a fundamental clash of religious and secular identities.[75] On the back cover of the UK edition of *Meursault*, an extract from *The New York Times* immediately recalls the demand for Daoud's "public execution."[76] In her review, Michiko Katutani focuses on how the rejection of religion is a principal element in the novel's plot, which in turn, "nudges us into a contemplation of Algeria's history and current religious politics."[77] *The Economist* reads the novel as a "lamentation for a modern Algeria gripped by pious fundamentalism," describing Daoud's book as a "brave [and] vertiginous response to a century of trauma."[78] For James Campbell of *The Wall Street Journal*, Daoud's novel "has an inescapable topical resonance, given the role played by political Islam in Algeria in recent times."[79] Meanwhile, in a review of Michel Houellebecq's *Soumission*, Adam Gopnik cites Daoud's novel as an instance of "French Muslims writ[ing] about French Muslim experience" (Daoud is of course neither French nor a Muslim), underlining how the author uses his novel to draw attention to the "degradation by political Islam" of a "free Algeria."[80] Finally, in his *Sunday Times* review, David Mills states how "Daoud has performed a great service for his country," taking Camus's "western classic" and using it "to illuminate the Algerian mind."[81] Adam Shatz's long review of the translated text is a nuanced account, but the subtitle to the piece adopts a binary culturalist lens, underlining how Daoud's novel is "caught between Islamist fervor and cultural flowering."[82]

By situating Daoud's novel within, or as emerging out of, the troubled context of the Black Decade, these commentators draw attention away from the self-conscious and critical focus of Daoud's literary texts, as well as some of his more nuanced journalism. Instead, *Meursault* is read, anachronistically, in the light of the embattled intellectual Daoud has become. While journalists and academic critics clearly wish to understand local factors involved in the production of a work of literature, they must also take care not to reproduce reductive ideas of the "local" in such a way that this then determines readings of a literary text or limits the scope of a text to refer to a historical event.[83] In their tendency to treat the text as a document, and its author as a spokesperson for contemporary Algeria, many of the above commentators remove the possibility that what the literary text does best is to open a dialogue between multiple representations of modern and contemporary Algeria and to encourage the reader to question these representations.[84] In its translation, reception, and presentation by a new audience—the beginnings of the consecration of *Meursault* as world literature—the literary status of Daoud's text is largely ignored. In the context of its English-language reception, Daoud's novel is privileged for its apparent ability to translate the violence of the Black Decade to Western audiences. As such, the text becomes a reified object of a discourse, or symbolic exchange, that thrives and survives on imagined cultures of violence.[85]

In his 2005 essay, "Who Needs an Idea of the Literary?," Harrison writes of the importance of "understand[ing] the shape and weight of ideas of the literary for particular readers," but also that "ideas of the literary have formed an integral part of the shifting conventions of authorship and reception."[86] Daoud offers us a prime example here of these shifting conventions. If critics have sought to place the figure of the author center stage, then authors such as Daoud have in turn used the literary text (albeit obliquely) to respond to these critical gestures and categorizations. In rewriting Camus's *L'Etranger*, Daoud plays with notions of authorship from the outset, as the oppositional *contre-enquête* challenges stable notions of authorship—a continuation of the interrogative stance the author began to explore in *La Préface du nègre*. In so doing, Daoud "frustrates" the way in which literary texts "refer" to historical events.[87]

In the context of the perception of an increased terrorist threat in France, coupled with threats made to writers, it would seem to be a truism to suggest that novels form part of the effort to "guarantee civil rights and freedom."[88] By framing the debate in this way, however, academic critics suppose that writers and commentators have a clear grasp on the bodies of power they seek to denounce or oppose. As Daoud's case demonstrates, the act of writing is not always a form of "dissent" from the status quo.[89] Daoud is, at the same time, complicit in perpetuating reductive and culturalist notions of opposition that propagate reductive stereotypes about the legacy of the violence of the Black Decade in Algeria. As with Camus, so with Daoud, it is not an easy task to delineate literary and journalistic discourses, especially when the popular reception of a novel relies upon fusing a fictional voice with that of its author. Yet, it is vital that we are cognizant of the risks we run of reproducing orthodoxies of opposition that perpetuate the political myth of a clash of civilizations and cultures—a myth many academic critics set out to scrutinize.

NOTES

1. Hiddleston, *Decolonising the Intellectual*, 205–49.
2. Valérie Orlando, *The Algerian New Novel: The Poetics of a Modern Nation, 1950–1979* (Charlottesville: University of Virginia Press, 2017), 32.
3. Hiddleston, *Writing After Postcolonialism*, 13; Orlando, *The Algerian New Novel*, 295, 287, 297.
4. Hiddleston, *Writing After Postcolonialism*, 158.

5. For the English translation, see Kamel Daoud, *The Meursault Investigation*, trans. John Cullen (London: Oneworld Publications, 2015).

6. Kevin Newmark, "Tongue-tied: What Camus's Fiction Couldn't Teach us About Ethics and Politics," in *Albert Camus in the 21st Century: A Reassessment of His Thinking at the Dawn of a New Millennium*, ed. Christine Margerrison et al. (New York: Rodopi, 2008), 107–20.

7. Sid Ahmed Semiane, "Le Fugitif," in Kamel Daoud, *Mes indépendances: Chroniques 2010–2016* (Arles: Actes Sud, 2017), 9.

8. Benkhaled and Vince, "Performing Algerianness," 243.

9. Kamel Daoud, *Ô Pharaon* (Oran: Editions Dar El Gharb, 2004).

10. Kamel Daoud, *La Préface du nègre* (Algiers: Editions Barzakh, 2008); *Le Minotaure 504* (Paris: Sabine Wespieser, 2011).

11. Hiddleston, *Writing After Postcolonialism*, 97.

12. Hiddleston, *Writing After Postcolonialism*, 116. The term "nègre" is widely used in French to describe a "ghostwriter," establishing a parallel between the invisible labour of the ghostwriter and that of enslaved or colonized Black subjects. Though common, its use has become increasingly controversial in France.

13. Hiddleston, *Writing After Postcolonialism*, 116.

14. In the original Algerian version of the text, the confusion between writer and fictional narrator is further stressed, as Haroun refers to the author of the offending piece of literature as *Albert* Meursault.

15. Daoud, *Meursault*, 15–16.

16. Daoud, *The Meursault Investigation*, 3–4.

17. Daoud, *Meursault*, 16; Daoud, *The Meursault Investigation*, 4.

18. Alice Kaplan, "'Meursault, contre-enquête' de Kamel Daoud," *Contreligne*, autumn 2015. http://www.contreligne.eu/2014/06/kamel-daoud-meursault-contre-en quete/#fn-4954-7

19. Daoud, *Meursault*, 68; Daoud, *The Meursault Investigation*, 47.

20. Daoud, *Meursault*, 14; Daoud, *The Meursault Investigation*, 2.

21. Lia Brozgal, "The Critical Pulse of the *Contre-enquête*: Kamel Daoud on the Maghrebi Novel in French," *Contemporary French and Francophone Studies* 20, no. 1 (2016), 39.

22. Daoud, *Meursault*, 74; Daoud, *The Meursault Investigation*, 52.

23. Daoud, *Meursault*, 79; Daoud, *The Meursault Investigation*, 57.

24. Daoud, *Meursault*, 105.

25. Daoud, *Meursault*, 109; Daoud, *The Meursault Investigation*, 79.

26. Harrison, *Postcolonial Criticism*, 79–81. Camus, *l'Etranger*, 9; Albert Camus, *The Outsider* trans. Sandra Smith (London: Penguin, 2012), 3.

27. Daoud, *Meursault*, 164; Daoud, *The Meursault Investigation*, 122.

28. Daoud, *Meursault*, 80; Daoud, *The Meursault Investigation*, 58.

29. Conor Cruise O'Brien, *Camus* (London: Fontana, 1970); Edward W. Said, "Albert Camus and the French imperial experience," in *Culture and Imperialism* (London: Vintage, 1994), 204–24.

30. Harrison, *Postcolonial Criticism*, 77.

31. Harrison, *Postcolonial Criticism*, 83. Others have read Camus's literary fiction as critically aware, especially as it moves from *L'Etranger*, published in 1942 to

the short stories in *L'Exil et le royaume* and *La Chute*, published in 1957 and 1956, respectively. See Colin Davis, "Camus, Encounters, Reading," in *Ethical Issues in Twentieth-Century French Fiction: Killing the Other* (Basingstoke: Macmillan Press, 2000), 64–85; see also, Colin Davis, "The Cost of Being Ethical: Fiction, Violence, and Altericide," *Common Knowledge* 9, no. 2 (2003), 241–53.

32. Said, *Culture and Imperialism*, 78–79; see also Harrison, *Postcolonial Criticism*.

33. Brozgal, "The Critical Pulse," 44.

34. Orlando, *The Algerian New Novel*, 295.

35. See chapter 1 for discussion of Mimouni and Boudjedra.

36. Amir Akef, "Un salafiste algérien émet une 'fatwa' contre Kamel Daoud," *Le Monde*, December 17, 2014. http://www.lemonde.fr/afrique/article/2014/12/17/un-salafiste-algerien-emet-une-fatwa-contre-kamel-daoud_4541882_3212.html

37. "Fausse polémique et vraie manipulation," *Algeria-Watch*, December 21, 2014. http://www.algeria-watch.org/fr/aw/hamadache_daoud.htm

38. Cited in Claire Devarrieux, "L'auteur Kamel Daoud visé par une fatwa. Un imam salafiste appelle au meurtre," *Libération Culture*, December 18, 2014, 25.

39. See François Menia, "Algérie: des artistes en quête de sécurité après la fatwa contre Kamel Daoud," *Le Figaro*, December 22, 2014. http://www.lefigaro.fr/livres/2014/12/22/03005-20141222ARTFIG00228-algerie-des-artistes-en-quete-de-securite-apres-la-fatwa-contre-kamel-daoud.php; Le HuffPost and AFP, "Kamel Daoud: une fatwa lancée contre l'écrivain déclenche l'indignation en Algérie," *Le Huffington Post*, December 17, 2014. http://www.huffingtonpost.fr/2014/12/17/kamel-daoud-fatwa-ecrivain-goncourt-meursault-contre-enquete-hamadache-ziraoui_n_6339970.html; Marion Cocquet, "Kamel Daoud sous le coup d'une fatwa," *Le Point.fr*, December 17, 2014. http://www.lepoint.fr/culture/kamel-daoud-sous-le-coup-d-une-fatwa-17-12-2014-1890421_3.php; see also Akef, "Un salafiste algérien."

40. For the Facebook post, see Le HuffPost and AFP, "Kamel Daoud"; see also, Sébastien Le Fol, "EXCLUSIF. Kamel Daoud: 'Mais pourquoi veut-il me tuer?,'" *Le Point.fr*, December 30, 2014. http://www.lepoint.fr/societe/exclusif-kamel-daoud-mais-pourquoi-veulent-ils-me-tuer-30-12-2014-1893138_23.php

41. See Meziane Abane, "L'écrivain Kamel Daoud gagne son procès contre un imam salafiste," *Le Monde*, March 8, 2016. http://www.lemonde.fr/afrique/article/2016/03/08/l-ecrivain-kamel-daoud-gagne-son-proces-contre-un-imam-salafiste_4878558_3212.html

42. Kamel Daoud, *Raïna Raïkoum: [chroniques]* (Oran: Dar El Gharb, 2002).

43. Daoud, *Mes indépendances*, 24, 121, 177; Kamel Daoud, *Chroniques: Selected Columns, 2010–2016*, trans. Elizabeth Zerofsky (New York: Other Press, 2018), 4, 85, 120.

44. James McAuley, "Why France Loves this Algerian Writer More than Algeria Does," *The Washington Post*, December 1, 2018. https://www.washingtonpost.com/world/europe/why-france-loves-this-algerian-writer-more-than-algeria-does/2018/12/01/d79f2807-8165-41c1-9b44-9c61ef6c974d_story.html

45. Noureddine Amara et al., "Nuit de Cologne: 'Kamel Daoud recycle les clichés orientalistes les plus éculés,'" *Le Monde*, February 11, 2016. http://www.lemonde.fr/idees/article/2016/02/11/les-fantasmes-de-kamel-daoud_4863096_3232.html

46. Kamel Daoud, "Cologne, lieu de fantasmes," *Le Monde*, January 31, 2016. http://www.lemonde.fr/idees/article/2016/01/31/cologne-lieu-de-fantasmes_4856694_3232.html

47. There were conflicting reports of what quickly became known as a series of (some claimed coordinated) "attacks" in Cologne and other cities across Germany. See "Cologne sex attacks: Women describe 'terrible' assaults," *BBC News*, January 7, 2016. http://www.bbc.com/news/world-europe-35250903. An initial lack of reporting of the incidents in the German press, on top of what was seen as an inadequate response by the police, led to accusations that the German "establishment" and "political elite" had tried to cover up the reported incidents for fear that they would have a negative effect on German chancellor Angela Merkel's liberal refugee policies; see, Gavin Hewitt, "Cologne attacks' profound impact on Europe," *BBC News*, January 11, 2016. http://www.bbc.com/news/world-europe-35261988. The sexual assaults in Cologne were also linked to other mass sexual assaults which had, for instance, taken place during and since protests related to the "Arab Spring" in Egypt in 2011. On this, see Patrick Kingsley, "80 sexual assaults in one day—the other story of Tahrir Square," *The Guardian*, July 5, 2015. http://www.theguardian.com/world/2013/jul/05/egypt-women-rape-sexual-assault-tahrir-square

48. Daoud, "Cologne, lieu de fantasmes."

49. Daoud, "Cologne, lieu de fantasmes."

50. Amara et al., "Nuit de Cologne."

51. Kamel Daoud, "The Sexual Misery of the Arab World," *The New York Times*, February 12, 2016. http://www.nytimes.com/2016/02/14/opinion/sunday/the-sexual-misery-of-the-arab-world.html

52. Adam Shatz, "The Daoud Affair," *LRB Online*, March 4, 2016. http://www.lrb.co.uk/2016/03/04/adam-shatz/the-daoud-affair

53. Daoud, "The Sexual Misery of the Arab World."

54. Adam Shatz, "Stranger Still," *The New York Times*, April 1, 2015. http://www.nytimes.com/2015/04/05/magazine/stranger-still.html; the letter and response were published in *Le Monde*; see "Kamel Daoud et les 'fantasmes' de Cologne, retour sur une polémique," *Le Monde*, February 20, 2016. http://www.lemonde.fr/idees/article/2016/02/20/kamel-daoud-et-les-fantasmes-de-cologne-retour-sur-une-polemique_4868849_3232.html

55. Shatz, "The Daoud Affair."

56. Fawzia Zouari, "Au nom de Kamel Daoud," *Libération*, February 28, 2016. http://www.liberation.fr/debats/2016/02/28/au-nom-de-kamel-daoud_1436364. There were other more vociferous attacks made on the collective of nineteen academics; Pascale Bruckner, for instance, coins the term "les fatwas de l'intelligentsia"; see "Défendons 'les libres-penseurs venus du monde musulman' contre les fatwas de l'intelligentsia," *Le Monde*, March 1, 2016. http://www.lemonde.fr/idees/article/2016/03/01/defendons-les-libres-penseurs-contre-les-fatwas-de-l-intelligentsia_4874077_3232.html

57. Benkhaled and Vince, "Performing Algerianness," 243.

58. Manuel Valls, "Soutenons Kamel Daoud!," *Facebook*, March 2, 2016. https://www.facebook.com/notes/manuel-valls/soutenons-kamel-daoud-/1002589256488085/

59. Gayatri Spivak, "Reading *The Satanic Verses*," *Public Culture* 2, no. 1 (1989), 79–99.

60. Daoud, *Mes indépendances*, 163; Daoud, *Chroniques*, 111.

61. Daoud, *Mes indépendances*, 163; Daoud, *Chroniques*, 112.

62. See Leperlier, *Algérie*, 94–107.

63. Benkhaled and Vince, "Performing Algerianness," 265.

64. See, for example, AFP, "L'Algérien Kamel Daoud lauréat du Goncourt du premier roman," *Le Point.fr*, May 5, 2015. http://www.lepoint.fr/culture/l-algerien-kamel-daoud-laureat-du-goncourt-du-premier-roman-05-05-2015-1926423_3.php; Philippe Douroux, "Goncourt de rattrapage pour Kamel Daoud," *Libération Culture*, May 6, 2015, 24. See also an earlier AFP report, "Kamel Daoud, dans la 'shortlist' du Goncourt, parle de l'Algérie au présent," *Le Point Culture*, October 28, 2014. https://www.lepoint.fr/culture/kamel-daoud-dans-la-shortlist-du-goncourt-parle-de-l-algerie-au-present-28-10-2014-1876463_3.php

65. Mohammed Aïssaoui, "L'hommage émouvant de Régis Debray à Kamel Daoud," *Le Figaro Culture Livres*, May 5, 2015. http://www.lefigaro.fr/livres/2015/05/05/03005-20150505ARTFIG00249-l-hommage-emouvant-de-regis-debray-a-kamel-daoud.php

66. Armelle Héliot, "Le fantoôme d'Albert Camus hante le festival d'Avignon," *Le Figaro*, July 22, 2015. http://www.lefigaro.fr/theatre/2015/07/22/03003-20150722ARTFIG00140-le-fantome-d-albert-camus-hante-le-festival-d-avignon.php

67. Gozlan, "Kamel Daoud," 64.

68. Julien Bisson, "Kamel Daoud et le désarroi de l'Algérie contemporaine," *Lire*, December 1, 2014, 12.

69. Benkhaled and Vince, "Performing Algerianness." See also McDougall, "Savage Wars?"

70. See "Kamel Daoud: 'Hamadache est instrumentalisé par les autorités pour me pousser à quitter l'Algérie,'" *Algérie Focus*, December 21, 2014. https://www.algerie-focus.com/2014/12/kamel-daoud-hamadache-est-instrumentalise-par-les-autorites-pour-me-pousser-a-quitter-lalgerie/

71. Daoud, "The Sexual Misery of the Arab World."

72. Claire Courbet, "Kamel Daoud: 'Le combat de Charlie Hebdo est aussi le mien,'" *Le Figaro*, January 12, 2015. http://www.lefigaro.fr/livres/2015/01/12/03005-20150112ARTFIG00246-kamel-daoud-le-combat-de-charlie-hebdo-est-aussi-le-mien.php

73. Alexandre Devecchio, "Kamel Daoud: 'pour gagner la guerre, il faut d'abord mener la bataille culturelle,'" *Le Figaro*, January 26, 2016. http://www.lefigaro.fr/vox/societe/2015/01/26/31003-20150126ARTFIG00330-kamel-daoud-pour-gagner-la-guerre-il-faut-d-abord-mener-la-bataille-culturelle.php

74. See my discussion in chapter 1.

75. Mundy, *Imaginative Geographies*.

76. Daoud, *The Meursault Investigation*, back cover.

77. Michiko Katutani, "Review: Kamel Daoud Interrogates Camus in 'The Meursault Investigation,'" *The New York Times*, May 28, 2015. http://www.nytimes

.com/2015/05/29/books/review-kamel-daoud-interrogates-camus-in-the-meursault-investigation.html

78. "Stranger and stranger," *The Economist*, May 30, 2015. http://www.economist.com/news/books-and-arts/21652251-biting-algerian-response-french-colonialism-stranger-and-stranger

79. James Campbell, "The Novelist as Murderer," *The Wall Street Journal*, May 29, 2015. http://www.wsj.com/articles/the-novelist-as-murderer-1432930737

80. Adam Gopnik, "The Next Thing," *The New Yorker*, January 26, 2016, 28. The relation between the French reception and marketing of Daoud's text, Houellebecq's *Soumission*, and Boualem Sansal's *2084* is not lost on some critics. See, for example, Nadia Ghanem, "Why Algerian Novelist Boualem Sansal's '2084' is a Sensation in France," *Arabic Literature (in English)*, October 6, 2015. http://arablit.org/2015/10/06/2084/

81. David Mills, "Camus condemned: a retelling of *L'Etranger* from the viewpoint of the murdered Algerian's brother is a tour de force," *The Sunday Times*, June 21, 2015, 39.

82. Shatz, "Stranger Still."

83. Referring to Théo D'Haen, Crowley shows how by capturing "historic and economic relationships of races and ethnicities" postcolonial narratives are privileged as lenses through which a certain "reality" can be depicted. Crowley, "Literatures in French Today," 418. See also Théo D'Haen, "World Literature, Postcolonial Politics, French-Caribbean Literature," in *Littératures francophones et politiques*, ed. Jean Bessière (Paris: Karthala, 2009), 64.

84. See Natalya Vince, "Literature as post-colonial reality? Kamel Daoud's *The Meursault Investigation*," *Fiction and Film for French Historians* 6, no. 4 (2016). http://h-france.net/fffh/maybe-missed/literature-as-post-colonial-reality-kamel-daouds-the-meursault-investigation/

85. Huggan, *The Postcolonial Exotic*, 29.

86. Harrison, "Who Needs an Idea of the Literary?," 7–8.

87. Harrison, "Who Needs an Idea of the Literary?," 13.

88. Orlando, *The Algerian New Novel*, 295, 287, 297.

89. Hiddleston, *Writing After Postcolonialism*, 13.

Chapter 5

Deconstructing Oppositional Criticism in Mustapha Benfodil's *Archéologie du chaos* (*amoureux*)

In her prizewinning book, *Your Fatwa Does Not Apply Here: Untold Stories from the Fight Against Muslim Fundamentalism*, the US-Algerian human rights lawyer and United Nations Special Rapporteur in the Field of Cultural Rights, Karima Bennoune presents the findings of several hundred interviews she conducted with artists, writers, journalists, and political activists across the Muslim world.[1] The daughter of the Algerian sociologist Mahfoud Bennoune (reportedly threatened in his classroom by one of the leaders of the FIS), Karima Bennoune begins her book with the alarming story of unknown assailants banging at the door of her father's apartment in Algiers. Coupled with an epilogue taken from Tahar Djaout's *Le dernier été de la raison* (1999) [*The Last Summer of Reason* (2007)], that tells of the fictional Boualem Yekker's resistance to a rising fundamentalism, Bennoune's book takes the Black Decade as the definitive starting point for recounting the stories of those threatened by Islamic fundamentalism.[2]

In an encounter with the Algerian journalist, writer, and political activist, Mustapha Benfodil, Bennoune writes about the violence he endured during the Black Decade, describing the "Islamist onslaught" faced by journalists, as well as the State censure of artists and writers, including Benfodil.[3] However, the polarizing and invidious discourse Bennoune's book both suggests and reiterates obscures Benfodil's complex literary response to the dominant conflict narrative of the Black Decade. By seeking to pit Algerian journalists and writers, such as Djaout and Benfodil, against "the rising tide of armed extremism," Bennoune imagines them, and their literary work, to take a firmly oppositional stance.[4] The reality is that both Djaout and Benfodil—along with many of the writers explored in the preceding chapters of this book—engage with recent history in a far more layered and deconstructive manner.[5]

In this chapter, I take Benfodil's landmark 2007 novel, *Archéologie du chaos [amoureux]* [Archeology of chaos (lovers)], as an example of how the writer develops avant-garde practices to move beyond the polarized conflict narrative of the Black Decade.[6] In so doing, I argue that reductive and polarizing narratives of power, of the kind we have seen throughout this book, have become subject to intensified scrutiny by Algerian artists and writers. Rather than replicate the binary discursive frameworks that many critics have deployed to understand Algerian literature (and in turn Algeria), I show how Benfodil's novel deconstructs dominant narratives of power upon which writers, publishers, critics, and Algerian citizens have relied for many years.

BETWEEN POLITICS AND AESTHETICS

Benfodil's *raison d'être* as a writer, artist, and political activist has, it would seem, always been to outplay and outdo dominant discursive frames. Difficult to describe as a novelist, journalist, playwright, or even simply a writer, Benfodil's work might best be described as existing between forms. Trained initially in mathematics, Benfodil switched to studying journalism at the beginning of the 1990s. In 1993, he was awarded the Prix spécial du jury aux 3e Poésiades de Bejaïa [Judge's Prize of the 3rd Annual Poetry Competition of Bejaïa] for the poem "À la santé de la République" [To the Health of the Republic], written in memory of the recently assassinated Djaout.[7] It was not until 2000 that his first novel, *Zarta! [The Deserter]*, was published as part of the initial releases by the newly established Algerian publishing house, Editions Barzakh.[8] After the publication of his first novel, Benfodil wrote several plays for the theater company Gare au Théâtre, based in Vitry-sur-Seine. In 2003, his second novel, *Les Bavardages du Seul [Mutterings of the Self]* was published, again by Barzakh, and was, in 2004, awarded the Prix du meilleur roman algérien [Prize for the Best Algerian Novel].[9] Also in 2003, Editions Casbah published *Les six derniers jours de Baghdad: journal d'un voyage de guerre [The Final Six Days of Baghdad: A War Diary]*, a short book collecting Benfodil's reports of a trip to Iraq made after the US-led invasion and just before the fall of the capital city to coalition forces.[10] Benfodil's *Archéologie* was published by Barzakh in 2007 and released in France in 2012 by the Marseille publisher, Al Dante. His most recent works include *Cocktail Kafkaïne*, a bilingual (English-French) volume of poems, and the novel *Body Writing*, both published in 2018.[11] Since the publication of *Archéologie*, Benfodil has taken to the streets to read passages from his work in various semi-informal performances, named "Lectures sauvages" [Wild Readings].[12] This multimodal dissemination, which some have viewed as the writer bringing the aesthetic into "collision" with the political, has attracted the attention of the Algerian authorities.[13] Even if the extent to which these practices can be deemed transformational remains to be seen, Benfodil is rare in our corpus in that the writer puts his body on the line in an attempt to bridge the gap between politics and literature.[14]

The writer's spontaneous readings are not the only occasion he has caused political controversy. In 2011, an art installation by Benfodil, entitled *Maportaliche/It Has No Importance*, which was exhibited at the Sharjah Biennial in the United Arab Emirates, was removed and the show's director was dismissed for allowing what the authorities saw as an offensive piece of work to be exhibited.[15] Written on a T-shirt worn by one of the mannequins which made up the installation was a graphic testimony of a woman who had been raped in Algeria during the violence of the 1990s. According to Bennoune, by citing the voices of the victims of the violence of the Black Decade, the installation was a form of journalism and had been misunderstood by those offended by the work.[16] However, as Benfodil himself articulated in a blog entry at the time, while the account was based in reality, it had already been performed in one of his previous plays. Rather than make claims to its journalistic or testimonial status, the author defends his work on the basis that "art is free to be impolite and impertinent."[17] At the center of Benfodil's artistic and literary expression is an effort to "provoke" the authorities through his use of obscenity, luring them into an explicitly theatrical space, demonstrating how they too maintain a shared performance of power.[18] In the attempt to frame art as a form of journalistic testimony, Bennoune reveals, as does the broader project of her book, an expectation she has of writers who have lived through a period of polarized conflict such as the Black Decade. If Bennoune's aim is to "[tell] the stories of those who have [. . .] faced the fire to battle extremism," her book asks very few questions about the complex political roots of fundamentalist violence and does little to acknowledge the invidious frame through which she articulates her interviewees' experiences.[19]

Whereas Bennoune's book breaks down the boundaries between art and journalism to seemingly write her own veiled testimony of the Black Decade, Benfodil's work playfully explores the lines between literature and journalism, obliquely casting his gaze back to the way testimonies of the Black Decade were framed and sold. *Zarta!*, written "sous les drapeaux" [under the sheets] while the author carried out his training for military service between August 1997 and February 1998, charts the journey of a journalist named Zen who secretly writes a column, "Conneriques" [Bullshit columns], while embedded in the Algerian army.[20] After Zen declares his desire to desert, his commanding officers imprison him deep in the Algerian desert and fake his death; his sole friend is a scorpion named Sheherayar to whom he recounts his story of his time in the "caserne" [barracks].[21] The novel tells a highly caricatured and unlikely story of the narrator's life, from the first-person account of the scorpion to a third-person account we are given of Zen once he returns to Algiers after being released from his internment. Changing perspective throughout, the narrative produces highly implausible scenarios. But the novel is also an unforgiving caricature of Algerian society, as well as a seeming parody of the kinds of commercialized testimonial literature that we discussed in the introduction and chapter 1. Zen writes a novel within the novel, also called *Zarta*, that is released in France during the 1990s under the title, *Le dernier cri de Z.B. avant son assassinat* [*The Final Scream of Z.B. Before his Assassination*], making its author a celebrity in France after the novel featured on the front page of *Paris Match*. While some might easily identify the mediatized trajectory of writers such as Mimouni, Boudjedra, and even Daoud in the above account, Benfodil might be accused of creating an overly homogenous or generalized image of Algerian literature produced during the 1990s, ignoring the more self-conscious uses of testimonial writing by the likes of Assia Djebar, Maïssa Bey, and Salim Bachi.

If *Zarta!* shows Benfodil adopting his own form of opposition to a body of testimonial literature produced during the 1990s, then his later novels show more explicit awareness of the dangers of homogenous classifications and the way in which writers, publishers, and commentators are complicit in perpetuating such generalizations. For Benfodil it is vital to stress that writers, publishers, and critics possess a degree of power to make aesthetic judgments and to have those views published in a potentially prominent space, but the author also seeks to show how the forces of the State are themselves complicit in imagining an "aesthetic regime" of power.[22] Indeed, unveiling the *performative* relationality between State and citizen is central to Benfodil's own experimental aesthetic and his desire to deconstruct forms of oppositional discourse that serve ultimately to reinforce the political status quo.

DECONSTRUCTING OPPOSITION: *ARCHÉOLOGIE DU CHAOS [AMOUREUX]*

In its reference to Michel Foucault's archaeological method, *Archéologie* interrogates what one might call the *épistème* of political contestation in contemporary Algeria—and the specific ways in which various narratives of the Black Decade have been shaped.[23] The deconstructive, fragmented, and frequently grotesque text studies in a far more overt and self-conscious manner the epistemological function of literature, as well as addresses the question of literature's place in the shared performance of power in contemporary Algerian society. If Benfodil challenges a testimonial literature that came to homogenize and regularize what many now understand as reductive narratives of the Black Decade, his work also highlights the failures of artists, writers, and protest groups to meaningfully contest the dominant spectacle of power in Algeria. In so doing, Benfodil deconstructs dominant narratives of opposition in contemporary Algeria and, in his performative practice, attempts to break out of the "zombified" state of discourse which had come to characterize post-1990s Algerian politics.[24]

While the new president, Abdelaziz Bouteflika, came to power with the promise of bringing an "end" to the violence of the Black Decade, he also presided over the creation of a series of laws that sought to take control of the conflict narrative of the 1990s. By deploying the language of the theater to frame the crisis years of the Black Decade, referring to the 1990s as a "tragédie nationale" [national tragedy], the authors of the Charter for Peace and National Reconciliation appeared to attribute a significant restorative power to the aesthetic—and, indeed, revealed the importance of what they saw as a performative relationality between the State and citizen.[25] This use of the theatrical lexis was telling not only of the Bouteflika government's reliance on the aesthetic but also of the way in which the State would continue to construct and consecrate its identity in an invisible dialogue with citizens and outside observers who increasingly relied upon the obfuscatory and nebulous tropes of *le pouvoir* or the "regime."[26]

Ever since the president became ill in 2005, rumors have circulated about his health. After suffering a stroke in 2013, the president was largely kept away from the public eye. Barely able to speak, he was infrequently aired on national television. In one broadcast, postproduction editing was required to give the appearance of the president constructing a coherent sentence, with the poorly executed cuts clearly visible to viewers.[27] If the mute and immobile president appeared to outsiders as encapsulating the "zombified" State, Algerians had become increasingly accustomed to this hastily cobbled together staging of Bouteflika and thereby increasingly aware that this "zombification" extended beyond the figure of the president and his immediate entourage.[28] Here, *le pouvoir* is understood as a broad group of politicians, military figures, and technocrats—including those involved in running State television.[29] Until the massive popular protests of the Hirak took hold in Algeria during the first months of 2019, this highly obscure and imprecise vision of the "regime" was where many Algerians' understanding of the "zombified" State ended (whether that was by conscious choice or unconscious coercion). Since Bouteflika was forced to step down in April 2019—and the arrest of many of the business people associated with his inner circle—the literal unraveling of the regime has allowed citizens to begin to dig beneath the *aesthetic* regime of power it relied upon in the years since the end of the Black Decade. It is, therefore, important that we understand the downfall of the president and his entourage as rooted in a longer history of artistic and literary activity that has deployed aesthetics to deconstruct the layers and languages of power in Algeria.[30]

Told through a series of "nested fictions," Benfodil's novel presents a sequence of interlocking and overlapping narratives, reflective of the obscure and frequently confusing state of discourse in Algeria.[31] The first layer of *Archéologie* is a fictional account of the life of Yacine Nabolci and his gang of fellow revolutionaries recounted in a book that is in the process of being written by its author Marwan K., whose own story we uncover in a series of diary entries that intersperse the text. After being killed in mysterious circumstances, Marwan's unfinished book is left for the reader to discover, before being made the center of a police investigation into the author's disappearance, conducted by the aging detective, Kamel El Afrite. Together with the inspector's notes, that make up the final third of Benfodil's text, is a manifesto discovered on the body of the writer—a manifesto that also features within Nabolci's story. In line with the archaeological method suggested in the book's title, the reader must progressively unearth and order the different layers of the story in their own narrative of the disjointed events. By publishing the unreliable notes of El Afrite, the reader is invited to make their own inquiries into the death of Marwan and the status of the literary text and manifesto found alongside his corpse.[32]

Not only is Benfodil's text a commentary on the worn-out realism of Algerian literature—and perhaps especially on the contestatory potential attributed to realist narratives more generally—it is at the same time a disjointed and fragmented account of the traumas of the Black Decade, as experienced by writers such as Marwan.[33] Inviting readers to write their own story of the death of the author is not simply a playful gesture toward Roland Barthes's famous essay; rather, Benfodil uses the intertext to pass commentary on the way in which Algerian literary texts were subjected to reductive readings throughout the Black Decade.[34] For Benfodil, Barthes's injunction to forget the author is both useful, in terms of reminding readers of the essential ambivalence of literary texts and problematic in that disregarding the author entirely would risk isolating the text from the political and social context of its production.[35] To comprehend the kind of work Benfodil wishes his text to do, we must remain conscious of its double-edged and sometimes contradictory nature. While the text is a pastiche of revolutionary groups who fail to understand power as part of a shared performance, Benfodil's own performative practice is aimed at disrupting the dominant spectacle of power that determines the outer limits of resistance and accommodation in contemporary Algeria.

Marwan's book begins with the story of the young and ambitious Nabolci, a revolutionary dreamer living in Algeria during the 1990s and key member of AGIR (the "Avant-Garde Intellectuelle Révolutionnaire" [Revolutionary Intellectual Avant-Garde]), a group of political activists whose aim is to "agir contre l'ordre narratif dominant'" [act against the "dominant narrative order"].[36] Benfodil's pastiche becomes increasingly clear as the other members of the group combine the names of their "gurus" and "griots" to make up their *noms de guerre*, Jamel Derrida, V'Laïd Navokov, Omar Rimbaud, Adlène Luis Borgès.[37] Transformed into the CIFS ("le Commando d'Insémination des Filles du Système" [The Commando for the Insemination of the Daughters of the System]), the principal mission of the group becomes to seduce and impregnate the daughters of a notorious elite of Algerian generals.[38] In a further iteration, the revolutionaries declare themselves to be a group of "Anartistes," whose aim is to "déconstruire l'ordre narratif national" [deconstruct the national narrative order] and whose doctrine is spelled out in the "Manifeste du Chkoupisme" discovered on the author's corpse and printed at the end of Benfodil's text—but also, of course, a diegetic object within the fictional tale.[39] The group initially espouses simplistic binary tropes of opposition, such as "la place naturelle de l'intellectuel est dans l'opposition" [the natural place of the intellectual is in opposition] and "il faut une oppsosition armée pour faire repartir ce régime" [we need an armed opposition to split this regime]; they also identify the elaborate apparatus of the State with the metonym "système," thereby reinforcing the obscurity and nebulous nature of their opposition.[40]

The manifesto is a clear pastiche of the contestatory stance of the young revolutionaries staged in Marwan's text. The term "Chkoupisme," which forms part of the title of the manifesto, hints at the stupidity and presumed failure of the demands being made within the political tract. Originating from the Algerian Arabic term for sea algae (foam, froth, or scum), "Choupki" refers to something that is rotten, lousy, or "fucked," to use a more vulgar terminology. The "Manifeste du Chkoupisme" might thus be translated as something akin to a "Manifesto of Rottenness" or a "Manifesto of Fuckery." As the tract progresses, however, its statements become at once more bizarre and more reflective of the deconstructive vision Benfodil has for the novel beyond the bounds of the written text:

> Il faut émouvoir, frapper, étonner, surprendre [. . .] faire entendre notre voix dans la Cité! [. . .] Il faut un théâtre-vérité. Pousser le happening à l'extrême. Produire un hyperréalisme de choc où chacun jouera son propre rôle. Il faut recruter les personnages dans la salle. [. . .] Il faut un changement qui s'opérerait comme une frappe chirurgicale, radicale, pour affranchir la société des tenailles du système. [. . .] Derrida avait fait de la déconstruction un paradigme de lecture. Nous faisons de la déconstruction un style de combat.[41]

> [We need to disturb, to strike, to surprise, to catch of guard (. . .) to make our voices heard in the City! (. . .) We need a theater-truth. To push audience participation to the extreme. To produce a hyperrealism of shock where everyone plays their own role. We must recruit the characters in the room. (. . .) We need a change that would act like a radical surgical strike to free society from the

pincers of the system. (. . .) Derrida made deconstruction a paradigm of reading. We make deconstruction a style of combat.]

In stressing the need to "deconstruct" the dominant spectacle of Algerian power, as well as morphing textual deconstruction into a "style de combat," the manifesto reaches well beyond the fictional tale or pastiche and serves as a rallying call to its Algerian readers. Further noting how literature has become a "fonctionnaire de la colère" [functionary of anger], subsumed within the existing spectacle of power, the manifesto stresses the limitations of all forms of language that risk being co-opted into the realms of the "langue officielle" [official language] or, its more widespread double, the "langue de bois" [waffle or doublespeak].[42]

Just as Daoud uses a diegetic reader to criticize the overly reductive reading practices of his Algerian protagonist, Benfodil deploys the figure of the literary "enquêteur" [investigator] to expose the "langue de bois" in the character of the detective, El Afrite, whose notes populate the final third of *Archéologie*. By replaying the story of the author through the eyes of the confused detective, the reader is invited to finally piece together Marwan and Nabolci's stories. Endlessly perplexed by the manuscript, and keen to treat the fictional story as material evidence in the death of its author, El Afrite decides to consult a literary professor friend, who reads the phallic symbols in Marwan's drawings and his constant references to an obscure "IL" as proof of his repressed homosexuality.[43] Ultimately, the detective uncovers the real identity of the elusive "IL"—these are the initials of Marwan's cousin, Ishtar Lahoud.[44] As Corbin Treacy stresses, El Afrite's efforts to unpick the complex layers of the text are reflective of the "slow and circuitous process" of "[d]econstructing the dominant narrative in Algeria."[45] Much like Daoud with his protagonist Haroun, Benfodil stages the complicated practice of learning to read literary texts, or narratives more generally; meanwhile, El Afrite's professor friend is ridiculed for his simplistic reading of the novel.

If El Afrite's reading allows him to glean an increasingly more nuanced interpretation of the facts, the inflexible framework of the police inquiry still takes the fictional text as its factual lens. In a passage which both ridicules the detective's investigative skills and reinforces the pastiche of the contestatory power of literature, El Afrite concludes that Marwan died after writing too much, too quickly:

Il était lancé dans une course effrénée contre la montre. Contre la mort [. . .] Et son cœur s'est arrêté sur une virgule. Arrêt cardiaque littéraire. Une virgule-précipice. Overdose littéraire. / Il avait trop écrit cette nuit-là. Il avait éprouvé jusqu'à l'épuisement de son pauvre cœur, sa mémoire tortueuse et son âme torturée. . . Il avait soulevé trop de couvercles, avalé trop de couleuvres, sorti trop de cadavres des placards... / Il avait écrit comme un forçat. Comme un forcené. / Il le disait lui-même: écrire tue.[46]

[He was in a frantic race against the clock. Against death (...) And his heart stopped on a comma. A literary cardiac arrest. A comma-on-the-precipice. Literary overdose. / He had written too much that night. He had continued to the point of the exhaustion of his poor heart, his tortuous memory and tortured soul.... He had lifted too many lids, swallowed too many insults, removed too many skeletons from the closet... / He had written like a slave. Like a madman. / He said it himself: writing kills.]

If the above passage is a tongue-in-cheek representation of the torturous process of writing, it is also a parody of the approach El Afrite takes to reading Marwan's text, ultimately framing it as an evidential account of the author's plight. The parody perhaps also extends to the way in which testimonial literature—and Algerian writing more generally—has been received by readers, journalists, and academic critics both during and since the end of the 1990s. Even if this passage might be read as a serious attempt to use a new fragmented literary form to rearticulate the traumatic events of the 1990s in their chaotic and incomplete nature, Benfodil's shift away from realism and toward a more experimental form is part of his desire to deconstruct the oppositional discourse that helps maintain the dominant spectacle of power in Algeria.

In both its textual form and extratextual performances, Benfodil's novel begins to broach the possibility of a new discourse, whose material outcome is far less certain. If the State seeks to co-opt its subjects in the ratification of its own obscurity, the instability of the State's idea of itself at the same time "enables the postcolonized subject to mobilize fluctuating and mobile subject-positions."[47] In moving beyond realist representation, and by deconstructing the performative relations of power in contemporary Algeria, Benfodil's novel both registers an increasing political awareness among citizens and draws the reader's attention toward the failure of the kinds of oppositional discourse articulated by groups such as AGIR and the CIFS. Benfodil's deconstructive style becomes increasingly evident with the development of the "Anartistes" and the "Manifeste du Chkoupisme," as the writer begins to gesture beyond the bounds of the written text.

"WILD READINGS"

In the wake of the publication of his *Archéologie* and in a seeming effort to deny the bounded nature of the text, Benfodil organized several unauthorized street readings in and around Algiers, which he entitled: "pièces détachées—lectures sauvages" [detached plays—wild readings].[48] These events were mirrored in Paris, where sections of the author's (and others') work were read aloud.[49] In and around Algiers, such public displays of dissent were met with increasing repression by the police. Benfodil's "lecture sauvage" at Tipasa, a town situated to the west of Algiers, led to his arrest and detention at a local police station.[50] In a television interview shown in 2003, the interviewer asks Benfodil who exactly he thinks reads his writing. He responds, after a pause, "personne" [nobody].[51] While words on the page may only work to unsettle the "ordre narratif dominant" within the bounds of the text, they offer no effective challenge to the dominant spectacle of power; it has, rather, been the performance of words beyond the text, the threat of their discursive and public enunciation, which has most unsettled the authorities tasked with policing the limits of the "shared language of power" in contemporary Algeria.[52]

In 2014, Benfodil recounts how he cofounded the group of political activists "Barakat!" ("Enough!," in Algerian Arabic) in opposition to the ailing Bouteflika running for a fourth term as president.[53] In his article, Benfodil explains the beginnings of his "wild readings" and the founding of the group which preceded "Barakat!," "Bezzzef" (along with Daoud and two other writers, Chawki Amari and Adlène Meddi). The author recounts how other groups came together to launch spontaneous artistic protests in the streets of Algiers in the run-up to the presidential elections in 2014. The group "Clacc" (the "Comité pour la libération de l'action culturelle et citoyenne" [Committee for the Liberation of Cultural and Civic Action]) organized spontaneous concerts in the space outside the Grande Poste in central Algiers; the group, Benfodil explains, was founded by Amazigh Kateb (the son of the celebrated Kateb Yacine) and Rihab Alloula (the daughter of Abdelkader Alloula, a playwright assassinated in 1994)—significant, perhaps, in the way the sons and daughters of more explicitly contestatory Algerian writers articulate less structured, more deconstructive modes of resistance. He also describes how in one of the first "wild readings" at the Salon international du livre (SILA) [International Book Fair], the group denounced the censorship of Mehdi El Djazaïri's novel, *Poutakhine*, which had been deemed to insult the president, inventing their very own pastiche "Prix de la Censure" [Prize for Censored Literature].[54] The main idea of the "wild readings," as Benfodil explains, was for the writer to simply read aloud fragments of his own work in public spaces; however, the embodied experience of the performances surprised even Benfodil:

> Depuis les Lectures sauvages, mon rapport à la Cité, à ma ville, Alger, à l'espace public, a complètement changé. Avant, j'étais dans un autre type de contrat avec ma société: j'écrivais comme on écrit des messages de détresse qu'on met dans une bouteille, et qu'on jette à la mer. [. . .] comme auteur, j'étais davantage

dans le schéma qui consistait à dire que l'écrivain est avant tout ses livres, et mes livres s'en sont trouvés chargés—ma littérature surtout—de tous ces cris que je n'arrivais pas à sortir. Mais à partir du moment où j'ai sorti mes textes pour leur faire "prendre l'air" (Léo Ferré, *Les Poètes*), j'ai commencé à écrire un autre texte, tout à fait inédit. Un texte écrit avec les cris et les trottoirs de ma ville. Depuis, mon regard sur ma "fonction," sur mon "status" d'écrivain, a été totalement chambardé. Je découvrais que des flics pouvaient m'embraquer juste parce que je déclamais de la poésie dans la rue. Oui, me faire embarquer juste parce que ma parole n'était plus confinée, emprisonnée dans un livre, dans une librairie ou une bibliothèque, mais qu'elle était incarnée, portée par un corps. Un corps qui dépassait désormais mes frontières organiques.[55]

[Since the Wild Readings, my relationship to the city, to my town, Algiers, to the public space, has completely changed. Before, I had a different sort of contract with my society: it was as if I was writing messages in bottles and throwing them out to sea. (. . .) as an author, I was viewed within a certain frame, seen as a writer who is before anything else his books, and my books—my literature in particular—were full of the cries that I couldn't let out. But from the moment I took my texts outside, to allow them to "breathe the air," I began to write a different, totally new text. This was a text written with the cries and sidewalks of my town. Since the Wild Readings, my understanding of my "function" and "status" as a writer has been turned upside-down. I discovered how the police were able to arrest me just for reciting poetry in the street. Yes, to detain me simply because my words were no longer confined, imprisoned in a book, a bookshop or a library, but rather my speech was performed, carried by a body. A body that would from now on exist beyond its own natural limits.]

As others came together under the banner of "Barakat!," Benfodil notes how his writing no longer felt like a "soliloque pathétique" [pathetic soliloquy], but was rather a "petite note dans une partition chorale. Une partition libertaire" [a small note in a choral score. A liberatory score].[56] In the way its language is embodied and carried in speech, Benfodil's novel pushes the boundaries of its own textuality in a deconstructive space which makes "Anartistes" of the readers who perform the text. If, on one level, the "wild readings" enact what, in *L'Archéologie du savoir*, Foucault names the "fonction énonciative" [enunciative function] of discourse, where with each reading a new meaning and political resonance of the text will emerge, the practice of reading aloud also tapped into something the authorities could not abide.[57]

Placed under arrest for performing readings in the streets, Benfodil came to understand Rancière's insight that "politics is the process of reconfiguring the ways in which subjects are heard and seen."[58] The "wild readings" were no longer dismissed as mere "noise," but counted as a viable and potentially threatening form of "speech" in an otherwise strictly policed discursive realm.[59] In launching the street performances, Benfodil was decoding a previously obscured political "aesthetics" and revealing this for citizens and commentators to see. In other words, he had diverted from an expected form of "dialogue"—a form that no longer maintained the "fantasy" of an impenetrable and nebulous "regime."[60]

Even within the body of Benfodil's 2007 text, there are signs that the language is beginning to break out of the typeface, with sketches, graffiti, and Arabic script. The text more generally is often interrupted, broken up, and peppered with poetry and lyrics, switching suddenly from direct to indirect speech or from the perspective of Nabolci to that of his author, Marwan. To attempt to read *Archéologie* is something of an undertaking in itself. Some of the more obvious deviations from the classic typed manuscript recall what Dina Al-Kassim terms the "calligraphic trope," which she claims challenges both "rhetorical discourses of the Arabo-Islamic tradition" and "the equally blinkered versions of modernity and history apparent in the rhetoric of the modern postcolonial State."[61] Of course, Al-Kassim's vision sets up yet another binary opposition between the "modern" State and the so-called "traditions" of Islam.[62] Nonetheless, these calligraphic experimentations anticipate the "wild readings," encouraging the reader to read aloud sections of the kaleidoscopic text or poetry. As Benfodil himself puts it, this is also a transgressive linguistic experimentation:

> Quand j'écris, j'invente une langue—même la langue française, je transgresse la grammaire, la syntaxe, les mots—après, oui, je suis dans cette famille de la langue française, mais c'est une langue que j'approprie à plusieurs niveaux. J'approprie en réinventant sa grammaire, donc je suis dans une autre grammaire; et puis c'est cette démarche qui consiste à intégrer dans le corps de la langue dominante des langues périphériques.[63]

> [When I write, I invent a new language—even in French, I transgress the grammar, the syntax, the words—thereafter, yes, I am in the family of the French language, but it's a language that I appropriate on multiple levels. I appropriate it by reinventing its grammar, so I am in another grammar; this is the process of integrating peripheral languages into the body of the dominant language.]

This incorporation of "des langues périphériques" within the body of a dominant language will remind us that the writer can never seek a simple escape from language, but, as Benfodil describes, must always project one through another. On one level, the author is clearly attempting to resolve the question of using French, stressing the way he integrates the once dominant colonial language into a multilingual grammar of a new language; but Benfodil also appears to capture Abdelkébir Khatibi's deconstruction of the notion of monolingualism. If, as Khatibi argues, there is "no such thing as absolute monolingualism," then one cannot understand bilingual writers as simply switching between the monolingual languages of French and Arabic. Transfiguring the common notion of "bilingualism" into the "bi-langue"— a kind of "double(d) tongue"—Khatibi stresses the way the Maghrebian writer or citizen speaks in multiple languages *at once*.[64] As Réda Bensmaïa has written of this notion of the "bi-langue," the question for Khatibi is not whether to write in one or the other language (Arabic or French): "Rather the point is to make visible another (infraliminal) level of writing *and thinking* that renders the dualistic opposition that has dominated Maghrebi literary production completely obsolete."[65] If we view this linguistic experimentation to prefigure Benfodil's multimodal performances, then perhaps the spoken language, the "bi-langue" of the street, presents the author with another way of deconstructing the kinds of "thinking" that reproduce limiting narrative frames. Here, Benfodil's performative practice doesn't simply challenge the imposed monolingualisms of colonial French, or indeed the Modern Standard Arabic of postindependence, but rather intersects and transforms the very binary discourse that would seek to pit one language against the other. If an obvious solution to breaking away from the dominant languages of French or Arabic might be found in the spoken language of *Darija*, or Algerian dialect, Benfodil never proposes a clear resolution to what he presents as an endless process of reinvention.

In the latest version of Mbembe's landmark essay, republished in his 2001 book *On the Postcolony*, the process of the rising of the masses, and of the demystification of the postcolonial *commandement*, is described in terms of the creation of "potholes of indiscipline on which the commandement may stub its toe."[66] Mbembe is highly skeptical about the possibility of inflicting violence on the material base of the *commandement*. And this may well hold true for Benfodil's novel and performances, which some critics have viewed as representative of a new "phase" of "revolutionary aesthetics" in Algeria.[67] However, the image of the pothole offers the prospect of a slightly different process of moving beyond political stagnation. Potholes are continually, but often unsatisfactorily, "patched up" or "filled in" by the authorities; they are irritating and therefore highly visible to the general population, but they are small and insignificant cracks in the road to the authorities or State.[68] Even though the "regime" clearly maintains a monopoly on violence (and this is reflected by the mysterious disappearance of the writer, Marwan, or the continued arrests of journalists and activists during the 2019 Hirak), there is always the possibility of a discursive recuperation of life through literature, or of the written text through performance.[69] This gives us hope, but it also affirms the imperative to chip away at the cracks in the road more quickly than the authorities can fill them in. If Benfodil's novel (and the failure of effective resistance within its pages) might initially reaffirm a degree of skepticism toward the contestatory power of the aesthetic, Benfodil's performances show how literature—and aesthetic interventions more generally—at the very least *begin* to deconstruct the spectacle of power, unveiling the "regime of unreality" and the manipulation and weaponization of the aesthetic that, as we see in the case of Algeria, remains *at the core of* the political.[70]

If writers like Benfodil set out to deconstruct the multilayered and complex languages of accommodation and resistance in contemporary Algeria, journalists and academic critics have played a crucial role in "packaging" Algerian writers in overly simplistic ways. Though not explicitly a work of literary criticism, Bennoune's *Your Fatwa Does Not Apply Here* appropriates literary texts and writers to advance factual understandings of Islam and secular opposition to it around the world. Although Bennoune admits she "cannot speak for" her interviewees, the interview-based approach nevertheless makes writers spokespeople for their compatriots.[71] And, even while Bennoune rejects Huntington's hypothesis of the post–Cold War clash of civilizations being played out between secularism and religion, the lawyer reproduces Huntington's polarizing language, as well as reductive understandings of a whole range of distinct conflicts, by reimagining "clashes *within* civilizations [. . .] between fundamentalists and their opponents everywhere."[72] By adopting such an encompassing framework, Bennoune's text universalizes experiences of violence that are distinct from specific moments of conflict. Like the popular reception of Daoud, Bennoune replicates binary "types" of contemporary Algerian identity, as her experiences of Islam during the polarized context of the Black Decade determine her presentation of an Islamist-secularist divide across the Muslim world.[73]

While Benfodil's experiences during the Black Decade influence both the writing of *Archéolgie* and his performative practice on the streets of Algiers, the text at the same time warns readers and commentators about their complicity in producing binary frameworks to conceive of the relations between "ruler" and "ruled," the all-powerful State and a downtrodden "revolutionary" avant-garde. Readers are thus encouraged to examine the more complicated configurations of, and opposition to, power in contemporary Algeria and to delve beneath the surface spectacle of the (supposedly) "zombified" State.

NOTES

1. Karima Bennoune, *Your Fatwa Does Not Apply Here: Untold Stories from the Fight Against Muslim Fundamentalism* (New York: W.W. Norton & Company, 2013).

2. Tahar Djaout, *Le dernier été de la raison* (Paris: Seuil, 1999); Tahar Djaout, *The Last Summer of Reason*, trans. Marjolijn de Jager (Lincoln: University of Nebraska Press, 2007).

3. Bennoune, *Your Fatwa*, 131–35.

4. Bennoune, *Your Fatwa*, 2.

5. For further discussion of Djaout's work, see Jane Hiddleston, "Rewriting Algeria, Past and Present: History and Cultural Politics in Two Novels by Tahar Djaout," in *The Fiction of History*, ed. Alexander Lyon Macfie (New York: Routledge, 2015), 149–61.

6. Mustapha Benfodil, *Archéologie du chaos [amoureux]* (Algiers: Barzakh, 2007/Marseille: Al Dante, 2012). Page references are to the Algerian edition, which is subsequently referred to in the body of the text as *Archéolgie*.

7. For a comparison of the two writers, see Mary Anne Lewis Cusato, "From Tahar Djaout's 'No' to Mustapha Benfodil's 'Enough!': Two Moments of Revolutionary Aesthetics in Contemporary Algerian Literature and Cultural Activism," *Expressions maghrébines* 17, no. 1 (2018), 103–17.

8. Mustapha Benfodil, *Zarta!* (Algiers: Barzakh, 2000). The title emerges from a mixture between the Algerian and French terms for "to desert."

9. Mustapha Benfodil, *Les Bavardages du Seul* (Algiers: Barzakh, 2003).

10. Mustapha Benfodil, *Les six derniers jours de Baghdad: journal d'un voyage de guerre* (Algiers: Casbah, 2003).

11. Mustapha Benfodil, *Cocktail Kafkaïne [Dark Poems]*, trans. Joe Ford (Bristol: Hesterglock Press, 2018); Mustapha Benfodil, *Body Writing* (Algiers: Barzakh, 2018), published in France with the title *Alger, journal intense* (Paris: Editions Macula, 2019).

12. Mustapha Benfodil, "Cherche flic pour lecture citoyenne à Tipaza . . . ," *El Watan*, August 16, 2009. https://www.djazairess.com/fr/elwatan/134732. Prior to this, in 2005, Benfodil had conducted a series of interviews published in a multimodal volume entitled *Alger nooormal*. The book, which is a photo-cum-music text, begins with a series of photographs of the city of Algiers taken by Jean-Pierre Vallorani and culminates in the interviews coordinated by Benfodil. Sound recordings of the city, music, and further interviews are included in the accompanying CD. See, Mohamed Ali Allalou and Aziz Smati (eds.), *Alger nooormal* (Paris: Françoise Truffaut Editions, 2005).

13. Treacy, "Writing in the Aftermath," 128.

14. The peaceful protests of the Hirak have already seen a radical transformation at the top of the government. Yet, many still doubt the extent to which they will see the wholesale transformation of all the factions of the "regime." For further discussion, see Ghazouane Arslane, "What is universal about the Algerian national 'Hirak'?," *Africa is a Country*, July 2019. https://africasacountry.com/2019/07/what-is-univer sal-about-the-algerian-national-hirak; Muriam Haleh Davis, Hiyem Cheurfa and Thomas Serres, "A Hirak Glossary: Terms from Algeria and Morocco," *Jadaliyya*, June, 2019. https://www.jadaliyya.com/Details/38734; Davis, "The Layers of History Beneath Algeria's Protests."

15. See Randy Kennedy, "Sharjah Biennial Director Fired Over Artwork Deemed Offensive," in the 'Arts Beat' blog of *The New York Times*, April 7, 2011. http://artsbeat.blogs.nytimes.com/2011/04/07/sharjah-biennial-director-fired-over-offensive-artwork/?partner=rss&emc=rss&_r=0. For an image of the offending artwork, see Lewis Cusato, "From Tahar Djaout's 'No,'" 110.

16. Bennoune, *Your Fatwa*, 134–35.

17. Mustapha Benfodil, "Algeria: Art about Rape of Women by Fundamentalist Armed Groups Censored," April 6, 2011. www.wluml.org/node/7089

18. Hiddleston, "'On peut apprendre de la littérature à se méfier,'" 61; Benkhaled and Vince, "Performing Algerianness," 265.

19. Bennoune, *Your Fatwa*, 2.

20. Mustapha Benfodil, "Post-scriptum: La petite histoire de *Zarta!*," in *Zarta!*, 217–19.

21. Shahryar is the king of Persia in the *Mille et Une Nuits*, who listens to Shéhérazade recount a story to him over a thousand and one nights.

22. Rancière, *The Politics of Aesthetics*, 14.

23. Michel Foucault, *L'Archéologie du savoir* (Paris: Gallimard, 1969), 262.

24. Mbembe, "Provisional Notes on the Postcolony," 4.

25. Ministère de l'Intérieur et des Collectivités Locales, *Charte pour la Paix et la Réconciliation Nationale*.

26. Davis and Serres, "Political Contestation," 106.

27. Treacy, "Writing in the Aftermath," 123–24.

28. Mbembe, "Provisional Notes on the Postcolony," 4.

29. Davis and Serres, "Political Contestation," 106.

30. See, for instance, Britta Hecking, "Algerian Youth on the Move. Capoeira, Street Dance and Parkour: Between Integration and Contestation," in *Algeria: Nation, Culture and Transnationalism 1988–2015*, ed. Patrick Crowley (Liverpool: Liverpool University Press), 184–202.

31. Alexandra Gueydan-Turek, "Figure of an Anartist: Keeping Local Francophone Literature Engaged with Mustapha Benfodil's Literature-action," *Contemporary French and Francophone Studies* 20, no. 1 (2016), 50.

32. The Arabic roots of the name El Afrite recall the demonic figure of the "ifrit" from Islamic mythology. Living in the underworld, the "ifrit" (a kind of jinn) is noted for its malevolent character. Thus, while we might understand the naive police inspector's role as, on the one hand, a useful idiot, El Afrite could also be seen as a more impish or sinister troublemaker. For further discussion of the "ifrit," see Amira El-Zein, *Islam, Arabs, and the Intelligent World of the Jinn* (New York: Syracuse University Press, 2009), 142.

33. Gueydan-Turek, "Figure of an Anartist," 50.

34. Roland Barthes, "La mort de l'auteur," in *Œuvres complètes*, vol. 3 (Paris: Seuil, 2002), 40–45.

35. As Derrida underlines, perhaps seeing the literary in "suspended" relation with reference is a more productive way of understanding the link between the text and the author. For a fuller discussion of Derrida's notion of "suspense," see Harrison, "Who Needs an Idea of the Literary?"

36. Benfodil, *Archéologie*, 59, 135. The name undoubtedly recalls the PAGS who, as I discussed in the introduction and chapter 1, served to further entrench a polarized discourse and accelerate the onset of the 1990s conflict; it is also reminiscent of the fictional left-wing terrorist organisation, *l'Avant-Garde prolétarienne*, that brings together a group of young friends during May 1968 in Jorge Semprún's *Netchaïev est de retour* (Paris: Lattès, 1987). Other elements of *Netchaïev* resonate with Benfodil's *Archéologie*, including the mysterious disappearance of the protagonist, the presence of a notebook, and a police detective who discovers the book after the protagonist's death. Semprún's novels, like Benfodil's, are also replete with intertextual references. For further discussion of *Netchaïev*, see Avril Tynan, "Life After Literature: Jorge Semprún's Narrative Afterlives," *Journal of Romance Studies* 20, no. 1 (2020), 139–57.

37. Benfodil, *Archéologie*, 64.
38. Benfodil, *Archéologie*, 87.
39. Benfodil, *Archéologie*, 118–19, 245–50.
40. See Davis and Serres, "Political Contestation," 105.
41. Benfodil, *Archéologie*, 246–49.
42. Benfodil, *Archéologie*, 250.
43. Benfodil, *Archéologie*, 206.
44. Benfodil, *Archéologie*, 236–37.
45. Treacy, "Writing in the Aftermath," 133.
46. Benfodil, *Archéologie*, 243–44.
47. Cecile Bishop, *Postcolonial Criticism and Representations of African Dictatorship: The Aesthetics of Tyranny* (Oxford: Legenda, 2014), 84.
48. See Mustpha Benfodil, "Algérie: de 'Bezzzef!' à 'Barakat!', écritures citoyennes," in *Penser la Méditerranée au XXIe siècle: rencontres d'Averroès #20*, ed. Thierry Fabre (Marseille: Editions Parenthèses, 2014), 189–99; see also the entries on Benfodil's blog about the series. http://mustaphabenfodil.canalblog.com/
49. The web-based World Amazigh TV has posted recording of these readings on the "Dailymotion" website: http://www.dailymotion.com/video/xas3kd_part-01-manifetse-du-chkoupisme_news.
50. See Benfodil, "Cherche flic."
51. Dominique Rabourdin and Mohamed Kacimi (dirs), "Vivre et écrire en Algérie," ARTE France Production, 2003.
52. Benkhaled and Vince, "Performing Algerianness," 265.
53. Benfodil, "Algérie: de 'Bezzzef!' à 'Barakat !.'"
54. See Mehdi El-Djazaïri, *Poutakhine: journal presque intime d'un naufragé* (Paris: Riveneuve, 2010).
55. Benfodil, "Algérie: de 'Bezzzef!' à 'Barakat!,'" 194–95.
56. Benfodil, "Algérie: de 'Bezzzef!' à 'Barakat!,'" 196.
57. Foucault, *L'Archéologie du Savoir*, 116–38.
58. Oliver Davis, *Jacques Rancière* (Cambridge: Polity, 2010), 91.
59. Rancière, *The Politics of Aesthetics*, 13.
60. Davis and Serres, "Political Contestation," 105.

61. Dina Al-Kassim, *On Pain of Speech: Fantasies of the First Order and the Literary Rant* (Berkeley: University of California Press, 2010), 222–23.

62. Benkhaled and Vince, "Performing Algeriannes," 243.

63. Personal interview with the author, Mustapha Benfodil, Algiers, April, 2014.

64. See Aldelkébir Khatibi, *Maghreb Pluriel* (Paris: Denoël, 1983); *Amour bilingue* (Montpellier: Fata Morgana, 1983); see also Derrida's discussion of his interactions with Khatibi in *The Monolingualism of the Other, Or, The Prosthesis of Origin*, trans. Patrick Mensah (Stanford: Stanford University Press, 1998), 7–8.

65. Réda Bensmaïa, "Multilingualism and National 'Traits,'" in *Experimental Nations, or, The Invention of the Maghreb* (Princeton: Princeton University Press, 2003), 103–04.

66. Achille Mbembe, *On the Postcolony* (Berkeley: University of California Press, 2001), 111.

67. Lewis Cusato, "From Tahar Djaout's 'No,'" 104.

68. The reader will recall Homi Bhabha's image of the "shreds and patches" of the nation-state. And, as Davis and Serres note, the "imagined communities and solidarities on which the nation-state was constructed" have been increasingly eroded because of the Algerian State's inability or unwillingness to constitute itself outside the obscure designation of *le pouvoir*. Davis and Serres, "Political Contestation," 106; Homi K. Bhabha, "DissemiNation: Time, Narrative and he Margins of the Modern Nation," in *The Location of Culture* (London: Routledge, 1994), 204.

69. On the detention of journalists and activists, see TV5MONDE and AFP, "Algérie: des journalistes et des militants arrêtés," *TV5MONDE*, October 8, 2019. https://information.tv5monde.com/afrique/algerie-des-journalistes-et-des-militants-arretes-325678

70. Rancière, *The Politics of Aesthetics*, 13.

71. Bennoune, *Your Fatwa*, 12.

72. Bennoune, *Your Fatwa*, 3.

73. Benkhaled and Vince, "Performing Algerianness."

Conclusion
Beyond the Language of Crisis and Conflict

If Edward Said's idea of the worldliness of literature, whereby the text is simultaneously circulating in and constituting the world, is a problem at the heart of all literature, then moments of conflict and crisis, such as the Black Decade, bring this question of the distance between literary representation and reality into sharp focus.[1] While I do not dispute the general tendency among writers, journalists, and academic critics examined in this book to situate texts in the political contexts in which they were produced, I do seek to bring into focus the ways writers and commentators use literature to advance often reductive and self-fulfilling visions about the world at a time of conflict. I have also sought to show how, since the end of the Black Decade, writers themselves develop a self-reflexive idea of literature's "worldliness" and its role in constructing conflict or contesting power.

By examining the literary work of Rachid Mimouni alongside his nonliterary writing, I illustrate the particular role played by testimonial literature during the political crisis of 1988–1992, in which the early conflict narrative of the Black Decade was forged in blunt opposition to political Islam and the FIS. I also situate this early period of conflict within the "global" move to categorize the post–Cold War political era in terms of a clash between cultural and religious identities.[2] As some historians and political scientists forged a reductive oppositional lens to advance a self-fulfilling idea of the "new world order," left-wing Algerian political parties such as the PAGS and RCD made their own self-fulfilling and polarizing narratives that hastened the descent into violence. While on the surface a literary text irreducible to the political logics of the ongoing crisis, Mimouni's novel diverged from the innovative style of his previous works and contributed to a new highly politicized genre of testimonial literature that emerged after 1993. In a not dissimilar way from the polarizing political narrative advanced by the PAGS and RCD, *La Malédiction* was at once constituted by, and reconstituted, the language of conflict and crisis that spread throughout Algerian society after October 1988 and before the outbreak of more extreme violence after 1992.

As we saw in the example of Kamel Daoud, the image of the embattled public intellectual pitted against that of a self-reproducing Islamist threat remains common currency in French and international receptions of the Algerian novel. While, in chapter 4, I read Daoud's literary work in isolation from his political and journalistic texts, I ultimately show how Daoud and his critics appropriate the literary text in order to fashion the writer in oppositional terms. In this respect, it becomes almost impossible to separate journalistic writing from literature, because one ultimately constitutes the visibility of the other. Here, the process of constructing the embattled public intellectual is very much like the way Mimouni fashioned himself as a firm opponent to Islamism in the early 1990s. Yet, Daoud's increased visibility is also a result of a "postcolonial exotic" of the global literary marketplace, in which *Meursault, contre-enquête* has become an "instant classic" of world literature and its author a "spokesperson" for the conflict years of the Black Decade.[3]

As I explore throughout *Writing the Black Decade*, self-conscious testimonial and literary forms among writers such as Assia Djebar and Maïssa Bey (in the case of testimonial literature), and Salim Bachi and Mustapha Benfodil (in the case of the novel), offer very different understandings of what it means to be a "spokesperson." If these writers explicitly reject the idea of *speaking for* or *on behalf of* their fellow Algerians, they also deploy literary form to explore the ways in which their works might be complicit in advancing a potentially reductive or Orientalizing conflict narrative of the Black Decade. Extending the examination of complicity to other moments of contemporary violence such as September 11, 2001, Salim Bachi reminds us of the continued presence, and dangers, of Huntington and Lewis's self-fulfilling political myth of the clash of civilizations.

In many ways, an embodiment of the (post-)conflict narrative he inaugurated at the end of the Black Decade, Bouteflika came to symbolize the static and "zombified" state of political discourse in Algeria, both because of the amnesty legislation he introduced and the ill health that came to dominate the final years of his rule. While initially framing his literary texts in the context of the revolutionary aesthetics adopted by a previous generation of Algerian writers, Habib Ayyoub seeks ultimately to break out of the inertia of the preapproved conflict narrative by drawing attention to the way citizens themselves perform and perpetuate a spectacle of power sanctioned by the authorities. By staging how groups of fictional citizens become caught up in the "intimate tyranny" of reproducing their own oppression, Ayyoub's later texts serve to illuminate Achille Mbembe's ideas about the "illicit cohabitation" between "ruler" and "ruled" and the consequent "*mutual* zombification" of political discourse.[4] In Mbembe's vision, grotesque caricatures of political leaders are not just an ineffective means of breaking free from the political status quo; rather, they serve to reinforce and "ratify" a *discursive* status quo.[5]

However, in the way they deconstruct the kinds of oppositional discourse Mbembe refers to, Benfodil's experimental work and performances prompt us to question the overly skeptical image of citizens ultimately trapped within a "zombie" State, as well as to reassess the effectiveness of the carnivalesque or the grotesque as a means of contesting the political status quo in Algeria. Thus, while the forced resignation of Bouteflika—and the arrest of those in his entourage—has led to a political shift in Algeria, the peaceful protests of the Hirak have at the same time engendered a discursive opening that forces us to revisit some of the claims made in Mbembe's 1992 essay. Indeed, Benfodil's novel, and accompanying "wild readings," is just one among the many examples of creative and artistic acts and groups that have persistently challenged the performance of power in contemporary Algeria.[6]

The peaceful protests, that have become widely known as the Hirak, began in February 2019 after it was announced president Bouteflika would run for a fifth term of office. Though protesters succeeded in forcing the president to resign in April 2019, they have continued to take to the streets in towns and cities across Algeria, conscious that the president was only the tip of an iceberg of corrupt ruling elites in the country. Fridays—the first day of the Algerian weekend—have been designated as "vendredire," a portmanteau that fuses the French words for "Friday" (*vendredi*) and "to say" (*dire*), while students take to the streets on Tuesdays.[7] In a recent piece on the protests, the historian Muriam Haleh Davis examines how the movement appropriates historical figures and images of Algerian nationalism to give the protests a revolutionary legitimacy. In this respect, the political and discursive opening of 2019 resembles that of 1989, when Chadli brought forward legislation to end one-party FLN rule. However, as Davis stresses, the organizers of the 2019 movement have been keen to maintain the "peaceful and orderly nature" of the protests, with many Algerians referring to the Hirak as "the revolution of smiles."[8]

Among those appropriated by protesters are previously occluded historical figures such as Messali Hadj and revolutionaries, like Ali La Pointe, whose image has been taken from the 1966 film that embodied him, *La Bataille d'Alger* [*The Battle of Algiers*], and is carried through the streets of the capital city.[9] Ultimately a *representation* of the real historical figure they refer to, posters and placards bearing Ali La Pointe's image reflect the way Algerians have always tended to creatively blur the boundaries between historical representation and reality. The return to humor is indicated in the name, "the revolution of smiles," but also in other forms of caricature, including the use of the grotesque to represent the violence of police officers, obese army generals or members of the ruling elite.[10] The Hirak has been both creative and critical, with protesters calling on aesthetic forms of expression as a means of undermining the political situation. If, as Davis notes, the Algerian authorities had a monopoly in "manufacturing [their own] legitimacy," then the Hirak has allowed previously localized struggles to unite around the symbols of the revolution and adopt carnivalesque forms of opposition that were previously subsumed within the realm of an all-powerful State.[11] To recall the words of the philosopher and sociologist of space, Henri Lefebvre, Algerians have moved from reproducing mere "representations of space" to engaging in an active "representational space" which "involves the appropriative transformation of objects in physical space."[12] Crucially, though, the discursive and representational opening of the Hirak has allowed Algerians to forge their own self-narrative that goes beyond the reductive stereotypes implicit or explicit in a language of crisis and conflict.

The linguistic wordplay and use of satire in some ways resemble Benfodil's text, which was apparently popular with young Algerians at the time of its publication in 2007. While initially disregarded as failed revolutionaries, the "Anartistes" of Benfodil's fictional *Achéologie du chaos [amoureux]* are later rehabilitated, and celebrated, by the writer as he sees them embodied in those citizens illicitly performing his texts in public.[13] It is impossible to say, of course, whether the cultural and literary expression has in any concrete way fostered the recent uprisings of the Hirak. In fact, given what I have argued throughout the book, it would probably be sensible to attenuate such celebratory claims about the power of art or literature. It is, however, important to recognize that different forms of cultural contestation and experimentation have existed across Algerian cities over the past thirty years, including what Brita Hecking has called the "more subtle forms of contestation [of] youth 'non-movements.'"[14] And, while opposition movements such as the Hirak have appropriated the historical symbols of the revolution, writers such as Benfodil do not simply inhabit or reconstitute that revolutionary narrative, but seek to continually question it. Thus, as Hiddleston suggests, rather than level a direct challenge to power, literature has been a space in which political futures can be experimented with and mapped out.[15]

Yet, others have gone further. For Pheng Cheah, theories of world literature, and of the world more generally, have tended to focus too much on space and not nearly enough on time. While many theorists of world literature have sought to stress how literature reflects or registers its production, circulation, and consumption in the capitalist marketplace, Cheah argues that such theories neglect how literature is "directly related to political struggles in the world" because it possesses a "world-making power," which is at its core a temporal process.¹⁶ Extrapolating from Lefebvre, Cheah underlines how the role of art is precisely to temporalize otherwise static, spatial representations of everyday lived existence to forge what Lefebvre calls a "representational space [that] influences the spatial practices of individual subjects when they become aware that they do not merely inhabit social space as passive subjects but can actively participate in making it."[17]

In her account of Djebar's return to writing during the 1990s, Mireille Calle-Gruber writes of the "resistance-conduction" of Djebar's writing.[18] Here, the text intersects the non-written, silent histories of the oppressed that begin to map out an unexplored future. Part of the work of listening Djebar *conducted* during her ten-year hiatus from writing during the 1970s was one of sitting across the languages of dialectal spoken Arabic and French, the language in which she was trained. This work of using the literary form to sit across languages, to stage Khatibi's "bi-langue," is also a work of writing a new "grammar," as Benfodil puts it.[19] If what the "bi-langue" reveals in Benfodil's writing is less a work of "colliding" with power or the political, and more one of deconstructing its multiple masks *from the street*, then our understanding of the way writers, or writing, "resist(s)" is altered. Whether conceived at the level of writing or *thinking*, dualistic or binary oppositions do not form part of the "grammar" of writing and resistance, as conceived by writers such as Benfodil and Djebar. Perhaps, therefore, our vision of Algerian literature—our "idea of the literary" in post-1990s Algeria—should be one of that emphasizes how literary form *intersects* social and political discourse, in a work of listening and conducting, that began with Assia Djebar's *Femmes d'Alger dans leur appartement* in 1980.

Finally, while there is a clear need to attenuate celebratory accounts of literature, such as those that prevailed throughout and since the 1990s, literature's "*suspended* relation to meaning and reference" offers a still "irreducible" space in which writers can work on literature itself, unveiling and reinventing the preexisting languages of accommodation and resistance associated with literary form and representational practice.[20] At the same time, the "resistance-conduction" that Calle-Gruber outlines in relation to Djebar's filmmaking and writing, is clearly part of a conversational, almost musical, exchange between writer and citizen. Just as Benfodil's extratextual performances recruit ordinary members of the public to read aloud his and others' work, Djebar uses film and literature to "conduct" a whole orchestra of voices from beyond the realms of the text. In other words, the literary text registers nonliterary phenomena, but it also projects itself back into the world and so, however subtly, has a role in defining what that world will be.

NOTES

1. Said, *The World*, 35.
2. Huntington, "The Clash of Civilizations?"; Lewis, "The Roots of Muslim Rage."
3. Huggan, *The Postcolonial Exotic*; Brouillette, *Postcolonial Writers in the Global Literary Marketplace*; Robin Yassin-Kassab, "The Meursault Investigation by Kamel Daoud review – an instant classic," *The Guardian*, June 24, 2015. https://www.theguardian.com/books/2015/jun/24/meursault-investigation-kamel-daoud-review-instant-classic
4. Mbembe, "Provisional Notes," 25, 4, my emphasis.
5. Mbembe, "Provisional Notes," 5.
6. In his interview, Benfodil mentions the Comité pour la libération de l'action culturelle et citoyenne, led by Amazigh Kateb and Rihab Alloula. In her piece, Davis notes the role of the National Committee for the Defense of the Rights of the Unemployed, as well as Benfodil's own "Barakat" movement from 2014. See Benfodil, "Algérie: de 'Bezzzef!' à 'Barakat!'"; Davis, "The Layers of History Beneath Algeria's Protests," 342.
7. Davis, "The Layers of History Beneath Algeria's Protests," 337.
8. Davis, "The Layers of History Beneath Algeria's Protests," 341.
9. Davis, "The Layers of History Beneath Algeria's Protests," 338.
10. Davis refers in particular to the work of the Algerian cartoonist, Dilem. Davis, "The Layers of History Beneath Algeria's Protests," 339.
11. Davis, "The Layers of History Beneath Algeria's Protests," 341–42.
12. Lefebvre, cited in Cheah, *What is a World?*, 86.
13. Benfodil, "Algérie: de 'Bezzzef!' à 'Barakat!.'"
14. Calling on Asef Bayat's theory of "non-movement," Hecking examines how street dance and parkour allow Algerian youths to "alter their relationship to public space," as they shift between "integration" and "contestation." See Hecking, "Algerian Youth on the Move," 186. See also, Asef Bayat, *Life as Politics: How Ordinary People Change the Middle East* (Stanford: Stanford University Press, 2010).
15. See Hiddleston, "'On peut apprendre de la littérature à se méfier,'" 61.
16. Cheah, *What is a World?*, 57.
17. Cheah, *What is a World?*, 85.
18. Calle-Gruber, "Eléments pour un portrait," 11.
19. Personal interview with the author, Mustapha Benfodil, Algiers, April 2014.
20. Harrison, "Who needs and Idea of the Literary?," 12–13.

Bibliography

Abane, Meziane. "L'écrivain Kamel Daoud gagne son procès contre un imam salafiste." *Le Monde*, March 8, 2016. http://www.lemonde.fr/afrique/article/2016/03/08/l-ecrivain-kamel-daoud-gagne-son-proces-contre-un-imam-salafiste_4878558_3212.html

AFP. "Kamel Daoud, dans la 'shortlist' du Goncourt, parle de l'Algérie au présent." *Le Point Culture*, October 28, 2014. https://www.lepoint.fr/culture/kamel-daoud-dans-la-shortlist-du-goncourt-parle-de-l-algerie-au-present-28-10-2014-1876463_3.php

AFP. "L'Algérien Kamel Daoud lauréat du Goncourt du premier roman." *Le Point.fr*, May 5, 2015. http://www.lepoint.fr/culture/l-algerien-kamel-daoud-laureat-du-goncourt-du-premier-roman-05-05-2015-1926423_3.php

Aïssaoui, Mohammed. "L'hommage émouvant de Régis Debray à Kamel Daoud." *Le Figaro Culture Livres*, May 5, 2015. http://www.lefigaro.fr/livres/2015/05/05/03005-20150505ARTFIG00249-l-hommage-emouvant-de-regis-debray-a-kamel-daoud.php

Aït-Aoudia, Malik and Séverine Labat, dir. *Algérie 1988–2000, autopsie d'une tragédie*. La Compagnie des Phares et Balises, 2005, DVD.

Akef, Amir. "Un salafiste algérien émet une «fatwa» contre Kamel Daoud." *Le Monde*, December 17, 2014. http://www.lemonde.fr/afrique/article/2014/12/17/un-salafiste-algerien-emet-une-fatwa-contre-kamel-daoud_4541882_3212.html

Al-Kassim, Dina. *On Pain of Speech: Fantasies of the First Order and The Literary Rant*. Berkeley: University of California Press, 2010.

Allalou, Mohamed Ali, and Aziz Smati, ed. *Alger nooormal*. Paris: Françoise Truffaut Editions, 2005.

Amara, Noureddine, et al. "Nuit de Cologne: «Kamel Daoud recycle les clichés orientalistes les plus éculés»." *Le Monde*, February 11, 2016. http://www.lemonde.fr/idees/article/2016/02/11/les-fantasmes-de-kamel-daoud_4863096_3232.html

Amis, Martin. "The Last Days of Muhammad Atta." *The Observer*, August 31, 2006. http://www.martinamisweb.com/documents/lastdays_one.pdf

Andrews, Chris and Matt McGuire. "Introduction: Post-Conflict Literature?" In *Post-Conflict Literature: Human Rights, Peace, Justice*, edited by Chris Andrews and Matt McGuire, 1–15. London: Routledge, 2016.

Anquetil, Gilles. "Deux romanciers algériens défient le FIS. Les Voltaire d'Alger." *Le Nouvel Observateur*, June 4–10, 1992: 133–34.

Aresu, Bernard. "Arcanes algériens entés d'ajours helléniques: *Le chien d'Ulysse*, de Salim Bachi." In *Echanges et mutations des modèles littéraires entre Europe et Algérie*, vol. 2, 177–87. Paris: L'Harmattan, 2004.

Arslane, Ghazouane. "What is universal about the Algerian national 'Hirak'?" *Africa is a Country*, July, 2019. https://africasacountry.com/2019/07/what-is-universal-about-the-algerian-national-hirak

Asseraf, Arthur. *Electric News in Colonial Algeria*. Oxford: Oxford University Press, 2019.

Assima, Fériel. *Une femme à Alger: Chronique du désastre*. Paris: Arléa, 1995.

Ayyoub, Habib and Amina Bekkat. "Entretien avec Habib Ayyoub." *Algérie Littérature/Action*, no. 57–58 (2002), 81–83. http://www.revues-plurielles.org/_uploads/pdf/4_57_12.pdf

Ayyoub, Habib. *Le désert, et après: suivi de le gardien*. Algiers: Editions Barzakh, 2007.

Ayyoub, Habib. *Le Gardien*. Algiers: Editions Barzakh, 2001.

Ayyoub, Habib. *Le Palestinien*. Algiers: Editions Barzakh, 2003.

Ayyoub, Habib. *Le Remonteur de l'horloge*. Algiers: Editions Barzakh, 2012.

Ayyoub, Habib and Joseph Ford. Personal interview with the author, Algiers, April, 2014.

Bachi, Salim. *Amour et aventures de Sinbad le Marin*. Paris: Gallimard, 2010.

Bachi, Salim. *Autoportrait avec Grenade*. Paris: Editions du Rocher, 2005.

Bachi, Salim. *La Kahéna*. Paris: Gallimard, 2003.

Bachi, Salim. *Le chien d'Ulysse*. Paris: Gallimard, 2001.

Bachi, Salim. *Le consul*. Paris: Gallimard, 2014.

Bachi, Salim. *Le dernier été d'un jeune homme*. Paris: Flammarion, 2013.

Bachi, Salim. *Le grand frère*. Paris: Editions du Moteur, 2010.

Bachi, Salim. *Le silence de Mohamet*. Paris: Gallimard, 2008.

Bachi, Salim. *Les douze contes de minuit*. Paris: Gallimard, 2006.

Bachi, Salim. "Le vent brûle." *Le Monde diplomatique*, January 1995. https://www.monde-diplomatique.fr/1995/01/BACHI/6009

Bachi, Salim. *Moi, Khaled Kelkal*. Paris: Grasset, 2012.

Bachi, Salim. "Moi, Mohamed Merah." *Le Monde des livres*, March 30, 2012. http://www.paperblog.fr/5477915/317-moi-mohamed-merah-article-de-salim-bachi-et-les-reactions/

Bachi, Salim. *Tuez-les tous*. Paris: Gallimard, 2006.

Bachi, Salim. *Un jeune homme en colère*. Paris: Gallimard, 2018.

Bahri, Deepika. *Native Intelligence: Aesthetics, Politics, and Postcolonial Literature*. Minneapolis: University of Minnesota Press, 2003.

Bakhtin, Mikhail. *Rabelais and his World*. Translated by Hélène Iswolsky. Bloomington: Indiana University Press, 1984.

Barthes, Roland. "La mort de l'auteur." In *Œuvres complètes*, vol. 3, 40–45. Paris: Seuil, 2002.
Bayat, Asef. *Life as Politics: How Ordinary People Change the Middle East.* Stanford: Stanford University Press, 2010.
Bayat, Asef. "Post-Islamism at Large." In *Post-Islamism: The Many Faces of Political Islam*, edited by Asef Bayat, 3–34. Oxford: Oxford University Press, 2013.
Baylee, Alek. "Maddah-Sartre." *Algérie Littérature/Action*, no. 6 (December 1996).
Bedjaoui, Youcef et al. *An Inquiry into the Algerian Massacres.* Geneva: Hoggar, 1999.
Beer, Gillian. "Representing women, re-presenting the past." In *The Feminist Reader: Essays in Gender and the Politics of Literary Criticism*, edited by Catherine Belsey and Jane Moore, 77–90. Basingstoke: Palgrave, 1989.
Belaghoueg, Zoubida. "Algérianisation du mythe de *l'Odyssée* et parodie de *Nedjma* dans *Le chien d'Ulysse* de Salim Bachi." *Synergies Algérie*, no. 3 (2008): 131–43.
Benfodil, Mustapha. "Algeria: Art about rape of women by fundamentalist armed groups censored." *Women Living Under Muslim Laws*, April 6, 2011. www.wluml.org/node/7089
Benfodil, Mustapha. "Algérie: de «Bezzzef!» à «Barakat!», écritures citoyennes." In *Penser la Méditerranée au XXIe siècle: rencontres d'Averroès #20*, edited by Thierry Fabre, 189–99. Marseille: Editions Parenthèses, 2014.
Benfodil, Mustapha. *Alger, journal intense.* Paris: Editions Macula, 2019.
Benfodil, Mustapha. *Archéologie du chaos [amoureux].* Algiers: Editions Barzakh, 2007/Marseille: Al Dante, 2012.
Benfodil, Mustapha. *Body Writing.* Algiers: Editions Barzakh, 2018.
Benfodil, Mustapha. "Cherche flic pour lecture citoyenne à Tipaza. . . ." *El Watan*, August 16, 2009. https://www.djazairess.com/fr/elwatan/134732
Benfodil, Mustapha. *Cocktail Kafkaïne [Dark Poems].* Translated by Joe Ford. Bristol: Hesterglock Press, 2018.
Benfodil, Mustapha. *Les Bavardages du Seul.* Algiers: Editions Barzakh, 2003.
Benfodil, Mustapha. *Les six derniers jours de Baghdad: journal d'un voyage de guerre.* Algiers: Casbah, 2003.
Benfodil, Mustapha. *Zarta!* Algiers: Editions Barzakh, 2000.
Benfodil, Mustapha and Joseph Ford. Personal interview with the author, Algiers, April, 2014.
Benjamin, Walter. *The Origin of German Tragic Drama.* London: Verso, 1985.
Benjamin, Walter. "Theses on the Philosophy of History." In *Illuminations*, edited by Hannah Arendt, 253–64. New York: Schocken Books, 1969.
Benkhaled, Walid, and Natalya Vince. "Performing Algerianness: The National and Transnational Construction of Algeria's 'Culture Wars'." In *Algeria: Nation, Culture and Transnationalism 1988–2015*, edited by Patrick Crowley, 243–69. Liverpool: Liverpool University Press.
Benkhaled, Walid. "Algerian Cinema Between Commercial and Political Pressures: The Double Distortion." *Journal of African Cinemas* 8, no. 1 (2016): 87–101.
Bennoune, Karima. *Your Fatwa Does Not Apply Here: Untold Stories from the Fight Against Muslim Fundamentalism.* New York: W.W. Norton & Company, 2013.

Bensmaïa, Réda. "Multilingualism and National 'Traits'." In *Experimental Nations, or, The Invention of the Maghreb*, edited by Anne-Emanuelle Berger, 99–148. Princeton: Princeton University Press, 2003.
Bey, Maïssa, and Martine Marzloff. *A Contre-silence*. Grigny: Parole de L'Aube, 1998.
Bey, Maïssa, and Rachid Mokhtari. "Maïssa Bey: «J'écris pour éviter les hurlements»." In Rachid Mokhtari. *La Graphie de l'horreur: essai sur la littérature algérienne (1990–2000)*, 148–49. Algiers: Chihab, 2002.
Bey, Maïssa. "Au commencement était la mer." *Algérie Littérature/Action*, no. 5 (November 1996).
Bey, Maïssa. "Le cri." *Algérie Littérature/Action* no. 9 (1997): 131–32.
Bey, Maïssa. *Nouvelles d'Algérie*. Paris: Grasset, 1998.
Bey, Maïssa. *Sous le jasmin la nuit*. La Tour-d'Aigues: L'Aube/Algiers: Editions Barzakh, 2004.
Bhabha, Homi K. "DissemiNation: Time, Narrative and he Margins of the Modern Nation." In *The Location of Culture*, 199–244. London: Routledge, 1994.
Bishop, Cecile. *Postcolonial Criticism and Representations of African Dictatorship: The Aesthetics of Tyranny*. Oxford: Legenda, 2014.
Bisson, Julien. "Kamel Daoud et le désarroi de l'Algérie contemporaine." *Lire*, December 1, 2014: 12.
Bonn, Charles. "Algérie." In *Littérature francophone. Tome 1: Le Roman*, edited by Charles Bonn and Xavier Garnier, 185–210. Paris: Hatier, 1997.
Bonn, Charles. "Littérature algérienne et conscience nationale: après l'indépendance." *Notre librairie*, no. 85 (1986): 29–38.
Bottici, Chiara, and Benoît Challand. "Rethinking Political Myth: The Clash of Civilizations as a Self-Fulfilling Prophecy." *European Journal of Social Theory* 9, no. 3 (2006): 315–36.
Boudjedra, Rachid. *FIS de la haine*. Paris: Denoël, 1992.
Boudjedra, Rachid. *Lettres algériennes*. Paris: Grasset, 1995.
Boudjedra, Rachid. *Timimoun*. Paris: Denoël, 1994.
Bourget, Carine. "Portrait of a Terrorist: Slimane Benaïssa and Salim Bachi's 9/11 Novels." In *The Star, The Cross, and The Crescent: Religions and Conflicts in Francophone Literature from the Arab World*, 141–60. Lanham: Lexington Books, 2010.
Bourget, Carine. "The Algerian Civil War: Rachid Boudjedra's *Le FIS de la haine*, Rachid Mimouni's *De la barbarie en général et de l'intégrisme en particulier*, and *Une enfance algérienne*." In *The Star, The Cross, and The Crescent: Religions and Conflicts in Francophone Literature from the Arab World*, 89–114. Lanham: Lexington Books, 2010.
Boussouf, Malika. *Vivre traquée*. Paris: Calmann Lévy, 1995.
Brand, Laurie. *Official Stories: Politics and National Narratives in Egypt and Algeria*. Stanford: Stanford University Press, 2014.
Brouillette, Sarah. *Postcolonial Writers in the Global Literary Marketplace*. Basingstoke: Palgrave, 2007.

Brozgal, Lia. "The Critical Pulse of the *Contre-enquête:* Kamel Daoud on the Maghrebi Novel in French." *Contemporary French and Francophone Studies* 20, no. 1 (2016): 37–46.
Bruckner, Pascale. "Défendons «les libres-penseurs venus du monde musulman» contre les fatwas de l'intelligentsia." *Le Monde*, March 1, 2016. http://www.lemonde.fr/idees/article/2016/03/01/defendons-les-libres-penseurs-contre-les-fatwas-de-l-intelligentsia_4874077_3232.html
Buffard-O'Shea, Nicole. "*Les Agneaux du Seigneur* de Yasmina Khadra et *Nouvelles d'Algérie* de Maïssa Bey: écrutures sans appel?" In *Subversion du réel: Stratégies esthétiques dans la littérature algérienne*, edited by Beate Burtscher-Bechter and Birgit Mertz-Baumgartner, 99–111. Paris: L'Harmattan, 2001.
Burns, Karin Garlepp. "The Paradox of Objectivity in the Realist Fiction of Edith Wharton and Kate Chopin." *Journal of Narrative Theory*, no. 29 (1999): 27–61.
Burtscher-Bechter, Beate. "'Donner la parole aux mots, et faire comme si demain était possible.' Mutisme et prise de parole dans les *Nouvelles d'Algérie* de Maïssa Bey." In *Subversion du réel: Stratégies esthétiques dans la littérature algérienne*, edited by Beate Burtscher-Bechter and Birgit Mertz-Baumgartner, 203–15. Paris: L'Harmattan, 2001.
Butler, Judith. *Precarious Life: The Powers of Mourning and Violence*. London: Verso, 2004.
Calle-Gruber, Mireille. "Eléments pour un portrait d'écrivain dans l'entrelangues." In *Assia Djebar ou la résistance de l'écriture*, 7–17. Paris: Maisonneuve et Larose, 2001.
Campbell, James. "The Novelist as Murderer." *The Wall Street Journal*, May 29, 2015. http://www.wsj.com/articles/the-novelist-as-murderer-1432930737
Camus, Albert. *L'Etranger*. Paris: Gallimard, 1942.
Camus, Albert. "L'Hôte." In *L'Exil et le royaume*, 81–99. Paris: Gallimard, 1957.
Camus, Albert. "Pour une trêve civile en Algérie." In *Essais*, edited by Louis Faucon and Roger Quilliot, 991–99. Paris: Gallimard, 1965 [1956].
Camus, Albert. *The Outsider*. Translated by Sandra Smith. London: Penguin, 2012.
Carroll, David. *Albert Camus the Algerian: Colonialism, Terrorism, Justice*. New York: Columbia University Press, 2007.
Caruth, Cathy. *Unclaimed Experience: Trauma, Narrative, and History*. Baltimore: Johns Hopkins University Press, 1996.
Casanova, Pascale. *The World Republic of Letters*. Cambridge: Harvard University Press, 2007.
Chaouat, Bruno. *Is Theory Good for the Jews? French Thought and the Challenge of the New Antisemitism*. Liverpool: Liverpool University Press, 2016.
Chaulet-Achour, Christiane. "Camus dans la presse algérienne des années 1985–2005." In *Albert Camus: l'exigence morale*, edited by Agnès Spiquel & Alain Schaffner, 141–61. Paris: Editions Le Manuscrit, 2006.
Chouaki, Aziz. *Les Oranges*. Paris: Mille et Une Nuits, 1997.
Chouaki, Aziz. "Le Tag et le Royaume." In *Albert Camus et les écritures algériennes: quelles traces*, edited by the Association "Rencontres méditerranéennes Albert Camus," 35–40. Aix-en-Provence: Edisud, 2004.

Cocquet, Marion. "Kamel Daoud sous le coup d'une fatwa." *Le Point.fr*, December 17, 2014. http://www.lepoint.fr/culture/kamel-daoud-sous-le-coup-d-une-fatwa-17-12-2014-1890421_3.php

"Cologne sex attacks: Women describe 'terrible' assaults." *BBC News*, January 7, 2016. http://www.bbc.com/news/world-europe-35250903

Courbet, Claire. "Kamel Daoud: «Le combat de Charlie Hebdo est aussi le mien»." *Le Figaro*, January 12, 2015. http://www.lefigaro.fr/livres/2015/01/12/03005-20150112ARTFIG00246-kamel-daoud-le-combat-de-charlie-hebdo-est-aussi-le-mien.php

Crowley, Patrick. "Literatures in French Today: Markets, Centres, Peripheries, Transition." *Australian Journal of French Studies* 50, no. 3 (2013): 410–25.

Crowley, Patrick. "Myth, Modernism, Violence and Form: An Interview with Salim Bachi." *Bulletin of Francophone Postcolonial Studies* 4, no. 1 (2013): 2–11.

Crowley, Patrick. "Mythologizing the City, Rethinking the Nation: Salim Bachi's Cyrtha Trilogy." In *Mediterranean Cities: Real and/or Imaginary*, edited by Federica Frediani, 267–84. Florence: Nerbini Editore, 2014.

D'Haen, Théo. "World Literature, Postcolonial Politics, French-Caribbean Literature." In *Littératures francophones et politiques*, edited by Jean Bessière, 63–73. Paris: Karthala, 2009.

Daoud, Kamel. "Cologne, lieu de fantasmes." *Le Monde*, January 31, 2016. http://www.lemonde.fr/idees/article/2016/01/31/cologne-lieu-de-fantasmes_4856694_3232.html

Daoud, Kamel. *Chroniques: Selected Columns, 2010–2016*. Translated by Elizabeth Zerofsky. New York: Other Press, 2018.

Daoud, Kamel. *La Préface du nègre*. Algiers: Editions Barzakh, 2008.

Daoud, Kamel. *Le Minotaure 504*. Paris: Sabine Wespieser, 2011.

Daoud, Kamel. *Meursault, contre-enquête*. Algiers: Editions Barzakh, 2013/Arles: Acted Sud, 2014.

Daoud, Kamel. *Ô Pharaon*. Oran: Editions Dar El Gharb, 2004.

Daoud, Kamel. *Raïna Raïkoum: [chroniques]*. Oran: Dar El Gharb, 2002.

Daoud, Kamel. *The Meursault Investigation*. Translated by John Cullen. London: Oneworld Publications, 2015.

Daoud, Kamel. "The Sexual Misery of the Arab World." *The New York Times*, February 12, 2016. http://www.nytimes.com/2016/02/14/opinion/sunday/the-sexual-misery-of-the-arab-world.html

Davis, Colin. "Camus, Encounters, Reading." In *Ethical Issues in Twentieth-Century French Fiction: Killing the Other*, 64–85. Basingstoke: Macmillan Press, 2000.

Davis, Colin. "The Cost of Being Ethical: Fiction, Violence, and Altericide." *Common Knowledge* 9, no. 2 (2003): 241–53.

Davis, Muriam Haleh, and Thomas Serres. "Political Contestation in Algeria: Between Postcolonial Legacies and the Arab Spring." *Middle East Critique* 22, no. 2 (2013): 99–112.

Davis, Muriam Haleh, Hiyem Cheurfa and Thomas Serres. "A Hirak Glossary: Terms from Algeria and Morocco." *Jadaliyya*, June, 2019. https://www.jadaliyya.com/Details/38734

Davis, Muriam Haleh. "The Layers of History Beneath Algeria's Protests." *Current History* 118, no. 812 (2019): 337–42.
Davis, Oliver. *Jacques Rancière*. Cambridge: Polity, 2010.
Demetz, Jean-Michel. "Tous les Rushdie du monde." *L'Express*, February 17, 1994: 74.
Derrida, Jacques. *The Monolingualism of the Other, Or, The Prosthesis of Origin*. Translated by Patrick Mensah. Stanford: Stanford University Press, 1998.
Devarrieux, Claire. "L'auteur Kamel Daoud visé par une fatwa. Un imam salafiste appelle au meurtre." *Libération Culture*, December 18, 2014: 25.
Devecchio, Alexandre. "Kamel Daoud: «pour gagner la guerre, il faut d'abord mener la bataille culturelle»." *Le Figaro*, January 26, 2016. http://www.lefigaro.fr/vox/societe/2015/01/26/31003-20150126ARTFIG00330-kamel-daoud-pour-gagner-la-guerre-il-faut-d-abord-mener-la-bataille-culturelle.php
"Dire l'indicible, nommer l'innommable. . . Mission impossible?," *Le Monde*, April 6, 2012. https://www.lemonde.fr/le-monde/article/2012/04/06/dire-l-indicible-nommer-l-innommable-mission-impossible_5984777_4586753.html
Djebar, Assia. *Algerian White*. Translated by David Kelley and Marjolijn de Jager. New York: Seven Stories Press, 2000.
Djebar, Assia. *Femmes d'Alger dans leur appartement*. Paris: Editions des Femmes, 1980.
Djebar, Assia. *La Disparition de la langue française*. Paris: Albin Mihel, 2003.
Djebar, Assia. *Le blanc de l'Algérie*. Paris: Albin Michel, 1995.
Djebar, Assia. *Oran, langue morte*. Paris: Actes Sud, 1997.
Djebar, Assia. *The Tongue's Blood Does Not Run Dry: Algerian Stories*. Translated by Tegan Raleigh. New York: Seven Stories Press, 2006.
Djebar, Assia. *Women of Algiers in their Apartment*. Translated by Marjolijn de Jager. Charlottesville: University of Virginia Press, 1992.
Djefel, Belaïd and Boussad Saïm. "Présentation," *Recherches & Travaux*, no. 76 (2010): 5–10.
Djemai, Abdelkader. *Camus à Oran*. Paris: Editions Michalon, 1995.
Douroux, Philippe. "Goncourt de rattrapage pour Kamel Daoud." *Libération Culture*, May 6, 2015: 24.
El Nossery, Névine. *Témoignages fictionnels au féminin: une réécriture des blancs de la guerre civile algérienne*. New York: Rodopi, 2012.
El-Djazaïri, Mehdi. *Poutakhine: journal presque intime d'un naufragé*. Paris: Riveneuve, 2010.
El-Zein, Amira. *Islam, Arabs, and the Intelligent World of the Jinn*. New York: Syracuse University Press, 2009.
Etcherelli, Claire. "Postface." In *Au commencement était la mer*, edited by Maïssa Bey, 153–55. La Tour-d'Aigues: L'Aube, 2003 [1996].
Evans, Martin, and John Phillips. *Algeria: Anger of the Dispossessed*. New Haven: Yale University Press, 2007.
Fanon, Frantz. *Les damnés de la terre*. Paris: Maspero, 1968 [1961].
"Fausse polémique et vraie manipulation." *Algeria-Watch*, December 21, 2014. http://www.algeria-watch.org/fr/aw/hamadache_daoud.htm

Fisher, Dominique. *Écrire l'urgence: Assia Djebar et Tahar Djaout*. Paris: L'Harmattan, 2007.
Ford, Joseph. "Rethinking *urgence*: Algerian Francophone literature after the 'décennie noire'." *Francosphères* 5, no. 1 (2016): 39–57.
Foucault, Michel. *L'Archéologie du savoir*. Paris: Gallimard, 1969.
Freytag, Gustav and Elias J. MacEwan. *Freytag's Technique of the Drama: An Exposition of Dramatic Composition and Art*. Amsterdam: Nabu Public Domain Reprints, 2013.
G.A. "Un écrivain contre la terreur islamiste. Mimouni le valeureux." *Le Nouvel Observateur*, October 7–13, 1993: 118.
Gafaïti, Hafid. "Between God and the President: Literature and Censorship in North Africa." *Diacritics* 27, no. 2 (1997): 59–84.
Gafaïti, Hafid. "Power, Censorship and the Press: The Case of Postcolonial Algeria." *Research in African Literature* 30, no. 3 (1999): 51–61.
Gafaïti, Hafid. "The Monotheism of the Other: Language and De/Construction of National Identity in Postcolonial Algeria." In *Algeria in Others' Languages*, edited by Anne-Emmanuelle Berger, 19–43. Ithaca: Cornell University Press, 2002.
Geesey, Patricia. "Violent Days: Algerian Women Writers and the Civil Crisis." *The International Fiction Review* 27, no. 1–2 (2000). https://journals.lib.unb.ca/index.php/IFR/article/view/7658/8715
Genette, Gérard. *Fiction et diction*. Paris: Seuil, 1991.
Ghanem, Nadia. "Why Algerian Novelist Boualem Sansal's '2084' is a Sensation in France." *Arabic Literature (in English)*, October 6, 2015. http://arablit.org/2015/10/06/2084/
Glucksmann, Raphael, David Hazan and Pierre Mezerette, dir. *Tuez-les tous! Rwanda: histoire d'un geénocide sans importance*. Dum Dum Films, 2004.
Gopal, Priyamvada. *Insurgent Empire: Anticolonial Resistance and British Dissent*. London: Verso, 2019.
Gopnik, Adam. "The Next Thing." *The New Yorker*, January 26, 2016: 28.
Gozlan, Martine. "Kamel Daoud contre l'idéologiquement correct." *Le Nouveau Marianne*, November 7, 2014: 64.
Gratton, Johnnie, and Brigitte Le Juez, ed. *Modern French Short Fiction: An Anthology*. Manchester: Manchester University Press, 1994.
Gross, Janice. "Albert Camus and contemporary Algerian playwrights: A shared faith in dialogue." In *Albert Camus, précurseur: Méditerranée d'hier et d'aujourd'hui*, edited by Alek Baylee Toumi, 127–40. New York: Peter Lang, 2009.
Gross, Janice. "The Tragedy of Algeria: Slimane Benaïssa's Drama of Terrorism." *Theatre Journal* 54, no. 3 (2002): 369–87.
Gueydan-Turek, Alexandra. "Figure of an Anartist: Keeping Local Francophone Literature Engaged with Mustapha Benfodil's Literature-action." *Contemporary French and Francophone Studies* 20, no. 1 (2016): 48–57.
Hadi, Amine Aït. "Carnaval à Sidi Bentayeb ou l'horloge de la discorde: Le Remonteur d'horloge de Habib Ayyoub." *L'Expression*, November 12, 2012. https://www.djazairess.com/fr/lexpression/163600

Harbi, Mohammed. "La tragédie d'une démocratie sans démocrates." *Le Monde,* April 1, 1994.
Harlow, Barbara. "Introduction." In *The Colonial Harem,* edited by Malek Alloula. Translated by Myrna Godzich and Wlad Godzich, x–xxii. Minneapolis: University of Minnesota Press, 1986.
Harrison, Nicholas. *Postcolonial Criticism: History, Theory and the Work of Fiction.* Cambridge: Polity Press, 2003.
Harrison, Nicholas. "Preface." *Paragraph* 28, no. 2 (2005): iii–vi.
Harrison, Nicholas. "Who Needs an Idea of the Literary?" *Paragraph* 28, no. 2 (2005): 1–17.
Harrison, Olivia. "Beyond France-Algeria: The Algerian Novel and the Transcolonial Imagination." In *Algeria: Nation, Culture and Transnationalism: 1988–2015,* edited by Patrick Crowley, 222–42. Liverpool: Liverpool University Press.
Heath, Malcolm. "Introduction." In *Poetics,* edited by Aristotle, vii–lxxi. London: Penguin, 1996.
Hecking, Britta. "Algerian Youth on the Move. Capoeira, Street Dance and Parkour: Between Integration and Contestation." In *Algeria: Nation, Culture and Transnationalism 1988–2015,* edited by Patrick Crowley, 184–202. Liverpool: Liverpool University Press.
Héliot, Armelle. "Le fantoôme d'Albert Camus hante le festival d'Avignon." *Le Figaro,* July 22, 2015. http://www.lefigaro.fr/theatre/2015/07/22/03003-2015072 2ARTFIG00140-le-fantome-d-albert-camus-hante-le-festival-d-avignon.php
Hewitt, Gavin. "Cologne attacks' profound impact on Europe." *BBC News,* January 11, 2016. http://www.bbc.com/news/world-europe-35261988
Hiddleston, Jane. *Assia Djebar: Out of Algeria.* Liverpool: Liverpool University Press, 2006.
Hiddleston, Jane. *Decolonising the Intellectual: Politics, Culture, and Humanism at the End of the French Empire.* Liverpool: Liverpool University Press, 2014.
Hiddleston, Jane. "'On peut apprendre de la littérature à se méfier': Writing and Doubt in the Contemporary Algerian Novel." *Contemporary French and Francophone Studies* 20, no. 1 (2016): 58–66
Hiddleston, Jane. "Rewriting Algeria, Past and Present: History and Cultural Politics in Two Novels by Tahar Djaout." In *The Fiction of History,* edited by Alexander Lyon Macfie, 149–61. New York: Routledge, 2015.
Hiddleston, Jane. *Writing After Postcolonialism: Francophone North African Literature in Transition.* London: Bloomsbury, 2017.
HuffPost and AFP. "Kamel Daoud: une fatwa lancée contre l'écrivain déclenche l'indignation en Algérie." *Le Huffington Post,* December 17, 2014. http://www.huff ingtonpost.fr/2014/12/17/kamel-daoud-fatwa-ecrivain-goncourt-meursault-contre -enquete-hamadache-ziraoui_n_6339970.html
Huggan, Graham. *The Postcolonial Exotic: Marketing the Margins.* London: Routledge, 2001.
Huntington, Samuel K. "The Clash of Civilizations?" *Foreign Affairs* 72, no. 3 (1993): 22–49.

Ibrahim-Ouali, Lila. "Maïssa Bey: «des mots sous la cendre des jours»: *Au commencement était la mer*. . . et *Nouvelles d'Algérie*." *L'Esprit Créateur* 40, no. 2 (2000): 75–85.
Jameson, Fredric. "Third-World Literature in the Era of Multinational Capitalism." *Social Text*, no. 15 (1986): 65–88.
Jauss, Hans Robert. *Toward an Aesthetic of Reception*. Translated by Timothy Bahti. Minneapolis: University of Minnesota Press, 1982.
Joffé, George. "National Reconciliation and General Amnesty in Algeria." *Mediterranean Politics* 13, no. 2 (2008): 213–28.
Just, Daniel. "The Politics of the Novel and Maurice Blanchot's Theory of the Récit, 1954–1964." *French Forum* 33, no. 1–2 (2008): 121–39.
"Kamel Daoud et les «fantasmes» de Cologne, retour sur une polémique." *Le Monde*, February 20, 2016. http://www.lemonde.fr/idees/article/2016/02/20/kamel-daoud-et-les-fantasmes-de-cologne-retour-sur-une-polemique_4868849_3232.html
"Kamel Daoud: «Hamadache est instrumentalisé par les autorités pour me pousser à quitter l'Algérie»." *Algérie Focus*, December 21, 2014. https://www.algerie-focus.com/2014/12/kamel-daoud-hamadache-est-instrumentalise-par-les-autorites-pour-me-pousser-a-quitter-lalgerie/
Kaplan, Alice. "«Meursault, contre-enquête» de Kamel Daoud." *Contreligne*, autumn 2015. http://www.contreligne.eu/2014/06/kamel-daoud-meursault-contre-enquete/#fn-4954-7
Katutani, Michiko. "Review: Kamel Daoud Interrogates Camus in 'The Meursault Investigation'." *The New York Times*, May 28, 2015. http://www.nytimes.com/2015/05/29/books/review-kamel-daoud-interrogates-camus-in-the-meursault-investigation.html
Kennedy, Randy. "Sharjah Biennial Director Fired Over Artwork Deemed Offensive." *The New York Times*, April 7, 2011. http://artsbeat.blogs.nytimes.com/2011/04/07/sharjah-biennial-director-fired-over-offensive-artwork/?partner=rss&emc=rss&_r=0
Kessous, Namaan and Andy Stafford. "Récit, Monologue et Polémique dans *Les Oranges* d'Aziz Chouaki." *ASCALF Yearbook*, no. 4 (2000): 168–178. http://sfps.org.uk/wp-content/uploads/2018/06/ASCALF-Yearbook-No.-4-28200029.pdf
Khatibi, Aldelkébir. *Amour bilingue*. Montpellier: Fata Morgana, 1983.
Khatibi, Aldelkébir. *Maghreb Pluriel*. Paris: Denoël, 1983.
Kingsley, Patrick. "80 sexual assaults in one day – the other story of Tahrir Square." *The Guardian*, July 5, 2015. http://www.theguardian.com/world/2013/jul/05/egypt-women-rape-sexual-assault-tahrir-square
Lacapra, Dominick. *Representing the Holocaust: History, Theory, Trauma*. Ithaca: Cornell University Press, 1994.
Laredj, Waciny. "La gardienne des ombres." *Algérie Littérature/Action*, no. 3–4 (September–October 1996).
Laroussi, Farid. "When Francophone Means National: The Case of the Maghreb." *Yale French Studies*, no. 103 (2003): 81–90.
Le Fol, Sébastien. "EXCLUSIF. Kamel Daoud: 'Mais pourquoi veut-il me tuer?'." *Le Point.fr*, December 30, 2014. http://www.lepoint.fr/societe/exclusif-kamel-daoud-mais-pourquoi-veulent-ils-me-tuer-30-12-2014-1893138_23.php

Leperlier, Tristan. *Algérie: les écrivains dans la décennie noire*. Paris: CNRS, 2018.
Lewis Cusato, Mary Anne. "From Tahar Djaout's 'No' to Mustapha Benfodil's 'Enough!': Two Moments of Revolutionary Aesthetics in Contemporary Algerian Literature and Cultural Activism." *Expressions maghrébines* 17, no. 1 (2018): 103–117.
Lewis, Bernard. "The Roots of Muslim Rage." *Atlantic Monthly* 266, no 3. (1990): 47–60.
Lewis, Mary Anne. "The Maghreb's New Publishing House: *les éditions barzakh* and the Stakes of Localized Publishing." *Contemporary French and Francophone Studies* 20, no. 1 (2016): 85–93.
Loch, Dietmar. *Jugendliche maghrebinischer Herkunft zwischen Stadtpolitik und Lebenswelt. Eine Fallstudie in der französischen Vorstadt Vaulx-en-Velin*. Weisbaden: VS-Verlag für Sozialwissenschaften, 2005.
Macey, David. "The Algerian with the knife." *Parallax* 4, no. 2 (1998): 159–67.
Margerrison, Christine. "Assia Djebar, Albert Camus et le sang de l'histoire." In *Algérie, vers le cinquantenaire de l'Indépendance*, edited by Naaman Kessous, Christine Margerrison, Andy Stafford and Guy Dugas, 161–82. Paris: L'Harmattan, 2009.
Marouane, Leila. *Ravisseur*. Paris: Julliard, 1998.
Martinez, Luis. *La Guerre civile en Algérie, 1990–1998*. Paris: Karthala, 1998.
Martinez, Luis. *The Algerian Civil War, 1990–1998*. Translated by Jonathan Derrick. New York: Columbia University Press, 2000.
Marx-Scouras, Danielle. "Portraits of Women, Visions of Algeria." In *The Cambridge Companion to Camus*, edited by Edward J. Hughes, 131–44. Cambridge: Cambridge University Press, 2007.
Mbembe, Achille. *On the Postcolony*. Berkeley: University of California Press, 2001.
Mbembe, Achille. "Prosaics of Servitude and Authoritarian Civilities." *Public Culture* 5, no. 1 (1992): 123–45.
Mbembe, Achille. "Provisional Notes on the Postcolony." *Africa: Journal of the International African Institute* 62, no. 1 (1992): 3–37.
McAuley, James. "Why France loves this Algerian writer more than Algeria does." *The Washington Post*, December 1, 2018. https://www.washingtonpost.com/world/europe/why-france-loves-this-algerian-writer-more-than-algeria-does/2018/12/01/d79f2807-8165-41c1-9b44-9c61ef6c974d_story.html
McDougall, James. *A History of Algeria*. Cambridge: Cambridge University Press, 2017.
McDougall, James. "Savage Wars? Codes of violence in Algeria, 1830s–1990s." *Third World Quarterly* 26, no. 1 (2005): 117–31.
Meddi, Adlène, and Mélanie Matarese, ed. *Algérie: la* nahda *des Lettres, la renaissance des mots*. Paris: Riveneuve Editions, 2015.
Mellal, Farid. "La violence de la réalité ne cède que très peu de place à la fiction dans ces récits." *La Tribune Culture*, September 23, 1998: 16–17.

Menia, François. "Algérie: des artistes en quête de sécurité après la fatwa contre Kamel Daoud." *Le Figaro*, December 22, 2014. http://www.lefigaro.fr/livres/2014/12/22/03005-20141222ARTFIG00228-algerie-des-artistes-en-quete-de-securite-apres-la-fatwa-contre-kamel-daoud.php

Metref, Arezki. "Camus sera-t-il un jour algérien?" *Ruptures*, no. 1 (1993): 30–31.

Metref, Arezki. "Quartiers consignés." *Algérie Littérature/Action*, no. 2 (June 1996).

Mika, Kasia. *Disasters, Vulnerability, and Narratives: Writing Haïti's Futures*. New York: Routledge, 2019.

Miliani, Hadj. *Une littérature en sursis? Le champ littéraire de langue française en Algérie*. Paris: L'Harmattan, 2002.

Mills, David. "Camus condemned: a retelling of *L'Etranger* from the viewpoint of the murdered Algerian's brother is a tour de force." *The Sunday Times*, June 21, 2015: 39.

Mimouni, Rachid. *De la barbarie en générale et de l'intégrisme en particulier*. Paris: Le Pré aux Clercs, 1992.

Mimouni, Rachid. *La Malédiction*. Paris: Stock, 1993.

Ministère de l'Intérieur et des Collectivités Locales. *Charte pour la Paix et la Réconciliation Nationale*. Algiers: MICL, 2006.

Mokeddem, Malika. *Des rêves et des assassins*. Paris: Grasset, 1995.

Mokeddem, Malika. *L'interdite*. Paris: Grasset, 1993.

Mokhtari, Rachid. *Le nouveau souffle du roman algérien: essai sur la littérature des années 2000*. Algiers: Chihab, 2006.

Mortimer, Mildred. *Women Fight, Women Write: Texts on the Algerian War*. Charlottesville: University of Virginia Press, 2018.

Mundy, Jacob. *Imaginative Geographies of Algerian Violence: Conflict Science, Conflict Management, Antipolitics*. Stanford: Stanford University Press, 2015.

Newmark, Kevin. "Tongue-tied: What Camus's fiction couldn't teach us about ethics and politics." In *Albert Camus in the 21st Century: A Reassessment of His Thinking at the Dawn of a New Millennium*, edited by Christine Margerrison et al., 107–20. New York: Rodopi, 2008.

O'Brien, Conor Cruise. *Camus*. London: Fontana, 1970.

Ochs, Edith. "Un lapsus dans la tête de Merah?" *The Huffington Post*, February 4, 2012. https://www.huffingtonpost.fr/edith-ochs/bachi-mohamed-merah_b_1399787.html

Orlando, Valérie. *The Algerian New Novel: The Poetics of a Modern Nation, 1950–1979*. Charlottesville: University of Virginia Press, 2017.

Orlando, Valérie. "The Truncated memories and fragmented pasts of contemporary Algeria: Salim Bachi's *Le Chien d'Ulysse*." *International Journal of Francophone Studies* 6, no. 2 (2003): 103–18.

Panagia, Davide. "'*Partage du sensible*': the distribution of the sensible." In *Jacques Rancière: Key Concepts*, edited by Jean-Philippe Deranty, 95–103. New York: Routledge, 2014.

Pears, Pamela A. *Front Cover Iconography and Algerian Women's Writing: Heuristic Implications of the Recto-Verso Effect*. Lanham: Lexington Books, 2015.

Pesle, O. and Ahmed Tidjani, trans. *Le Coran*. Paris: Editions Larose, 1948.

Quayson, Ato. "Periods versus Concepts: Space Making and the Question of Postcolonial Literary History." *PMLA* 127, no. 2 (2012): 346–47.
Quilligan, Maureen. *The Language of Allegory: Defining the Genre*. London: Cornell University Press, 1979.
Rabourdin, Dominique, and Mohamed Kacimi, dir. "Vivre et écrire en Algérie." ARTE France Production, 2003.
"Rachid Boudjedra, 'Dire l'urgence'." *El Moudjahid*, March 20, 1994, Centre culturel algérien, Paris.
Rahal, Malika. "1988–1992: Multipartism, Islamism and the Descent into Civil War." In *Algeria: Nation, Culture and Transnationalism 1988–2015*, edited by Patrick Crowley, 81–100. Liverpool: Liverpool University Press.
Rahal, Malika. "Fused Together and Torn Apart: Stories and Violence in Contemporary Algeria." *History & Memory* 24, no. 1 (2012): 133–34.
Rancière, Jacques. *The Politics of Aesthetics: The Distribution of the Sensible*. Translated by Gabriel Rockhill. London: Continuum, 2004.
Remzi, Ali. "Salim Bachi: Les quêtes fertiles d'un écrivain." *La Dépêche de Kabylie*, July 20, 2010. http://www.depechedekabylie.com/cuture/84737-salim-bachi-les-quetes-fertiles-dun-ecrivain.html
Resnais, Alain, dir. *Hiroshima mon amour*. Argos Films, 1959.
Rice, Alison. *Polygraphies: Francophone Women Writing Algeria*. Charlottesville: University of Virginia Press, 2012.
Roberts, Hugh. *The Battlefield Algeria 1988–2002: Studies in a Broken Polity*. London: Verso, 2003.
Rosello, Mireille. *The Reparative in Narratives: Works of Mourning in Progress*. Liverpool: Liverpool University Press, 2010.
Rothberg, Michael. *Multidirectional Memory: Remembering the Holocaust in the Age of Decolonization*. Stanford: Stanford University Press, 2009.
Rothberg, Michael. "Seeing Terror, Feeling Art: Public and Private in Post-9/11 Literature." In *Literature after 9/11*, edited by Ann Keniston and Jeanne Quinn, 123–42. New York: Routledge, 2008.
Roy, Jean. "Boudjedra se dresse contre la barbarie." *L'Humanité*, January 7, 1994. Centre cultural algérien, Paris.
Said, Edward W. *Culture and Imperialism*. London: Vintage, 1994.
Said, Edward W. *Orientalism*. New York: Vintage, 1978.
Said, Edward W. *The World, the Text, and the Critic*. Cambridge: Harvard University Press, 1983.
Sanson, Hervé. "Moins qu'une nahda, plus qu'un «air de flute»." In *Algeérie: la nahda des Lettres, la renaissance des mots*, edited by Adlène Meddi and Mélanie Matarese, 14–21. Paris: Riveneuve Editions, 2015.
Sanyal, Debarati. *Memory and Complicity: Migrations of Holocaust Remembrance*. New York: Formham University Press, 2015.
Sartre, Jean-Paul. *Qu'est-ce que la littérature?* Paris: Gallimard, 1948.
Semiane, Sid Ahmed. "Le Fugitif." In *Mes indépendances: Chroniques 2010–2016*, edited by Kamel Daoud, 7–12. Arles: Actes Sud, 2017.
Semprún, Jorge. *Netchaïev est de retour*. Paris: Lattès, 1987.

Shattuck, Roger. "The Doubting of Fiction." *Yale French Studies*, no. 6 (1950): 101–108.
Shatz, Adam. "Stranger Still." *The New York Times*, April 1, 2015. http://www.nytimes.com/2015/04/05/magazine/stranger-still.html
Shatz, Adam. "The Daoud Affair." *LRB Online*, March 4, 2016. http://www.lrb.co.uk/2016/03/04/adam-shatz/the-daoud-affair
Silverstein, Paul. "An Excess of Truth: Violence, Conspiracy Theorizing and the Algerian Civil War." *Anthropological Quarterly* 75, no. 4 (2002): 643–74.
Simon, Catherine. "L'écrit-survie de Maïssa Bey." *Le Monde*, October 17, 1997. https://www.lemonde.fr/archives/article/1997/10/17/l-ecrit-survie-de-maissa-bey_3775463_1819218.html
Soler, Ana. "Un espace littéraire empreint de violence: *Nouvelles d'Algérie* de Maïssa Bey." In *Diversité littéraire en Algérie,* edited by Najib Redouane, 97–116. Paris: L'Harmattan, 2009.
Souaïdia, Habib. *La sale guerre: le témoignage d'un ancien officier des forces spéciales de l'armée algérienne.* Paris: La Découverte, 2001.
Spivak, Gayatri Chakravorty. *A Critique of Postcolonial Reason.* Cambridge, Mass.: Harvard University Press, 1999.
Spivak, Gayatri Chakravorty. "Can the Subaltern Speak?" In *Marxism and the Interpretation of Culture*, edited by Cary Nelson and Lawrence Grossberg, 271–313. London: Macmillan, 1988.
Spivak, Gayatri Chakravorty. "Reading *The Satanic Verses*." *Public Culture* 2, no. 1 (1989): 79–99.
"Stranger and stranger." *The Economist*, May 30, 2015. http://www.economist.com/news/books-and-arts/21652251-biting-algerian-response-french-colonialism-stranger-and-stranger
Stora, Benjamin. "Deuxième guerre algérienne? Les habits anciens des combattants." *Les Temps Modernes*, no. 580 (1995): 242–61.
Stora, Benjamin. *La guerre invisible: Algérie des années 90.* Paris: Presses Sciences Po, 2001.
Stora, Benjamin. "La tragédie algérienne des années 1990 dans le miroir des films de fiction." *La Pensée du Midi* 3, no. 9 (2002): 32–43.
Tarnero, Jacques. "Merah n'est pas un héros de roman." *Causeur*, April 2, 2012. http://www.causeur.fr/merah-n%e2%80%99est-pas-un-heros-de-roman-16861
Temlali, Yassin. "Discussion avec Rachid Mokhtari sur la violence dans la littérature algérienne." In *Algérie, Chroniques Ciné-Littéraires de Deux Guerres*, 53–62. Algiers: Editions Barzakh, 2011.
Temlali, Yassin. "Salim Bachi: «un romancier et non un témoin»." In *Algérie: Chroniques Ciné-Littéraires de Deux Guerres*, 91–100. Algiers: Editions Barzakh, 2011.
Todd, Olivier. *Albert Camus: une vie.* Paris: Gallimard, 1996.
Touati, Amine. "Peurs et mensonges." *Algérie Littérature/Action*, no. 1 (May 1996).
Toumi, Alek Baylee. "Albert Camus entre la mère et l'injustice." In *Albert Camus et les écritures algériennes: quelles traces* edited by the Association "Rencontres méditerranéennes Albert Camus," 143–78. Aix-en-Provence: Edisud, 2004.

Toumi, Alek Baylee. "Albert Camus, l'algérian(iste): genèse d'«Entre la mère et l'injustice»." In *Albert Camus et les écritures algériennes: quelles traces,* edited by the Association "Rencontres méditerranéennes Albert Camus," 81–91. Aix-en-Provence: Edisud, 2004.
Treacy, Corbin. "L'Effet Barzakh." *Contemporary French and Francophone Studies* 20, no. 1 (2016): 76–83.
Treacy, Corbin. "Writing in the Aftermath of Two Wars: Algerian Modernism and the Génération '88." In *Algeria: Nation, Culture and Transnationalism 1988–2015,* edited by Patrick Crowley, 123–39. Liverpool: Liverpool University Press.
TV5MONDE and AFP. "Algérie: des journalistes et des militants arrêtés." *TV5MONDE,* October 8, 2019. https://information.tv5monde.com/afrique/algerie-des-journalistes-et-des-militants-arretes-325678
Tynan, Avril. "Life After Literature: Jorge Semprún's Narrative Afterlives." *Journal of Romance Studies* 20, no. 1 (2020): 139–57.
Valls, Manuel. "Soutenons Kamel Daoud!" *Facebook,* March 2, 2016. https://www.facebook.com/notes/manuel-valls/soutenons-kamel-daoud-/1002589256488085/
Vihalem, Margus. "Everyday aesthetics and Jacques Rancière: reconfiguring the common field of aesthetics and politics." *Journal of Aesthetics & Culture,* 10, no. 1 (2018), 1506209. doi: 10.1080/20004214.2018.1506209
Vince, Natalya. "In Amenas – a history of silence, not a history of violence." *Textures du temps,* January 20, 2013. http://texturesdutemps.hypotheses.org/576
Vince, Natalya. "Literature as post-colonial reality? Kamel Daoud's *The Meursault Investigation.*" *Fiction and Film for French Historians* 6, no. 4 (2016). http://h-france.net/fffh/maybe-missed/literature-as-post-colonial-reality-kamel-daouds-the-meursault-investigation/
Weimann, Gabriel. "The Theater of Terror: The Psychology of Terrorism and the Mass Media." In *The Trauma of Terrorism: Sharing Knowledge and Shared Care, An International Handbook,* edited by Yael Danieli, Danny Brom and Joe Sills, 379–90. Binghamton, NY: Haworth Maltreatment and Trauma Press, 2005.
Yassin-Kassab, Robin. "The Meursault Investigation by Kamel Daoud review – an instant classic." *The Guardian,* June 24, 2015. https://www.theguardian.com/books/2015/jun/24/meursault-investigation-kamel-daoud-review-instant-classic
Yous, Nesroulah. *Qui a tué à Bentalha?* Paris: La Découverte, 2000.
Zirem, Youcef. "Entre l'enfer et la rasion." *La Nation,* August 15–21, 1995, 21.
Zouari, Fawzia. "Au nom de Kamel Daoud." *Libération,* February 28, 2016. http://www.liberation.fr/debats/2016/02/28/au-nom-de-kamel-daoud_1436364

Index

Abane, Meziane, 116n41
academic criticism, 1, 6, 69, 78, 99, 106, 114, 129, 134, 139. *See also* academic literary criticism
academic literary criticism, 2, 6, 8, 13–14, 16, 19, 21–22, 43, 46, 52, 89, 104–5
Actes Sud, 99
Aïssaoui, Mohammed, 110, 118n65
Aït-Aoudia, Malik, 55n39
Akef, Amir, 116n36
Algerian army, 3–6, 9, 37–38, 111–12, 123, 142
Algerian independence, 3, 15, 19, 25n30, 48, 66, 69, 96n3, 103
Algerian newspapers: *Algérie Actualité*, 27n83; *El Watan*, 27n83; *La Nation*, 27n83; *Le Quotidien d'Oran*, 106, 111
Algerian War of Independence (1954-62), 5–6, 8–9, 14, 18–19, 37–38, 40, 50, 77, 87, 89, 92, 99, 101, 103
Algeria-Watch, 105
Algérie Littérature/Action, 45, 58n96
Al-Kassim, Dina, 132, 137n61
Allalou, Mohamed Ali, 135n12
allegory, 38, 48, 63, 69, 86–88, 96. *See also* national allegory
Alloula, Abdelkader, 130

Alloula, Rihab, 130, 144n6
Amara, Noureddine, 116n45, 117n50
Amari, Chawki, 130
Amis, Martin, 81n54
Andrews, Chris, 12–13, 16, 27nn73, 76, 28n97
Anquetil, Gilles, 53n3
Antigone, 47–48
Arab Spring, 108, 117n47
Aresu, Bernard, 79n18
Aristotle, 56nn40, 54
Armée islamique du salut [Islamic Salvation Army] (AIS), 4, 24n19
Arslane, Ghazouane, 135n14
Asseraf, Arthur, 7, 25n36
Assima, Fériel, 17, 29nn102–3, 54n8
Atta, Mohammad, 81n54
avant-garde, 22, 122, 126, 134
Ayotallah Ali Khomeni, 11
Ayyoub, Habib, 19, 21–22, 85–96, 96n2, 97nn9, 20, 98nn30, 46, 140

Bachi, Salim, 19, 21, 61–78, 79nn9, 17, 80nn20, 48, 81n53, 82nn81, 86, 85, 99, 124
Bahri, Deepika, 18, 29n110, 140
Bahti, Timothy, 54n6
Bakhtin, Mikhail, 87, 89, 91–92, 97nn14, 23, 98nn31–32

Balibar, Etienne, 58n72
Barthes, Roland, 126, 136n34
Bayat, Asef, 31n124, 144n14
Baylee, Alek. *See* Toumi, Alek Baylee
Bedjaoui, Youcef, 24n21
Beer, Gillian, 18, 30n113
Bekkat, Amina, 96n1
Belaghoueg, Zoubida, 63, 79n15
Benameur, Samia. *See* Bey, Maïssa
Bendjedid, Chadli, 3–4, 141
Benfodil, Mustapha, 7, 19, 20, 22, 121–34, 135nn6, 12, 136nn17, 20, 137nn36, 56, 138n63, 140–43, 144nn6, 19
Benjamin, Walter, 38, 55n30, 79n13, 81–82n70
Benkhaled, Walid, 5, 8, 23n2, 24nn9, 29, 25n44, 26nn49, 60, 27n77, 28n88, 29n105, 31nn127–29, 37, 40, 53n4, 55nn15, 36, 56n42, 57n64, 77, 80n39, 81n51, 83n89, 95, 97n11, 98nn34, 52, 115n8, 117n57, 118nn63, 69, 136n18, 137n52, 138nn62, 73
Benmahdjoub, Abdelaziz. *See* Ayyoub, Habib
Bennoune, Karima, 121, 123, 134, 134n1, 135nn3–4, 136nn16–19, 138nn71–72
Bennoune, Mahfoud, 121
Bensmaïa, Réda, 133, 138n65
Bentalha, 4
Berger, Anne-Emanuelle, 25n30
Berlin Wall, 11
Bessière, Jean, 119n83
Bey, Maïssa, 7, 21, 33–34, 44–50, 52–53, 57nn68–70, 58nn74, 96, 59nn97, 104, 63, 65, 67, 69, 77, 85, 124, 140
Bhabha, Homi, K., 26n60, 138n68
the binary, 5, 22, 25n30, 33, 35, 38–39, 44, 53n5, 62–64, 70, 72, 74, 86, 91–92, 110–11, 113, 122, 127, 132–34, 143
Bishop, Cécile, 137n47
Bisson, Julien, 118n68

Blanchot, Maurice, 42
Bonn, Charles, 25n41, 29n100, 36, 54n6, 55nn23–25, 78n5, 97n13
Bottici, Chiara, 27n67, 55n19, 82n75
Boudiaf, Mohamed, 4, 63–65
Boudjedra, Rachid, 33–36, 40–42, 53nn1–2, 64, 77, 86, 105–6, 112, 116n35, 124
Bourdieu, Pierre, 58n72
Bourget, Carine, 54n14, 55n22, 71–72, 81nn52–53
Boussouf, Malika, 29n106, 54n8
Bouteflika, Abdelaziz, 1, 10, 20, 125, 130, 140–41
Brand, Laurie, 10, 26nn59–61
Brom, Danny, 82n76
Brouillette, Sarah, 56n46, 144n3
Brozgal, Lia, 103, 105, 115n21, 116n33
Bruckner, Pascale, 117n56
Buffard-O'Shea, Nicole, 57n66
Burns, Karin Garlepp, 54n7, 58n84
Burtscher-Bechter, Beate, 52, 57n66, 58n92, 59nn97, 105
Butler, Judith, 81n69

Calle-Gruber, Mireille, 56n44, 143, 144n18
Calmann-Levy, 29n106
Campbell, James, 113, 119n79
Camus, Albert, 8–9, 13–15, 22, 28nn85, 94, 67, 79n10, 80n33, 99–105, 113–14, 115nn26, 31
Caruth, Cathy, 50, 58n91
Casanova, Pascale, 79n12
Challand, Benoît, 27n67, 55n19, 82n75
Chaouat, Bruno, 74, 82nn72–73
Charlie Hebdo, 110, 112
Charte pour la paix et la réconciliation nationale [Charter for Peace and National Reconciliation], 10, 39, 125
Chaulet-Achour, Christiane, 14, 27n83
Cheah, Pheng, 23n5, 142–43, 144nn12, 17
Cheurfa, Hiyem, 135n14
Chihab Editions, 30n118

Chouaki, Aziz, 15, 28nn89, 93, 77
Clash of civilizations, 11, 17, 19–20, 35–36, 40, 61, 71, 77–78, 80n23, 112–14, 134, 139–40
Cocquet, Marion, 116n39
Cold War, 11–12, 35–36, 61, 134, 139
colonialism, 68, 89, 103
complicity, 16, 40, 44, 53, 57n63, 61–63, 68–69, 72, 74, 78, 91–92, 96, 114, 124, 134, 140
Concorde civile [Civil Concorde], 10
Conflict narrative, 3, 12, 18, 33–34, 41, 44, 53, 62–63, 68, 78, 88, 96, 110, 122, 125, 139–40
Courbet, Claire, 118n72
Crowley, Patrick, 24n9, 27n71, 30nn118–20, 63, 78n8, 79nn9, 19, 80nn28, 50, 81n55, 82n82, 98n27, 119n83, 136n30
Cullen, John, 115n5
culture war. *See* clash of civilizations

Danieli, Yael, 82n76
Daoud, Kamel, 7, 19, 22, 25n34, 99–114, 115nn5, 28, 116nn42–43, 117nn46, 53, 118nn60, 76, 119n80, 124, 128, 130, 134, 140
Davis, Colin, 116n31
Davis, Muriam Haleh, 26n60, 30n122, 93, 95, 98nn40, 50, 135n14, 136nn26, 29, 137nn40, 60, 138n68, 141–42, 144nn6, 11
Davis, Oliver, 137n58
decolonization, 99
Delacroix, Eugène, 56n50
Demetz, Jean-Michel, 53n3
Denis, Benoît, 97n4
Deranty, Jean-Philippe, 23n8
Derrick, Jonathan, 26n52
Derrida, Jacques, 3, 58n72, 70, 127–28, 136n35, 138n69
Devarrieux, Claire, 116n38
Devecchio, Alexandre, 118n73
D'Haen, Théo, 119n83
Dilem, 144n10

Djaout, Tahar, 4, 34, 54n9, 121–22, 135n2
Djebar, Assia, 21, 28n94, 33–34, 40–45, 49, 53, 54n12, 56nn44, 60, 57nn61, 64, 63, 65, 67, 77, 85, 87, 124, 140, 143
Djefel, Belaïd, 13, 27n78
Djemaï, Abdelkader, 27n83
Douroux, Philippe, 118n64
Dugas, Guy, 28n94
Durand, Gilbert, 51

The Economist, 113
écriture de l'urgence [emergency writing], 16, 34, 43, 50
Editions Al Dante, 122
Editions Alpha, 30n118
Editions Apic, 30n118
Editions Barzakh, 19, 85, 89, 122
Editions Casbah, 30n118, 122
Editions *de minuit*, 24n24
Editions *du Seul*, 17
Editions Gallimard, 62
Editions Grasset, 75
Editions Julliard, 17, 29n106
Editions Stock, 37
El Djazaïri, Mehdi, 130, 137n54
elections: 1991–92, 1, 3–5, 33, 35, 55n15; 1999, 10; 2014, 20, 130
Eliot, T. S., 16
El Nossery, Névine, 13, 27n77, 29nn100–101, 43, 50, 54n8, 56nn57–58, 58n93, 59n100
El-Zein, Amira, 136n32
Etcherelli, Claire, 58n74
Evans, Martin, 4, 24nn14, 22, 26n57, 82n80

Fabre, Thierry, 137n48
Facebook, 105–6, 116n40
Fanon, Frantz, 18, 30n114, 85–86, 96n3
Fisher, Dominique, 24n20, 54n9
Ford, Joseph, 29n100, 135n11
Foucault, Michel, 124, 131, 136n23, 137n57

Frediani, Federica, 78n8
French newspapers: *Le Figaro*, 110, 112; *Le Monde*, 6, 76, 82n79, 105, 107–8, 117n54; *Le Monde diplomatique*, 63, 69; *Le Nouveau Marianne*, 7, 111; *Le Point*, 106
Freytag, Gustav, 76, 82n85
Fromentin, Eugène, 42
Front de l'Eveil islamique salafiste [Salafist Islamic Awakening], 105
Front de libération nationale [National Liberation Front] (FLN), 3–5, 28n87, 37, 53n1, 89, 141
Front islamique du salut [Islamic Salvation Front] (FIS), 4–5, 24n19, 33, 35, 37, 53n1, 55n15, 58n72, 86, 121, 139
fundamentalism, 13, 15, 19, 33, 35–37, 43–44, 73, 75, 79n10, 113, 121, 123, 134

Gafaïti, Hafid, 16, 25n30, 28nn95–96, 30nn115–16, 59n99
Garnier, Xavier, 29n100
Geesey, Patricia, 13, 27n79, 29n100, 54n8
Geisser, Vincent, 35, 82n75
Genette, Gerard, 54n6
Ghanem, Nadia, 119n80
Gide, André, 42
Glucksmann, Raphael, 81n53
Godzich, Myrna, 57n67
Godzich, Wlad, 57n67
Gopal, Priyamvada, 83n90
Gopnik, Adam, 113, 119n80
Gozlan, Martine, 25n35, 118nn67
Gratton, Johnnie, 57n62
Gross, Janice, 28n94, 55n39
Grossberg, Lawrence, 54n12
the grotesque, 13, 21, 86–93, 95–96, 124, 141–42
Groupe islamique armée [Armed Islamic Group] (GIA), 4, 7, 9, 14, 24n19, 75, 82n80, 111–12

Gueydan-Turek, Alexandra, 136nn31–33

Hadi, Amine Aït, 94, 98n45
Hadj, Messali, 8, 141
Hamadache, Abdelfatah, 105–6, 108, 110–11
Harbi, Mohammed, 55n39
Harlow, Barbara, 57n67
Harrison, Nicholas, 3, 18, 24nn10–12, 29n109, 30n112, 41, 56n49, 80n49, 104, 114, 115nn26, 31, 116n32, 119nn86–87, 136n35, 144n20
Harrison, Olivia, 89, 98nn27–28
Haut Comité d'Etat [High State Committee] (HCE), 4, 10
Hazan, David, 81n53
Heath, Malcolm, 56n40
Hecking, Britta, 136n30, 142, 144n14
Héliot, Armelle, 110–11, 118nn66
Hellal, Selma, 19
Hewitt, Gavin, 117n47
Hiddleston, Jane, 18, 29n109, 30nn114–17, 39, 41–42, 56nn41, 51, 57n65, 66, 80nn29–30, 86, 90, 96n3, 97nn4, 19, 98n29, 101, 114nn1–4, 115n13, 13, 119n89, 135n5, 136n18, 142, 144n15
Hirak, 20, 30n122, 125, 133, 135n14, 141–42
Hiroshima, 72–73
Hitchcock, Alfred, 72
Houellebecq, Michel, 113, 119n80
Huggan, Graham, 56n46, 119n85, 144n3
Hughes, Edward J., 27n80
Huntington, Samuel P., 11–12, 20, 26nn62–65, 36, 40, 54n13, 61, 77, 134, 140, 144n2
Hussein Saddam, 11

Ibrahim-Ouali, Lila, 50, 58nn74, 90, 80n42
Iranian Revolution (1979), 12

Islam, 11, 14, 20, 31n124, 35–37, 44, 46, 54n9, 100, 105–9, 111, 132, 134
Islamism. *See* political Islam
Islamophobia, 108
Isreal-Palestine conflict (1948), 90

Jager, Marjolijn de, 56n45, 135n2
Jameson, Fredric, 97n3
Jauss, Hans Robert, 54n6
Joffé, George, 26n56
Just, Daniel, 42, 56n56, 88

Kacimi, Mohamed, 137n51
Kaplan, Alice, 102, 115n18
Kateb, Amazigh, 130, 144n6
Kateb, Yacine, 18, 67, 80n31, 85, 96n3, 99, 103, 130
Katutani, Michiko, 113, 118n77
Kelkal, Khaled, 75, 82n79
Kelley, David, 56n51
Keniston, Ann, 82n78
Kennedy, Randy, 136n15
Kessous, Namaan, 28n89
Khadra, Yasmina, 87
Khatibi, Adbelkébir, 57n67, 132–33, 138n69, 143
Khelladi, Aissa, 45–46
Kingsley, Patrick, 117n47

Laâbi, Abdellatif, 97n4
Labat, Séverine, 55n39
Lacapra, Dominique, 39
La Découverte, 24n24, 29n99
La Pointe, Ali, 141
Laredj, Waciny, 57n71
Laroussi, Farid, 29n100, 54n8, 78n5
Le Boucher, Dominique, 51, 59n98
lectures sauvages. *See* Wild Readings
Lefebvre, Henri, 142–43, 144n12
Le Fol, Sébastien, 116n40
Le Juez, Brigitte, 57n62
Leperlier, Tristan, 17, 25n30, 29nn105–7, 52, 53nn3–5, 54n11, 58n72, 59n107, 118n62
Levinas, Emmanuel, 81n69

Lewis, Bernard, 11–12, 20, 26n63, 140, 144n2
Lewis, Mary Anne, 30n119, 97n25
Lewis Cusato, Mary Anne, 135n7, 136n15, 138n67
Lire, 111
Loch, Dietmar, 82n79

MacEwan, Elias J., 82n85
Manicheism, 19, 25n30
Margerrison, Christine, 28n94, 115n6
Marouane, Leïla, 17, 29nn106–8, 54n8
Marsa Editions, 45
Martinez, Luis, 9–10, 24n28, 26n52
Marx-Scouras, Danielle, 13–14, 27n80–81
Marzloff, Martine, 57nn68–69, 58n83, 59n98
Matarese, Mélanie, 30n120, 97n26
Mbembe, Achille, 19, 30nn121–23, 86, 92–93, 95, 97nn5, 24, 133, 136nn24, 28, 138n66, 141, 144nn4–5
McAuley, James, 116n44
McDougall, James, 3, 9, 23n1, 24nn13, 27, 25n42, 26nn47, 51, 27n71, 55n34, 80n39, 87, 97nn11–12
McGuire, Matt, 12–13, 16, 27nn73, 76, 28n97
Meddi, Adlène, 30n120, 97n26, 130
Mellal, Farid, 57n66
Menia, François, 116n39
Mensah, Patrick, 138n64
Merah, Mohammed, 76, 78
Merkel, Angela, 117n47
Mertz-Baumgartner, Birgit, 57n66
Metref, Arezki, 27n83, 57n71
Mezerette, Pierre, 81n53
Mika, Kasia, 31n128
Miliani, Hadj, 23n2
Mills, David, 113, 119n81
Mimouni, Rachid, 20–22, 31n124, 33–42, 45–46, 53nn1–3, 54n8, 55nn16, 38, 64, 68, 77, 86, 105–6, 112, 116n35, 124, 139–40
modernity, 5, 35, 92, 109, 132

Mokeddem, Malika, 54n8
Mokhtari, Rachid, 30n120, 49, 58n88
Morocco, 30n122
Mortimer, Mildred, 13, 27n79
Mosteghanemi, Ahlem, 90
Mouvement islamique algérien [Algerian Islamic Movement] (MIA), 24n19
Mouvement National pour la Renaissance [National Movement for Renaissance] (MNR), 55n15
Mouvement pour la Societé et la Paix [Movement for Society and Peace] (MSP), 55n15
Mundy, Jacob, 4, 11–12, 24nn18, 26nn61, 66, 27nn68–70, 113, 118n75
myth(s), 47–48, 61–62, 64–65, 67–71, 75, 77–78, 80n23; about Algerian society and/or culture, 3, 21, 53–54n5, 64, 68, 96, 114

national allegory, 46, 48, 85, 90, 96n3
Nelson, Cary, 54n12
Newmark, Kevin, 100, 115n6
New York Times, 108, 113
Nezzar, Khaled, 29n99

O'Brien, Conor Cruise, 104–5, 115n29
Ochs, Edith, 83n91
Orientalist stereotypes, 6–7, 11, 17, 41, 107, 140
Orlando, Valérie, 79n15, 99, 114nn2–3, 116n34, 119n88

Palestine, 90
Panagia, Davide, 23n8
Paris Match, 124
Parti communiste algérien [Algerian Communist Party] (PCA), 12
Parti de l'avant-garde socialiste [Party of the Socialist Avant-Garde] (PAGS), 12, 40, 56n43, 137n36, 139–40
Pears, Pamela, 17, 29n104
Pesle, O., 97n17

Phillips, John, 4–5, 24nn14, 22, 26n57, 82n80
pied-noir, 15
Plato, 2
political Islam, 5, 12, 15, 31n124, 33, 35–36, 51, 87, 100, 105, 111–13, 139–40
postcolonial criticism, 3, 18
postcolonial studies. *See* postcolonial criticism
protests: April 2014, 20, 130; February 2019, 1, 20, 141; October 1988, 3, 66–69, 85, 93, 140. *See also* Hirak

Quayson, Ato, 18, 30n111
Quilligan, Maureen, 38, 55n30, 58n82
Quinn, Jeanne, 82n78

Rabourdin, Dominique, 137n51
Rahal, Malika, 12, 21, 25nn30, 45, 26n45, 27nn71–72, 31n125, 40, 56n43
Raïs, 4
Raleigh, Tegan, 56n59
Ramadan, 35
Rancière, Jacques, 2, 23n6, 86, 93–94, 98nn38–39, 131, 136n22, 137n59, 138n70
Rassemblement pour la culture et la démocratie [Rally for Culture and Democracy] (RCD), 12, 139–40
recidivism, 8–9, 13, 15, 21, 38, 55n32, 65, 68, 71, 77, 81n51, 89
Redouane, Najib, 57n66
Remzi, Ali, 78n6, 80n40
Resnais, Alain, 72–73, 81n56
Rice, Alison, 31n126, 46, 58n73
Roberts, Hugh, 5, 9, 24nn15, 26, 26nn53–55
Rockhill, Gabriel, 23n6
Rosello, Mireille, 13, 27n74
Rothberg, Michael, 48, 58n85, 75, 82n78
Roy, Jean, 6, 25n33
Ruptures, 27n83

Rwandan genocide, 81n53

Said, Edward W., 2, 23, 25n32, 31n130, 104–5, 115n29, 116n32, 139, 144n1
Saïm, Boussad, 13, 27n78
Salon international du livre [International Book Fair] (SILA), 97n25, 130
Sansal, Boualem, 119n80
Sanson, Hervé, 97n26
Sanyal, Debarati, 57n63, 82nn71, 74
Sartre, Jean-Paul, 18, 30n114, 85–86, 93, 96n3
Schaffner, Alain, 27n83
Sebbar, Leila, 48
secularism, 5, 15, 100, 108, 110–13, 134
Semiane, Sid Ahmed, 100, 115n7
Semprún, Jorge, 137n36
September 11, 2001, 12, 21, 61–62, 71–72, 81n54, 140
Serres, Thomas, 26n60, 93, 95, 98nn34, 52, 135n14, 136nn26–29, 137nn40, 60, 138n68
Shattuck, Roger, 42, 56n55, 88, 97n16
Shatz, Adam, 108–9, 113, 117nn52, 55, 119n82
Sills, Joe, 82n76
Silverstein, Paul, 7–8, 25nn38–40
Simon, Catherine, 6, 25n33
Smati, Aziz, 135n12
Smith, Sandra, 115n26
Soler, Ana, 51–52, 57n66, 58n92, 59nn106–8, 80n42
Souaïdia, Habib, 24n24, 29n99
Spiquel, Agnès, 27n83
Spivak, Gayatri Chakravorty, 18, 29n110, 30n110, 41, 54n12, 56n49, 118n59
Stafford, Andy, 28nn89, 94
the State, 2, 8, 10–11, 13–14, 20–22, 24n19, 33, 37, 39–40, 44, 48, 51, 86–87, 89–90, 92–93, 95, 97n25, 103, 105–6, 121, 124–25, 127, 129, 133, 138n68, 141–42

Stora, Benjamin, 8–10, 14, 16, 25n43, 26nn46–48, 27n82, 29n98, 55n39
The Sunday Times, 113

Tahrir Square, 108
Tamazight, 1
Tarnero, Jacques, 83n91
Temlali, Yassin, 29n101, 61, 77, 78nn1, 7, 80nn25, 36, 82n87, 83n88
terrorism, 5, 13, 51, 63, 71, 73–75, 77–78, 112, 114. *See also* fundamentalism
testimonial literature, 6–7, 13, 17, 20–21, 33, 36–37, 42–45, 47–50, 52–53, 58n95, 61–65, 68, 70, 77–78, 124, 129, 139, 140
testimony, 5, 8, 16, 63, 67–69, 123, 140. *See also* testimonial literature
Tidjani, Ahmed, 97n17
Todd, Olivier, 27n83, 28n87
Touati, Amine, 57n71
Toumi, Alek Baylee, 14–15, 28nn84, 94, 57n71
Toumi, Khalida, 14
tradition, 5, 108
tragédie nationale [national tragedy], 10, 39, 96, 125
tragedy, 10, 39–40, 43–44, 56n40, 76. *See also* tragédie nationale [national tragedy]
trauma, 39, 50, 53, 69, 73, 113, 126, 129
Treacy, Corbin, 30n120, 97n25, 128, 135n13, 137n45
Twitter, 106
Tynan, Avril, 137n36

Vallorani, Jean-Pierre, 135n12
Valls, Manuel, 109, 117n58
Vietnam, 72
Vihalem, Margus, 23n7
Vince, Natalya, 5–6, 8, 24nn9, 29, 25nn31, 44, 26nn49, 60, 27n77, 28n88, 29n105, 31nn127–29, 37, 40, 53n4, 55nn15, 36, 56n42, 57n64,

77, 80n39, 81n51, 83n89, 95, 97n11, 98nn34, 52, 115n8, 117n57, 118nn63, 69, 119n84, 136n18, 137n52, 138nn62, 73
Virole, Marie, 45
Voinchet, Marc, 111

Wall Street Journal, 113
Weimann, Gabriel, 75, 82nn76–77
Wild Readings, 22, 122, 129–32, 141
women's writing, 13, 17–18, 21, 29n100, 34, 43, 48, 54n8

world literature, 113, 140, 142
World Trade Centre, 72

Yassin-Kassab, Robin, 144n3
Yous, Nesroulah, 4, 24n24, 29n99

Zekri, Khalid, 97n4
Zerofsky, Elizabeth, 116n43
Zéroual, Liamine, 10
Zirem, Youcef, 27n83
Zouari, Fawzia, 108–9, 117n56

About the Author

Joseph Ford is Lecturer in French Studies at the Institute of Modern Languages Research, School of Advanced Study, University of London.

His research focuses on contemporary French and Francophone literature and culture, with specific interests in Algeria. He has broad research interests in postcolonial studies, migration, world literature, and literary translation. His articles on Salim Bachi, Mustapha Benfodil, and Albert Camus have appeared in several journals, including the *Irish Journal of French Studies*, *Francosphères*, and the *Bulletin of Francophone Postcolonial Studies*, among others. He is the editor and translator of a bilingual edition of Mustapha Benfodil's poetry, *Cocktail Kafkaïne*, which appeared with Hesterglock Press in 2018.

www.ingramcontent.com/pod-product-compliance
Lightning Source LLC
Chambersburg PA
CBHW032150010526
44111CB00035B/1430